THE ITALIAN THEATRE

Fêtes vénitiennes, after a painting by Watteau.

THE
ITALIAN
THEATRE

** **

FROM THE CLOSE OF
THE SEVENTEENTH CENTURY

BY

JOSEPH SPENCER KENNARD

Benjamin Blom
New York

First published by Rudge, 1932
Reprinted 1964, by Benjamin Blom, Inc., New York 52.
L.C. Catalog Card No.: 64-14709

Printed in U.S.A. by
NOBLE OFFSET PRINTERS, INC.
NEW YORK 3, N. Y.

AS A TRIBUTE
TO THE LOVING CO-OPERATION
OF MY WIFE
E. H. K.
THIS WORK IS GRATEFULLY DEDICATED

FOREWORD

METASTASIO *was the most genial and famous artist of his time. His melodrama was the last and finest fruit of the Renaissance.* Goldsmith *wrote in* The Bee *that any English manager could fill his theatre by putting on his bills "Written by Metastasio." The same was true everywhere in Europe.*

Goldoni is the world's best loved and most popular writer of comedies.

Alfieri's passionate tragedies directed a national political movement, a fact which entitles him to glorious remembrance.

Timid, pallid Niccolini spoke in a whisper. Yet so vital was his literary production, so intense his patriotic purpose, that he swayed a whole generation. The simplicity and grandeur of his career have scarcely a parallel in literary history.

Harbinger of Romanticism, reviver of the Commedia dell' Arte, Gozzi was praised, translated, and imitated in France, England, and Germany. He personified and agonized in the crumbling of the old aristocratic Venetian order.

It was not by accident that almost at the same time these writers appeared among a people who had not yet given the full measure of their genius in melodrama, comedy, or tragedy. Under a diversity of temperament and of literary accomplishment they have certain traits of resemblance.

As novelist, poet, and playwright, D'Annunzio is the most discussed of modern writers. Monti was an authoritative exponent of classicism. Foscolo composed some of the most perfect Italian verses ever written. The plays of these dramatists, with those of the Pindemonte brothers, Pellico and Manzoni must be read in order to understand the Risorgimento. *Benelli, Giacosa, Rovetta and Pirandello have occupied a large space in European and American dramatic criticism.*

J. S. K.

New York
November, 1931

CONTENTS

CHAPTER I

PAGE 3

METASTASIO'S LIFE:

Metastasio was first applauded, then neglected. It is time to assign him his proper place among Italian poets: In our first notice of him, he stands on a stone pillar extemporizing poetry: When ten years old, is adopted by Gianvincenzo Gravina: Is often required to improvise, which injures his health: He visits Naples: Is given the clerical title of *Abaté,* and for the rest of his life wears the *Abaté* dress: Gravina dies, leaving Metastasio a legacy: He studies law in Naples and writes poetry: He meets the actress Marianna Bulgarelli called Romanina, who falls in love with him: Metastasio lives with her in Rome: He gives up a legal career and becomes a playwright: Music is the essence of Metastasio's genius: His mysterious love-affair in Rome: Metastasio accepts position of *Poeta Cesareo* at the court of Vienna, where he avoids court ceremonies and lived with an Italian family: Metastasio's best work produced during his first ten years in Vienna: His failing health, early senility: Marianna is unhappy; dies and leaves her fortune to Metastasio: Metastasio grieves for her, but is comforted by Countess d'Althan, who centers her life on his welfare: Metastasio visits her twice every day: Countess d'Althan dies; Metastasio grieves: Metastasio refuses invitations to return to Italy: Lives with the Martinez family, to whom he leaves his fortune: His last years were unhappy: His friendship for Farinello: Metastasio was the trusted confidant of several good women: Metastasio always preserved religious appearances: Dies, after a short illness, over eighty years old.

CHAPTER II

PAGE 41

METASTASIO: HIS TIME AND HIS WORK:

Italian *Settecento* literature was first unduly condemned, and afterwards unduly praised: It is now time for an unprejudiced consideration: After the council of Trent, Italy was submerged in obscurantism: Literature was a pastime, religion was formality, and all social or political initiative was smothered: Arcadia, though justly ridiculed, had some merit: Metastasio selected the "canzonetta" form for his verse, which is the best Italian poetry of the period: The evolution of the Italian melodrama and opera: Metastasio's plays: *Dido* is the first truly Metastasian drama; the model is Virgilian: It is followed by *Siroe, Ezio,* and *Alessandro: Artaserse* shows Metastasio's progress: *Olimpiade* is most typical of Metastasio's first Viennese manner: *La Clemenza di Tito* is Metastasio's most admired drama, but *Temistocle* contains *Metastasio's* most complex and complete character, while *Attilio Regolo* is the unsurpassed blossom of this sort of tragedy. This greatest of Metastasio's works was first performed in Poland: Women's place in Italian Eighteenth Century society is mirrored in Metastasio's plays: The place and importance of the Italian highborn ladies, their influence through their *salotti,* and their emotions, are truthfully described: Metastasio's own career is an example of what feminine influence could accomplish: An analysis of Metastasio's feminine heroines: Metastasio has many qualities of a great tragic poet: The only rival to Tasso's *Gerusalemme Liberata* is Metastasio's verse.

CHAPTER III   PAGE 63

GOLDONI'S VENICE:

The evolution of acting as a regular profession: Early professional comedians preferred improvisation to memorized recitation: Improvisations and masks are characteristic of the "Art Comedy": These comedians created a few personages, and made them famous: For more than two centuries Italian improvised comedy amused the courts of Europe: In the second half of the eighteenth century, this form of Italian drama had almost disappeared: The statue of Goldoni in the *Piazzette dei Mercanti* in Venice: Goldoni belongs to Venice: The spirit of revolt which swept through Europe found its echo in Venice: To measure the importance of Goldoni's theatre, one must understand the Venice of which his work is the reflection: Venice and the eighteenth century is a fascinating theme with many variations: Underneath exterior magnificence there was senile decay: The great aristocracy was dissolved: Venice was the most orderly city in Europe: Many magnificent public festivals in which the entire populace participated: Chief among these was the festival *della Senza* (the Ascension), undoubtedly the most splendid spectacle performed in Europe: All Venetian life was theatrically inclined: Private entertainments almost rivalled the public festivals in magnificence: The Venetian lady of fashion: Gambling was the supreme vice of Venetian society. One gambled everywhere and at all hours of the day and night: All classes in Venice wore masks: The *cavalier servente* was a Venetian institution: The Venetian country "House party": The gondola played a very important part in the Venetian eighteenth century life: Goldoni ignored the Catholic Church in his plays: Worldliness of the nuns and priests: Prevalence in this Venetian society of *Abbés* of dubious charms and cunning ways.

CHAPTER IV   PAGE 81

GOLDONI AND HIS PLAYS:

Goldoni was a true Venetian, and this Venetian atmosphere furnishes the foundation of his plays: Goldoni's plays show that he was a marvelous observer but was unable to generalize: His satire is softened by his good nature: He vividly described the world in which he lived: His religious attitude is typically Italian: He respects appearances, but goes no farther: In his comedies, Goldoni severely judged the aristocracy, but regarded the bourgeois family with indulgence: He did not invent his types, which he completes by showing the same character in many plays: His Pantalone, the most ancient of the Masks, is Goldoni's favorite character: Goldoni's female characters are many and varied, and some of them are unsurpassed: Goldoni tried to reform the comedy, and partly succeeded: Goldoni hated militarism and loathed war: In Goldoni's social plan, the family is the nucleus of society: He admired the medical profession, and highly respected lawyers: He knows and loves the lower classes and asks for them fair play.

CHAPTER V   PAGE 96

Carlo Gozzi: His Life and Times:

Jealousy of Goldoni inspired Carlo Gozzi's plays: Gozzi and Goldoni contrasted: Gozzi begins writing poems when only nine years old: Is appointed a Government Secretary in Dalmatia: Writes a cynical description of his family's misfortune: The new Venetian Academy named "I Granelloni": Writes *La Tartana degli influssi,* a malicious attack on Goldoni: Composes an ignoble lampoon on Goldoni, *Il Teatro Comico*: Gozzi's first *fiaba* is performed (1760): Gozzi falls in love with the actress Teodora Ricci: Detail of quarrel between Gozzi and Gratarol: The *Memorie* describes Gozzi's increasing melancholia and misfortunes: Nievo's *Confessioni* describes this cruel moment in the history of Venice with the coming of the French: Sad end of Carlo Gozzi.

CHAPTER VI   PAGE 105

The Plays of Carlo Gozzi:

Gozzi's plays secured the attention of his audience, but did not interest Italian readers: To German and English critics, Gozzi is the harbinger of Romanticism: To Italians, Gozzi's fantasy is the product of his surfeited memory: The *Masks* of Gozzi and Goldoni contrasted: In his *fiabe* Gozzi opened wide the doors of wonderland: The fickle Venetians were glad to see Goldoni parodied: Gozzi's Venetian plays made vulgar caricatures of real people: But they also contain some valuable motives: *The Pretty Green Bird* is the best of the *fiabe*: Though the story is complex, it is an interesting play: His comedy *Turandot,* written in verse and prose, has been widely praised: Gozzi failed to produce a true work of art. The invasion of foreign ideas distressed and distorted his mental balance. Gozzi presumed to oppose the onward march of new ideas, and failed.

CHAPTER VII

THE SETTECENTO BEFORE ALFIERI:

Influence of the French classical tragedy during the eighteenth century in Italy: Maffei's *Merope,* the only successful tragedy before Alfieri: The tragedies of Conti, Verris, Landi, and Gozzi: The work of Ringhieri and Varano: Ducal patronage of the theatre: Gigli's *Don Piloni*: Nelli: Types of Italian comedy of the eighteenth century: The Lachrymose Drama, importation of French and English sentimentality: Life and works of De Gamerra: Influence of this type of drama on later forms.

CHAPTER VIII

LIFE OF VITTORIO ALFIERI:

Political importance of Alfieri's tragedies: Alfieri was a neglected child, a lonely boy: Through fault of his tutor Alfieri hated study: Read little except French novels, and admired French plays: Obtained commission in the army, and during next six years was restless, vain, and idle: Traveled almost everywhere in Europe: In the Netherlands, falls in love with a married woman: In Turin, he begins an intense system of reading: In London, becomes entangled in a love-affair, and fights a duel with the husband: In Madrid, has a fight with his valet, Elia: After much wandering, returns to Turin, and becomes *cavalier servente* to the beautiful wife of the Marquis of Priero: In 1775, his tragedy *Cleopatra* is performed in Turin: In 1777 he begins his life-long attachment to Countess d'Albany, wife of the Young Pretender, who was a brute and a drunkard: The story of Alfieri's semi-royal amours: Countess d'Albany leaves her husband and lives with Alfieri until his death: Her meanness of character contrasts strangely with Alfieri's extravagant praise of her: Her *salon* in Paris was the resort of many famous men and women: Alfieri fiercely loves liberty, yet could not comprehend the French Revolution: Though a military officer, he never fought for his own country: Has several love-affairs, and ignores the love made to Countess d'Albany by the painter François Xavier Fabre: She wept when Alfieri died, and married Fabre: The rhetorical eloquence of Alfieri's tragedies entitles him to be ranked among the great Italian writers.

CHAPTER IX

ALFIERI'S TRAGEDIES:

Alfieri lacked poetical discernment, but his patriotic emotion burned fiercely: His tragedies answered to Italian aspirations for freedom: Alfieri aspired to rank among the greatest Italian poets: Alfieri's passionate patriotism was limited to his writings;

he never drew his sword: More than he loved liberty, Alfieri hated tyranny: In his first tragedy, *Filippo*, tyranny is personified: In all his tragedies, Alfieri paints his personages with the color of his own soul: His plays follow classical models: *Saul* is Alfieri's masterpiece: Saul is torn by contrary passions. He struggles with God, he struggles also with himself: Saul is mad, but he possesses a majesty that inspires compassion and admiration: *Mirra* is Alfieri's final masterpiece: The drama lies in the horrified struggle of a chaste soul with an unclean obsession: It is a horrible yet pitiful picture: Alfieri's theatre had a political importance which surpassed its artistic worth: His appeals are trumpet calls: Alfieri is greater than his work; his own people understood him and magnified merits.

CHAPTER X   PAGE 166

GIOVANNI BATESTA NICCOLINI:

The contrast between Niccolini's frail body and the great work he accomplished is almost unparalleled in literary history: When he was graduated from the University of Pisa, he was penniless: In 1807, he became professor of history at the *Accademia* in Florence: In fifteen years, Florence saw many changes in government under foreign rulers: But Niccolini was always writing and plotting for the freedom of his country: His great hatred was for the political power of the Church of Rome: His intellectual combat preserved him from other desires: His lifelong attachment to the actress Maddalena Pelzet: When old and sad he settled at the house of Carlotta Cortellini: Niccolini did not trust the promises of political liberty of Pope Pius IX: He was not in sympathy with Cavour, Mazzini, or Garibaldi: He died in 1860, and was buried at Santa Croce.

CHAPTER XI   PAGE 181

THE PLAYS OF NICCOLINI:

In all his plays Niccolini sought for an historical basis for his ideal of Italy's independence: Niccolini was morbidly sensitive to criticism of his plays: Niccolini's real début was his play *Nabucco*: It is intended to be an historical picture of Napoleon: As a political pamphlet, *Nabucco* has sincerity and courage: In the dispute between classicism and romanticism, Niccolini never seems to have made up his mind: Both schools claimed him: Some of his plays are called classic and others are called romantic: His play *Antonio Foscarini* was hailed as a masterpiece: There are many incongruities and inconsistencies in this play; but passion and patriotism give it reality and beauty: The play *Giovanni da Procida* was violently discussed, praised, and blamed: Niccolini's next tragedy, *Lodovico Sforza*, is one of his best works: Niccolini poured out his soul and some of the speeches are truly eloquent: Its theatrical performance was prohibited: His tragedy *Arnaldo da Brescia* had an enormous success; it was hailed as a gospel of liberty, justice, and nationalism: Its characters are symbols: The complex conditions of Italy are discussed by Pope Adrian, by Arnaldo, the Emperor Frederic, and many others: The author of *Arnaldo,* though unmolested in Tuscany, would have been imprisoned or murdered elsewhere in Italy: Niccolini's last tragedy, *Mario e i Cimbri,* printed after his death, does not answer to the sublimity of its aims.

CHAPTER XII   PAGE 196

AN OUTLINE OF POLITICAL EVENTS IN ITALY:

The contribution of Bonaparte to the Italian State: Italy after Napoleon's fall: The Congress of Vienna: Reaction in Italy: Oppression of political prisoners: Election of Pope Pius IX: Beginnings of an organization for a united and independent Italy: Garibaldi's "Thousand": Recovery of Rome: The Italian *Risorgimento*: Patriotism among the dramatists: Growth of Romanticism: Alfieri, Foscolo, Mazzini, Niccolini: The realism of D'Annunzio, Verga, and De Roberto: The work of Gazzaletto, Battaglia, and the end of the historical drama: Giacometti's *La Morte Civile*: The patterning of comedy after Goldoni: The work of Giraud and the French influence.

CHAPTER XIII   PAGE 209

MINOR DRAMATISTS:

Vincenzo Monti: his verses in connection with the new Italian State: His life in Rome: His poem *Bassvilliana*: His enthusiasm for Napoleon: His family: His tragedies: *Aristodemo, Caio Gracco*: Monti as a writer of tragedy: Giovanni Pindemonte: his ancestors, early life, marriage: Influence of the French upon his writing: His *I Baccanali*: His *Ginevra di Scozia*: *Cincinnatus,* his most classical play: Ippolito Pindemonte: his life: Influence of Rousseau and Pascal: His *Armino*: Ugo Foscolo: His *I Sepolcri,* a glorification of his country: His birth and youth: His career in politics: Exiled to foreign lands: His death in poverty: The popularity of his *Ajace* among the literati: His *Ricciarda*: Silvio Pellico: early life, journalistic adventures, political activities and imprisonment: The great success of his play, *Francesca da Rimini*: His lighter tragedy, *Eufemio da Messina*: Allessandro Manzoni: his early and uneventful life: His marriage: Influence of Romanticism and religion on his plays: His *Conte di Carmagnola*: Influence of Schiller: His second tragedy *Adelchi*: Carlo Marenco: his *Pia dei Tolomei*: The patriotism of his *Arnaldo da Brescia*: Paolo Ferrari: his realistic comedies of social life: *Roberto Vighlius, Cause ed effeti, Il Ridicolo*: His reliance on Goldoni: His best plays: *La Satira e Parini, Goldoni e le sue sedici commedie nuove.*

CHAPTER XIV
PAGE 249

Gabriele D'Annunzio: The Man and His Plays:

Gabriele D'Annunzio is the most discussed of modern writers; the world watches him; the world applauds him as novelist, poet and playwright: In all his writings, his characters are puppets, each reflecting some phase of his own personality: With himself as the subject, he became the world's most successful publicity agent: D'Annunzio's last rôle is in Franciscan garb, and his motto "silentium" has become vocal over all the world: D'Annunzio's tragedies are simple in their structure. Their characters are dominated by lust, ambition, or cruelty. They are mere tools in the hands of Fate, and the lower nature always triumphs: D'Annunzio's plays present magnificent descriptions unsurpassed in any language: There is no real psychoanalysis: Primitive emotion requires no delicate investigation: D'Annunzio's play *Gioconda* deals with the familiar social triangle. It reflects Italian characters, manners, and social atmosphere: In his *Francesca da Rimini,* D'Annunzio has transformed Dante's sweet sinner into a fiery amazon who brandishes deadly weapons: She is filled with sensual desire: The play is full of brutal violence: D'Annunzio's fame will rest on *La Figlia di Jorio* when his other plays are forgotten: In D'Annunzio's masterpiece there is throbbing life: On his *Fedra* D'Annunzio has lavished æsthetic beauties: This classical mosaic, containing many fragments of antique plays, is drowned in the verbosity of episodes.

CHAPTER XV
PAGE 269

Modern Dramatic Representations of the Tuscan Contado:
The Giostre, Bruscelli and Maggi:

Names of rural dramatic representations vary according to the part of Italy where they are given: The chief names are *Giuochi, Giostre, Bruscelli,* and *Maggi*: *Maggio,* the most frequently used, celebrates the return of the Springtime, and is very ancient: In Siena the Bruscello is a form of theatrical art given in rustic style and language: The music of the *Maggio* is always a slow song in four verses of eight beats: At first the *Maggio* was recited in the open country, without stage or curtain: Now it is sometimes given in theatres: The *Maggi* are either heroic, historic, or spiritual: The subjects of these dramas are paladins, saints, and martyrs: The *Maggio* is a fragment of history arranged in dialogue: The *Maggio* avails itself of the marvelous and the spectacular, all performed in the most realistic manner: Celestial and diabolic personages, strange animals, and even Divinity, are among the actors; especially the devil, who frequently takes a comic part: In the *Maggio* innocence and justice always triumph: For the rustic the *Maggio* is the mirror of life and of history.

Living survivals of the sacred drama are found everywhere in southern Italy: Sometimes they are mute, frequently they are spoken: Usually it is a procession which issues from the church, passes through the streets, and returns to the church: Christmas, the Last Supper, the Crucifixion and Resurrection are most often represented. At Arzans near Naples there is an elaborate performance of the Annunciation: Elsewhere they celebrate the festivals of the patron saints. In some parts of northern Italy they still arrange processions in which the Madonna and the saints appear in masquerade: At Sordevolo a *Passione* is magnificently performed every five years by about four hundred persons: Also in Sardinia like customs survive: The festival of the *Rua* of Vicenza is a singular blending of the sacred and profane: The celebrated procession of *Gesu morto* is given at Prato every third year: A similar *Processione* is still held at Grassina and at Galluzzo near Florence.

CHAPTER XVI   PAGE 286

Some Contemporary Italian Dramatists:

Sem Benelli: His reaction from the imitative theatre of the past and the dawn of "Teatro di Poesia": His *La Maschera di Bruto, Tignola, La Cena delle Beffe, L'amore dei tre re, Mantellaccio, L'Arzigogolo*, and *Ali*: Giuseppe Giacosa: success of his *La Partita a scacchi*: His *Il Trionfo d'Amore*: His *Tristi Amori* as a picture of Italian provincial life: His most profound and original play, *Come le foglie*: His *I Diritti dell Anima* a psychological play: His *Il piu forte*: Gerolamo Rovetta: His *Romanticismo*, dealing with the Italian *Risorgimento*, a great success: His *Papa Eccellenza*: Luigi Pirandello: Profound change in the Italian post-war drama marked in his plays: His *Six Characters in Search of an Author* with the thesis that personality as generally understood is an illusion: His *Henry IV* preaches the confusion of personality and pretense: His pre-eminence among internationally known Italian dramatists.

BIBLIOGRAPHY

A complete bibliography of the matters here considered would require more than a large volume, even if such a compilation were possible. The titles here selected, together with the various supplementary bibliographies will probably suffice for most readers. The two works by A. d'Ancona, on the Italian theatre and the Italian literature are most important, and have been invaluable to the author.

ADEMOLLO, A. *Intorno al teatro drammatico italiano dal* 1550 *in poi.* "Nuova Antologia," 1881. *Il Carnevale di Roma nei secoli XVII e XVIII.* Rome, 1883. *Una Famiglia di comici italiani nel secolo decimotavo.* Florence, 1885. *I teatri di Roma nel secolo decimosettimo.* Pasqualucci, Roma, 1888.

AMBRA, Lucio d'. *Le théâtre contemporain en Italie.* "La rev. d'art dramatique," ANNÉE 17, p. 273–286. "La rev. d'art dramatique," Paris, 1902. N. S., v. 5, pp. 345–350.

ANCONA, A. d'. *Origini del teatro italiano.* Turin, 1891. 2 VOLS. *Manuale della letteratura italiana.* (With Orazio Bacci.) Florence, 1904–1908. 6 VOLS.

ANTOLINI, Patrizio. *Notizie e documenti Farrarese.* Ferrara, 1889. ATTI., v. 2, p. 33.

BARTOLI, Francesco. *Scenari inediti della commedia dell'arte.* Firenze, Sansoni, 1880. *Notizie istoriche de' comici italiani che fiorirono intorno all'anno MDL fino a'giorni presenti.* Padua, 1782. 2 VOLS.

BASCHET, Armand. *Les Comédiens italiens à la cour de France sous Charles IX, Henri III, Henri IV et Louis XIII.* Paris, 1882.

BERRET, Paul. *Des Conditions de representation de la comédie latine.* "Rev. d'art dramatique." Paris, 1899. N. S., v. 7, p. 174.

BLACK, John. Translation from the French of Goldoni's *Memoirs.* London, 1814. 2 VOLS. Same, abridged, with essay by W. D. Howells. Boston, 1877.

BROCCHI, Virgilio. *Carlo Goldoni a Venezia nel secolo XVIII.* Bologna, 1907.

BROGNOLIGO, G. *Nel Teatro di C. G.; Il Cavaliere e la Dama; Le Femmine puntigliose; La guerra.* Naples, 1907.

BROSSES, Le Président des. *Lettres familières écrites d'Italie en* 1739 *et* 1740. Fourth edition. Paris, 1885. 2 VOLS.

BUCKLEY, Eric R. *The Staging of Plays* 300 *years ago.* "Gentlemen's Mag.," London, 1901. v. 291, pp. 288–297.

CAMPARDON, E. *Les Comédiens du Roi de la Troupe Italienne pendant les deux derniers siècles.* Paris, 1880. 2 VOLS.

CAPRIN, Giulio. *La Commedia dell'arte al principio del secolo XVIII.* "Rivista teatrala italiana." Naples, 1905.

CARDUCCI. *I Corifei della Canzonetta nel secolo XVI.* VOL. XVIII in Antologia di Critica Letterari Moderna.

CASANOVA de Seingalt, J. *Mémoires écrites par lui-même.* Nouvelle édition collationnée sur l'édition originale de Leipsick. Paris, no date. 8 VOLS.

CASTELNUOVO, A. *Una Dama Veneziano del secolo XVIII.* Nuovo Antologia, Jan., 1882.

CHAMBERS, E. K. *The Mediæval Stage.* Oxford, 1903. 2 VOLS.

CLODEL, Judith. *Le théâtre italien.* NOUV. REV., N.S. Paris, 1900. Pp. 601–612.

CUMAN, Arpalice. *La riforma del teatro comica italiano e Carlo Goldoni.* "L'Ateneo Veneto." ANNO 22, V. 2, p. 293; ANNO 23, V. 1, p. 80; V. 1, p. 197.

DEJOB, Charles. *Les abbés,* etc. "Rev. prolit. et litt. Rev. Blue. Paris, 1898. SER. 4, V. 10.

DIDEROT, D. *De la poésie dramatique* (1758). Garnier, Paris, 1875.

DOUHET. *Dictionnaire des Mystères.* Paris, 1854.

DURAND. *Le culte catholique dans ses cérémonies,* etc. Méguignon, Paris, 1868.

FAINELLI, Vittorio. *Chi era Pulcinella?* Gior. Stor. d. lett. Ital. Torino, 1909. v. 54, p. 59.

FUNCK, Brentano. *Les théâtres dans l'ancienne France.* "Minerva," Paris, 1902. v. 4, p. 526.

GANTHERON, René. *Le théâtre italien en France.* SÉRIE 2, TOME 35, pp. 307–343.

GHERARDI, E. *Le théâtre italien de Gherardi.* Paris, 1721.

GIACOMO, Salvatore, di. *Cronaca del teatro San Carlino, 1738–1884.* Trani; V. Vecchi, 1895. (Collezione Storica Napoletani, v. 1.)

GRIMM, Le Baron de. *Correspondance littéraire, etc.* (1753–1790). Paris. 16 VOLS.

HASTINGS, Charles. *The Theatre.*

HAWKINS, F. *Annals of French Stage.* Chapman and Hall, London, 1884. 2 VOLS.

HILLEBRAND, K. L. *Des Conditions de la bonne comédie.* Durand, Paris, 1863. *Études historiques et Études italiennes.* Frank, Paris, 1868.

JULLEVILLE, Louis Petit de. *Les Mystères.* Hachette, Paris, 1880. 2 VOLS. *La Comédie et les Moeurs en France au Moyen Age.* L. Cerf, Paris, 1885–1886. *Histoire de la littérature française,* VOL. I, M. A. *Histoire du théâtre en France.* Paris, 1880–1889.

LEROY, Onésime. *Études sur les Mystères.* Hachette, Paris, 1837. *Histoire comparée du théâtre.* Paris, 1844.

LUCAS, Hippolyte. *Histoire philosophique et litt. du théâtre.* 1862. 2 VOLS. in 1.

LUNGO, Isadoro Del. *Medio evo dautesco sul teatro.* "Nuovo Antologia." v. 98, p. 23.

MAGNIN, Charles. *Les origines du Théâtre moderne.* Hachette, Paris, 1838. "Journal des Savants," 1848, p. 199; 1849, p. 14; 1860, p. 537.

MANTZIUS, Karl. *A history of Theatrical Art.* VOLS. I AND 2. "Middle Ages and the Renaissance." VOL. 2.

MARCHESI, G. B. *I Romanze dell'abate Chiari.* Bergamo, 1900.

MASI, Ernesto. *La Vita e le opere di C. G.* Bologna, 1880. *La Vita, i tempi, gli amici di Francesco Albergati.* Bologna, 1878.

MENGHINI, Mario. *Bibliografia del dramma It.* "Rivista della Biblioteche." Firenze, 1896. VOL. 6, pp. 65–77.

MÉRIL, Edelestand du. *Histoire de la comédie.* Didier, Paris, 1864. *Origines latines du Théâtre moderne.* Franck, Paris, 1849. *Dictionnaire des Myst.*

Molière. Cf. M. A. D. Regnier's collection, *Les Grands Ecrivains de la France.* "Molière."

Molmenti, P. G. *La Storia di Venezia nella vita privata dalle origini alla caduta della republica.* Fifth edition, profusely illustrated. vol. i, *La Grandezza;* vol. ii, *Lo Splendore;* vol. iii, *Il Decadimento.* Bergamo, 1910.

Muratori. *Annali d'Italia.* Venice, 1848. vol. vii.

Morice, E. *Historie de la Mise en Scène,* etc. Paris, 1836.

Neri, Achille. *Carlo Goldoni.* Pavia, 1907. *Bibliografia goldoniana.* Giorn. degli eruditi e curiosi. Padua, 1883. vol. iii.

Ortolani, Giuseppe. *Della Vita e dell'arte di C. G.* Venice, 1907.

Parfaict, Frères. *Histoire de l'ancien théâtre italien depuis son origine en France jusqu' à sa supression en l'année* 1697. *Suivie des extraits ou canevas des meilleurs pièces italiennes qui n'ont jamais été imprimées.* Paris, 1767.

Parma (City of Parma). *Esposizione, Litt. del Teatro a Parma.* "L'illustrazione italiana," Milano, 1913. anno 40. pp. 308–309.

Petit de Julleville. See Julleville.

Rabany, Charles. *C. G. Le théâtre et la vie en Italie au XVIIIe siècle.* Paris, 1896.

Rasi, Luigi. *I Comici italiani, Biografia, Bibliografia, Iconografia.* Florence. vol. i, 1897; vol. ii, 1905.

Rayer. *Histoire universelle du Théâtre.* Franck, Paris, 1869.

Ricci, Corrado. *I teatri di Bologna nei secoli* 17. "Storia aneddotica." Bologna, 1888.

Riccoboni, Luigi. *Histoire de théâtre italien depuis la decadence de la comédie latine.* Delormel, Paris, 1728. *Histoire de l'ancien théâtre italien.* Paris, 1730. 2 vols. *An historical and critical account of the theatres in Europe.* London, 1741.

Ruggeri, Luigi. *L'Archiconfraternita del Gonfalone.* Roma, 1866.

Sacchetti, Renzo. *Le théâtre italien.* "Rev. d. rev." vol. 30, p. 611.

Saint-Evremond. *De la Comédie Italienne.* Paris, 1777.

SAINTSBURY, George. *Short History of English Literature*. London, 1908.

SANCTIS, Francesco di. *Storia della letteratura italiana*.

SAVIOTTI, Alfredo. *Feste e spectacoli nel seicento*. "Gior. Storia della letteratura italiana." VOL. 41, p. 42.

SCALA, Flaminio. *Il Teatro delle favole rappresentative,* etc. Venice, 1611. Collection of 50 scenarios.

SCHERILLO, Michele. *L'Opera Buffa Napoletana*. Milano, 1916.

SEICENTO (seventeenth century). *La Vita Ital^{ne} Nel Seicento*. Firenze, 1894; Milano, 1895.

SEMAR, John. *Pre-Shakespearean Stage*. Florence, 1913.

SEPET, Marius Cyrille Alphonse. *Le drame chrétien au Moyen Age*. Didier, Paris, 1878. *Origines catholiques du théâtre moderne*. P. Lethielleux, Paris, 1901.

SOLERTI, Angelo. *Le origini del melodramma*. Fratelli Boca, Torino, 1903. *Gli Albori del Melodramma*. Remo Sandron, Milano, 1904–1905. 3 VOLS. Is chiefly a collection of plays. *Musica, Ballo e Drammatica alla Corte Medicea, dal 1600 al 1637*. Bemporad, 1905.

SOUBIERS, Albert. *Le Théâtre italien,* etc. Paris, 1910.

STENDHAL. *La vie de Metastasio*.

TAMMASO, Niccolò. *Storia civile della Letteraria*. Turin, 1872.

TIPALDO, G. di. *Biografia degli Italiani illustri*. Venice, 1837.

VATASSO, Marco. *Per la storia del Dramma sacro in Italia*. Tip. Vaticana, Roma, 1903.

LIST OF ILLUSTRATIONS

VOLUME II

The plates either face the page designated or are grouped after it.

Frontispiece: Fêtes vénitiennes, after a painting by Watteau.

Metastasio   *page*   3

Ruzzante (1525)   32

Fiorinette (1533)

Coviello (1550)

Harlequino (1570)

Spavento (1577)

Isabella (1600)

Beltrame (1613)

Tabarin (1618)

Goldoni   81

Masked Actors: Coviello and a Sicilian   88

Gozzi   96

Mezzetin, after a painting by Watteau   104

Tartaglia (1620)   112

Orazio (1645)

Narcisino (1650)

Biscegliese (1680)

La Cantatrice (1694)   *Le Notaire* (1725)   *Polichinelle* (1820)

LIST OF ILLUSTRATIONS

Leandre (1850)   112

Gianduja (1858)

Alfieri   134

Niccolini   166

Monti   208

Foscolo   221

Pellico   227

Manzoni   230

D'Annunzio   248

The Italian Theatre

Metastasio

CHAPTER I

METASTASIO'S LIFE

Metastasio was first applauded, then neglected. It is time to assign him his proper place among Italian poets: In our first notice of him, he stands on a stone pillar extemporizing poetry: When ten years old, is adopted by Gianvincenzo Gravina: Is often required to improvise, which injures his health: He visits Naples: Is given the clerical title of *Abaté*, and for the rest of his life wears the *Abaté* dress: Gravina dies, leaving Metastasio a legacy: He studies law in Naples and writes poetry: He meets the actress Marianna Bulgarelli called Romanina, who falls in love with him: Metastasio lives with her in Rome: He gives up a legal career and becomes a playwright: Music is the essence of Metastasio's genius: His mysterious love-affair in Rome: Metastasio accepts position of *Poeta Cesareo* at the court of Vienna, where he avoids court ceremonies and lived with an Italian family: Metastasio's best work produced during his first ten years in Vienna: His failing health, early senility: Marianna is unhappy; dies and leaves her fortune to Metastasio: Metastasio grieves for her, but is comforted by Countess d'Althan, who centers her life on his welfare: Metastasio visits her twice every day: Countess d'Althan dies; Metastasio grieves: Metastasio refuses invitations to return to Italy: Lives with the Martinez family, to whom he leaves his fortune: His last years were unhappy: His friendship for Farinello: Metastasio was the trusted confidant of several good women: Metastasio always preserved religious appearances: Dies, after a short illness, over eighty years old.

METASTASIO was applauded, admired, almost worshipped during his lifetime. He has since been neglected; and his conception of life, philosophic ideal, and style of literature have been scorned. Both these judgments need revision. The time has come for assigning to Metastasio his proper place among Italian poets.[1]

Pietro Armando Dominico Trapassi was born in Rome, January 3, 1698. He was the fourth child of Felici Trapassi and Francesca Galasti. Our first notice of him is the story of his encounter with Gianvincenzo Gravina, in the piazza dei Cesarini. A boy of ten stands on a stone pillar, extemporizing poetry to a group of his playfellows. Two elderly gentlemen, on their way to the Farnese Palace, listen. One of these is the famous jurist Gianvincenzo Gravina. "The child was pretty; his voice was beautiful; the verses followed each other with singular facility. Gravina was astonished at the ease and grace of the improvisation," and bade him come to his house next morning.[2]

On this visit, by the "vivacity of his eye and that peculiar gentleness which, during the course of his long life, everywhere won the hearts of those who came near him," he so won Gravina's heart that he adopted the boy. The anecdote suggests later readjustment. Would the elderly and cautious Gravina, a master in Roman Law, the Arcadian, have acted so impulsively? The boy's improvisation was not an extraordinary feat. Improvisations are not rare in Italy. Young people frequently join in playful *stornelli,* singing improvised strophes, each beginning with the name of a flower, each a coy defiance, an amorous challenge, a witty rebuke, or other device of rustic love-making. Something more must have attracted Gravina's attention. The two sons of Felice Trapassi were his pupils; and it is probable that the scholarly Gravina discerned Pietro's unusual gifts, and hoped to acquire fame for himself by proxy.

Pietro Trapassi was ten years old when he was transplanted from home-like surroundings to the chill atmosphere of classical studies and a grave bachelor's propriety. Gravina translated the name of "Trapassi" into its Greek equivalent "Metastasio," from *meta* and *stao* meaning change from one place to another, as the Italian *trapasso.* Of the throbbing street life of Rome, of the sun and shade that constitute a boy's happy days, he henceforth knew nothing.[3] Through the monotony of long days, he was drilled in treatises of ancient law and in unabridged Latin and Greek grammars. At dinner, he listens to Gravina's learned guests discoursing on the law. He is often required to amuse the audience by repeating Latin poetry, or improvising poems.[4]

Metastasio certainly resented the strain inflicted on body and spirit by this practice of improvisation. The scene may be thus reconstructed: a subject is chosen, then someone sits at the spinetta or clavicembalo and plays slow chords, while the boy meditates. He begins slowly; painfully he delivers his first lines; then his voice rises louder; his utterance is more rapid; his gesture more ample; his poetical frenzy is restrained only by habits of courtly grace. When the last words have been spoken, the exhausted boy, pale and panting, sits on the chair brought to him.[5]

For improvisation, cavalier Perfetti[6] and Corilla Olimpica had been crowned in the Capitol with Petrarch's laurel wreath; and not a voice had been raised to denounce the desecration. With the exaggeration that often characterizes these pseudo-paternal affections, Gravina was proud of his pupil's success. He did not note the growing pallor and frequent coughing. But he immediately stopped Metastasio's improvisation when warned by donna Anna Francesca Pinelli di Sangro, a young girl who afterwards married Prince Pignatelli di Belmonte.

Gravina took Metastasio to visit his native Roggiano in Calabria. Stopping in Naples, the famous Hellenist and his pupil were warmly welcomed. Great houses opened their doors to such guests. Metastasio improvised eighty stanzas at one sitting! At the Duke of Limatola's palace, he was the central figure in a group of young, pretty, high-born girls. Two of these were to exert a lasting influence on Metastasio's life. One of them, already a widow, mother of five children, though only twenty years old, donna Marianna Pignatelli, Countess d'Althan, will play a first rôle in Metastasio's amorous career; the other, donna Francesca, probably saved his life when she made Gravina promise that the boy should not improvise. She insisted that he be sent to her family residence at Massa di Somma, where Metastasio recovered from incipient lung trouble.

When Gravina returned to Naples, Metastasio remained with Gregorio Caroprese at Scalea. Caroprese taught Metastasio to think; also, he took the boy boating, hunting, tramping. Metastasio never forgot the little room where the sound of the breaking waves had lulled him to sleep. He remembered the rowboats, and the boys with whom he had studied, and Caroprese's little dog—all joyful oases in the monotony of his boyhood.

Metastasio resumed his law study in Rome. In 1717, he published a volume of short poems which contained his first dramatic attempt, *Il Giustino*. Gravina obtained for him the title of *Abaté*. Such a clerical title imported slight religious bonds, and was the first step towards advancement in many professions, and especially in church or state employment. An *abaté* wore becoming and not expensive clothes. Among a crowd of noblemen gorgeous in embroidered diamond-buttoned coats and waistcoats, with dangling swords, and a double gold chain supporting a watch and tinkling trinkets, their movements embarrassed by the long heavy cloak, and the beplumed hat perched on their enormous wigs, the contrast of the *abatino's* simple elegance shone in relief. His coat and waistcoat of soft black material, his tight silk knee-breeches, the short cloak hanging gracefully from one shoulder, on his head a cocked hat daintily poised on curly hair, or small wig, were well adapted to set off the slender figure of a youthful *abaté* as he bends over a lady's hand, stoops at her feet, or renders some slight service to one of these rulers of *settecento* society.[7] Metastasio "never afterwards discarded this garb"; also "he took the first tonsura and the four minors." Metastasio did not intend to become a priest, though he obtained a pension of 300 *scudi*.

Gravina died on January 6, 1718, leaving a legacy to Metastasio, who shortly after moved to Naples. He remembered those aristocratic circles, benevolent patrons, and beautiful patronesses. "To be a great lawyer there," writes a contemporary, "means to be wealthy and powerful." And Metastasio wanted to be honored and wealthy. He found a place with one of the best lawyers of Naples, Giovanantonio Castagnola.[8] His biographers relate that Metastasio was admitted into the Arcadian assembly during Gravina's lifetime. They forget the feud between partisans of Crescimbeni and Gravinians. The annals of Arcadia show that Metastasio was admitted on April 15, 1718, three months after Gravina's death, when the dying man's words of apology and for reconciliation had been answered by the Arcadian Custode.[9] On May 29, 1718, at a solemn assembly of Arcadia held to commemorate Gravina, in the place from which Gravina had departed in wrathful humiliation, his pupil delivered a poem in terza rima, *La strada della gloria,* in honor of his memory. The poem is not a cold and stupid thing, as alleged by a foreign critic.

Metastasio's biographer says his income amounted to 40 *scudi* per month, adding that "this sum sufficed for his expenses; the more so, as he was alien to all sorts of games, especially from those termed *'di resto,'* and from dissipation and debauchery."

Biographies represent Castagnola as a gruff lawyer who forbade his clerk to write or read poetry. Why then did he admit the poet to his studio? Metastasio's poems were dedicated to important personages, were read or recited at fashionable gatherings. Castagnola surely knew that Metastasio was courting Giambattista Vico's daughter Luisa, and composing immortal love songs for her.[10]

Everyone asked for the name of the author of *Gli Orti Esperidi.* Signora Marianna Benti Bulgarelli, "La Romanina," who had sung the part of Venus, "spent much money to discover the name of the poet." Yet Metastasio's name was printed in full letters at the end of the dedicatory epistle to Princess Borghese di Sulmona, which prefaced the book of *Gli Orti Esperidi.* Marianna Bulgarelli wished to attract the author of a successful play. A woman of social distinction, an actress and famous singer, and a patroness of musicians and singers, she naturally wanted to exhibit and lionize Metastasio.[11] Romanina's intellect and her aspirations were superior to those of contemporary actors. Ambitious she was, but not vain. With the first evidence of failing beauty, in place of mere theatrical applause, she desired a salon, to be the central figure in a gallery of famous persons. Marianna Bulgarelli was her own mistress in a fine house; and she owned a creditable husband who lent her benevolent assistance. Her salon was already provided with composers, poets, singers, a few noblemen, and a bodyguard of older celebrities, Scarletti, Porpora, Vinci, Leo, and other composers. A list of Romanina's guests is also the roll of the best known Neapolitan names in the world of music. Metastasio, the applauded author of *Gli Orti Espridi,* the protégé of Prince Borghese and of Princess di Belmonte, was worth taking pains to secure.

Many critics discuss the exact nature of Metastasio's relation with Romanina. Was it love? Was it only affection on one side and gratitude on the other? And if it was "love," what kind of love? That Marianna Bulgarelli offered hospitality to her protégé and his family, and asked Metastasio to return to Rome and live with her and her husband, and that he accepted, rather discredits the suggestion of a secret amour. It was not unusual for a bachelor to dwell with a family of friends. The anonymous biographer writes: "Here then was Metastasio, dwelling with Romanina in a union of the most enviable concord, a union which never varied until her death."[12] Romanina wanted Metastasio to live with her; and to make sure of him, she presently removed from Naples to Rome. The anonymous biographer writes that Metastasio was not inclined to give up the legal career, and that Marianna Bulgarelli persuaded him to make one household of both families, as she wanted to live quietly on the fruit of her past activities and give up singing. Naples meant for Metastasio the probability of wealth and honor from the legal profession, but Rome offered the possibility of some papal office and leisure for the composition of poetry and greater intimacy with Marianna. The two families settled in Rome in a house in via del Corso. How Metastasio spent these years is unknown. He certainly wrote plays for the *Teatro delle Dame,* or Aliberti.

Romanina's care of Metastasio's physical welfare and poetical career was the most important factor of his success. But for her assistance, he would have plodded on in Castagnola's office, possibly winning a position in the Neapolitan "Curia," scribbling occasional poetry, and basking in the sunshine of aristocratic patronage. In Rome, Romanina introduced him to the world behind the curtain; she taught him his craftsmanship; she awoke his ambition for public applause; and she stirred his musical talent.[13]

Metastasio's success and popularity are due chiefly to the music of his poetry. Music is the essence of his genius. All praise to Romanina for leading him to Porpora as a pupil, for introducing him to the best composers of the grand Neapolitan school, for singing to him and for him, for surrounding him with the best singers, and for thus revealing his talent to himself and to others. Metastasio took to music as a bird takes to flying. He learned to sing, and was educated in the intricacies of musical composition. He could read the most complicated scores and sing the vocal parts of each, and could also compose canons.[14]

In Metastasio's biography, 300 *scudi* is said to have been paid for each one of his dramas, a considerable sum for a bachelor of regular habits, already provided with an income through Gravina's bounty. An *abaté* was not expected to squander money on his apparel. The memoirs of Goldoni offer some information; and Benedetto Marcello's *Teatro alla Moda,* a full picture of that microcosm of intrigue and gossip, vanity and caprice, which lived and quarreled behind the curtain, and with which Metastasio had to contend.[15]

Critics have sought mysteries in this eventless life. In Venice, there was some sort of idyll, which left no trace. But in Rome, something serious happened. About this so-called "mystery," the anonymous biographer gives this reticent account: "Free from all care, Metastasio resumed his relations with Arcadia and with old friends, and made many new ones with persons of great distinction, as he was everywhere invited and appreciated for his amiable character, his humility, and his polite manners. His good heart, however, got him into sad trouble. I cannot and must not narrate the cause, as some persons concerned are still living. I can only say that his polite partiality for a certain person produced, against him and against her, slanders that were only with great difficulty silenced. They were stirred again when he was in Vienna, with a renewal of his grief; but then prudently smothered by means of Cardinal Gentili, to whom he applied, as we will show in due time. The unnamed person having afterwards *taken a resolution,* there was an end to this thing." Does this mystery explain Metastasio's voluntary exile to Vienna? It may have been the cause of his never returning to Italy.[16]

In 1729, Metastasio received from Vienna a letter signed by Prince Pio di Savoia of the Imperial Chapel, offering him the post of *poeta cesareo* at the court of Charles VI. This offer was not unexpected. Metastasio knew that his friends were seeking it for him. When a great lady provided for her protégés, she also asserted her own social importance. Princess di Belmonte secured the assistance of her sister-in-law, the all-powerful Countess D'Althan. The Countess remembered the gifted boy whom she had seen in Naples years ago; the poet remembered the beautiful Countess, and was pleased to thank her for her patronage.[17]

The *poeta cesareo,* Apostolo Zeno, was eager to leave the damp and cold, the ceremonies and the intellectual vacuity of Vienna. He pined for his own sunlit Venice, his congenial occupation of collecting medals and books and of directing his "Giornale dei Letterati."[18] On being asked by Charles VI to name his successor, he probably mentioned Metastasio's name, either because Countess D'Althan asked him to or because he realized that Metastasio could achieve great success. Metastasio gladly accepted the invitation, though he claimed that 3000 Florins, the salary offered, was inadequate. No tie of affection, no moral bond, restrained Metastasio from accepting the splendid offer that came from Vienna. There was perhaps an urgent reason for his departure. When we know more about that mystery of his Roman amours, this reason may be better understood. Reticent hints in his letters suggest this as one reason for his leaving Rome.[19]

To reconstruct the moral, intellectual, and social conditions in the Imperial Viennese court-life that surrounded Metastasio, that Vienna of Eastern barbarism and Western scepticism, of bigotry and debauchery, would be an interesting historical study. But, for our purpose, such historical reconstruction would be only an *hors-d'oeuvre,* since Metastasio was not greatly influenced by his surroundings. He lived with an Italian family, and refused to learn German. He avoided court ceremonies, made friends with Italians, and finally, when he again fell in love, it was with an Italian.

Metastasio is sometimes represented as an idle and servile courtier. The rare idleness of a man who has left material for fifteen big volumes of poetry and prose, the idleness of a poet who, like Molière, like Flaubert, like Manzoni, like many great writers, found it necessary laboriously to correct and revise his work before he could produce such apparently facile poetry! The charge of servility is not consistent with the fact that he refused all titles offered him by Maria Theresa.

Metastasio produced the larger and the better part of his work during his first ten years in Vienna. Then the impulse died out: and, when the placid waters of court life were ruffled by the great war, when Maria Theresa, absorbed in the most difficult task that ever faced a princess and a mother, forgot to give orders to her court poet, when Metastasio's unheroic soul was shaken by vague apprehensions, his health and his intellectual energy gave way. Early senility was the price paid for his intellectual precocity.

As the dreary years passed, he wrote with increasing difficulty; but he never refused an offer, never grumbled at the Imperial avarice that offered no respite to such a faithful servant. Metastasio's daily life was as uneventful as any such long and splendid career could be. His love for Marianna Bulgarelli and his attachment for Countess D'Althan are stressed because there is so little else to relate. There is also very little positive knowledge about these two romances. Metastasio carefully shielded from curiosity and malice the two women who gave him the best of their hearts and lives.[20]

When, after the agony of parting, she faced the dull reality of absence, Romanina, like all married women who will neither abandon their position nor renounce their love, was most unhappy. Was it Metastasio's fault? He wrote her gentle, considerate letters, recalling the past and refusing to hold out impossible hopes for the future. A younger or a more passionate woman might have sacrificed position and reputation to follow him; but Romanina was middle-aged and sensible; she cared for many things besides her young friend or lover. So she remained in Rome, chafed, and became jealous and exacting. She did not follow Metastasio to Vienna; but she purposed to send her husband there. Time passed, she grew more dissatisfied with herself and with Metastasio, and her letters were more pressing. Oh, the sad story of these incompleted amours. Remorse has its compensations which are unknown to regret.

That Metastasio tried to soften the definitive parting is evident from his letters. In one letter he writes, "read the third act, scene three, of my *Adriano,* observe the character of the emperor as he describes himself, and you will find mine." Metastasio tries to make her realize that the heart of a poet is revealed in his writings. The letter continues: "You see that I know myself; but that is not enough to correct me. This obstinacy is a fault that torments me, without compensation of joy; I realize well that though I cannot get rid of it, it forces me to speculate on the tyranny exerted by our body over our soul. Why, when my reason, discoursing calmly and seriously, is persuaded that these excessive doubts and hesitations are but useless, tormenting, miserable errors, an impediment to my work, why can I not shake them off and enact the resolution, so many times asserted to myself, to doubt no more? . . . The consequence is clear, because the machinery of this our imperfect dwelling leads us to conceive things as coloured by the colour they assume on their way before reaching our mind: just as the sunbeams appear to our eyes either yellow, green, or crimson, according to the colour of the glass or drapery through which they filter to illumine the place we are in. Hence it is evident that men do not act in accordance with reason, but through mechanical impulse; and they afterwards adapt their reason to the impulsive action. If it were not so, all those who think well must act well; and we see just the contrary. Be not vexed if I write philosophy to you. You know I have no one else to talk to; and then, as I write, I recall to my mind this same sort of talk in which we spent together so many many happy hours." It is a clear statement of his mental position and a considerate manner of telling a woman that she has lost the power to sway his actions. Why should Metastasio alone be condemned because he cannot love forever the woman who had captured his youthful affections? Metastasio's detractors seem to believe that faithfulness to such a love is the rule and not the exception among artists.

Then, suddenly, came news of Romanina's death. He did not conceal his grief, but retired to his rooms and nursed his sorrow— perhaps his remorse. Metastasio's affection was not the love that Romanina desired from him. He therefore refused to accept the inheritance that she left him. He directed his brother Leopold to convey it to Romanina's husband. Leopold grumbled and quarreled with Domenico Bulgarelli, who married a second wife after

Metastasio had generously given him the fortune of his first wife. Perhaps this indecorous quarrel disinclined Metastasio to return to Italy. He also ordered his brother to burn all his letters to Roma-nina, as he had destroyed all her letters to him. Even if some of these epistles should be found, they would not reconstruct the psychology of a situation and of a mentality so different from any modern instance.

The grief caused by one Marianna was assuaged by another Marianna. It was Metastasio's fortune that the love of good women should smooth his life's asperities. Each was named Marianna. Marianna Pignatelli, Countess d'Althan, may have been the first dream of the youthful poet who in Naples saw her splendour of youth and beauty. Then she went the way of court favour, and perhaps of Imperial preference. As the boy ripened into manhood, the image of the lady may have acquired that "crystallization" which Stendhal has so aptly defined; and, when he became *poeta cesareo* through the aid of this great lady, loving gratitude was added to youthful romance. In Vienna, Metastasio was surrounded by a court of dazzling splendour and of aristocratic rigidity. When he felt chilled by the lack of that "gentilezza"—supreme virtue of the high-born in Italy—he rejoiced to find friendship from the lady who first had smiled on his boyish triumphs.

Though humbly born, Metastasio equalled Countess d'Althan in that refinement of manners, politeness, and courtesy which distin-guished them from the proud, bigoted, Viennese court. Metastasio paid homage to his benefactress; she encouraged his devotion; and they became indispensable to each other. When Metastasio was nursing his grief for Romanina's death, Countess d'Althan did a brave thing: she went openly to visit and comfort him. She carried him away to her country seat in Moravia; she arranged for him little concerts, in which her son played the violin to Metastasio's singing. Her life was centered on his welfare. Yet they respected appearances. He always mentions her with her title, kisses her hand, and observes the elaborate forms of politeness then required. Every letter, even the simplest note exchanged between them, was destroyed.[21]

Twice every day he visits his lady-love; first, immediately after hearing mass in the morning, and a longer visit in the evening. There is something very sweet and delicate in this twenty-four years of unpresuming devotion. Romance at twenty has been often sung; who will tell the beauty of that more enduring love that soothes the worries and softens the afflictions of growing age and declining health? Metastasio's health was never good, though he lived to a very old age. He was subject to nervous spasms something like convulsions, which physicians could not cure. Countess d'Althan kept him in the country either on her estates in Moravia or in some other place of *villeggiatura*. When Countess d'Althan died, Metastasio was as sorely afflicted as such a nature could be. After this bereavement, he writes to Princess di Belmonte, "So many favours received, so many and so great qualities admired, a service, a habit, a friendship of twenty-four years, are ties that cannot be severed without a terrible shock." Later he writes, "The wound is as yet intolerant of any medical assistance . . . Day by day I realize that my loss cannot tolerate any compensation. . . ."

Why did not Metastasio return to Italy? Landau declares that Metastasio, having become a German subject, did not care to leave Vienna. Every manifestation of the poet's feelings, every expression of his letters, belies this assertion, though many influential Italians entreated him to return, and a Pope condescended to express this wish. He writes: "Everything cannot be told, yet, believe me, I never give up the idea of seeing Naples again." He explains his refusal by philosophical arguments such as "the object over which persuasion works is the soul not the body. Hence neither Demosthenes nor Cicero will persuade a steeple to change its place." He speaks of his health, of affairs that require his presence —all plausible excuses to account for his attachment to the place where he has built his nest. A slave to regular hours, an assiduous reader of the classics, content with a few learned friends, such a change would mean havoc in all Metastasio's dearest habits. Probably the splendour of court life also attracted him. Other unspoken motives may have kept him from Rome. The quarrel between his brother and Domenico Bulgarelli? That mysterious love-affair? Was the unnamed lady now dead? Any hypothesis will do, since Metastasio hides his real feelings.[22]

In the same manner, a veil surrounds his relations with the Martinez family, especially with a third Marianna, daughter or sister to the poet's host. Neither the not impossible hypothesis of a paternity nor the absurd idea of a senile attachment is required to account for Metastasio's fondness for a girl whom he had known from her childhood. The Martinez family appreciated the honor and the financial advantage of having such a guest. They copied the letters that Metastasio sent to Italy. Many of these letters were preserved, and afterwards given or sold to the Viennese Biblioteca. This devotion of the whole family, and especially of the young woman who smiled on and cared for the aged poet, explains the generosity of Metastasio's will bequeathing them a respectable fortune.

Metastasio's last years were not happy. The glory which haloed his name, the terms "divine poet," "Italian Sophocles," royal and imperial gifts, election to membership in many academies, visits from grand personages, could not soothe his sensitive heart. He was discouraged, lonely. He shared in the afflictions of the Imperial family.[23] Metastasio had found Maria Theresa an apt pupil, learning Italian from him and acting in plays he composed for her. This noble Queen, whom Europe admired and feared, this excellent mother of many children, still found time for granting him a kind word, a little present, an increase of salary. After the Empress' death, Metastasio appeared quite changed. By his letters, the change does not appear to have been so sudden, but to have come very early, with frequent allusions to his age, to his difficulty in accomplishing his tasks. To the very end he translated, and discussed his favorite classics with a few intimate friends, especially Count Perlas and Count Canale. He never relaxed in his affectionate correspondence with the friends whom he had left in Italy. With Princess di Belmonte he constantly exchanged letters. His correspondence with his brother Leopold was frequently unpleasant, but ever kind and considerate. His affection for Farinello retained some of its early boyish vivacity. Farinello's brilliant career in Spain, he followed with eager delicacy. Yet their friendship lasted not *malgré que* but *parce que* they were separated. Metastasio is never so unlike himself as when he endeavors to tune his harp to Farinello's note. When, after the storms of his chequered career, Farinello settled in Bologna and, with many noisy relations, lived the spacious life of a country gentleman, he invited Metastasio to join him. What a tragic ending to their long friendship! The "twin brothers" had led such different lives, had developed such different characters, that their continued friendship was mainly due to separation. Farinello was a man of action, of intrigue, and of that vanity that does duty for ambition, and that had nothing in common with Metastasio's refined delicacy, his dislike for courtly gatherings, his scholarly habits.

Metastasio was the trusted confidant, delicate friend, of good and superior-minded women. There were ties of reliance and deep sympathy between him and Romanina, even though the more passionate element prevailed. Countess d'Althan was certainly a world-wise woman. Knowing life's scandals, she appreciated the delicacy, the spiritual companionship of her elderly friend. Even his last affection for a third Marianna has a charm of delicate vagueness. Kindly he supervised her education, provided for her, expecting and asking little from her in return.[24]

This Marianna Martinez remains a connecting link between the musical world of Metastasio and that new world of music which was then dawning. As he sat at the same table, Joseph Haydn, who taught her harmony and was often a guest in the Martinez household, may have learned precious musical lessons from Metastasio. The pupil of Porpora, the composer of several symphonic pieces, had certainly something to say to the young musician who, living under the same roof, was honoured by the friendship of the court-poet of European fame. Metastasio's memoirs and letters show him calmly awaiting the end of a life that contained little wrongdoing and much glory.[25]

Metastasio preserved religious appearances without attaining deep religious experience. The dogmas of his faith scarcely influenced his conduct of life. He attended mass, he wrote several religious poems, but he was not inspired by religious fervour. He said that it was less trouble to accept the dogmas of the church than to discuss them. He writes, "some philosophy and much patience" help one through every trouble. He advises Daniele Florio "to wash himself free from the prejudices one is apt to learn in books, by the practical knowledge of the great book of the world." Had any one told him of Alfieri's indignation at seeing him paying homage at the coach window of a princess, Metastasio would have smiled, surprised. Reverence to Imperial power was to him an undiscussed duty. With the same humility, he accepted the special benediction sent him by Pope Pius, who was then a visitor at the Imperial Court.

The story which shows Metastasio, dying with his own paraphrase of the *Miserere* on his lips, is probably apocryphal: the verse as quoted is unlike his style. He was more than eighty, had never been strong, had aged prematurely. Death came kindly after a short illness. The Martinez family inherited his fortune, his furniture, and the precious legacy of his letters, which they either sold or gave to the Viennese archives.[26]

NOTES

CHAPTER I

Chronology

1698 Birth of Pietro Trapassi, son of Felice Trapassi, a native of Assisi, and Marianna Galasti, a native of Bologna.

1709 Giambattista Gravina takes the boy to live with him. Changes his name to Metastasio.

1712 Metastasio goes to Scalea in Calabria and there studies philosophy under Gregorio Caroprese. On his way through Naples he has great success with his improvisation, and meets Princess di Belmonte and Countess d'Althan.

1714 Metastasio adopts the title and garb of *abaté,* which he never discarded. He is also admitted into Arcadia with the name of Artino Corasio.

1718 Death of Gravina, who bequeaths part of his fortune to Metastasio.

1720 Metastasio goes to Naples and finds employment with Giovanantonio Castagnola.

1722 By order of the Viceroy of Naples, Metastasio writes the serenata *Gli Orti Esperidi.*

1724 to 1727 His attachment to Marianna Bulgarelli. Composes *La Galatea l'Angelica, la Didone, il Siroe.*

1727 to 1730 *Ezio, il Catone, la Semiramide, l'Alessandro, l'Artaserse.*

1730 He leaves for Vienna.

1731 *l'Adriano,* which is considered first of his second and best manner.

1732 *il Demofronte, la Clemenza di Tito,* and *Attilio Regolo* (the last was not represented until ten years later) *l'Olimpiade, il Giuseppe Riconosciuto.*

1734 Death of Marianna Bulgarelli. Metastasio renounces inheritance in favor of her husband.

1736 *Achille in Sciro, il Ciro riconosciuto, il Temistocle*

1739 *la Zenobia.*

1740 After the death of Emperor Charles VI, interruption of work by Metastasio. End of his best manner.

1744 *l'Ipermestra*

1751 *Il Re Pastore*

1752 *l'Eroe Cinese*

1755 Death of Countess d'Althan for 25 years his patroness.

1756 *Nitteti*

1762 *Trionfo di Clelia*

1765 *Romolo ed Ersilia*

1782 12 April, death of Metastasio.

BIBLIOGRAPHY

Vita | dell'Abaté | Pietro Metastasio | Poeta Cesareo | aggiuntivi | Le Massime e Sentenze-estratte dalle sue opere | Firenze, 1799 | nella stamperia di Filippo Stecchi | Con approvazione. (Abbreviation V. P.M.)

Opere | di | Pietro Metastasio | Volume Unico, Trieste | Sezione Letterario Artistica del LLOYD AUSTRIACO | 1857. (Ab. Op. P.M.)

Studies of the Eighteenth Century in Italy, by Vernon Lee | London, W. Satchell & Co. | 12 Tavistock Street, Covent Garden | 1880. (Ab. V. L.)

Letterature Italiana, Francesco De Sanctis | Napoli, Morando, 1879 | Nuovi Saggi Critici, Francesco De Sanctis | Napoli, Morando. (Ab. DS.)

Storia Letteraria d'Italia | Scritta da una Societa di Professori, Tullio Concari, Prof. di Lettere Italiane nel R. Istituto Tecnico di Milano | IL SETTECENTO | casa Editrice Francesco Vallardi | Milano-Napoli-Firenze. (Ab. Sett.)

La Vita Italiana | del | Settecento | Conferenze tenute a Firenze nel 1859, | da R. Bonfadini, Is Del Lungo, Fratelli Treves, edit. (Ab. V. I.)

Francesco Albergati e i sui tempi, | E. Masi | Bologna | (Ab. E. M.)

Ferdinando Nunziante, | Metastasio a Napoli, | in Nuova Antologia 15 Agosto. 1 Settembre 1895. (F. N.)

Lettere disperse ed inedite di P. M. per cura di Giosuè Carducci Bologna | 1883. (Ab. Carducci)

Lettere disperse ed inedite di P. M. raccolte da C. Antona Traversi con appendice di diversi scritti sul Metastasio. (C. An.)

Manuale | della Letteratura Italiana, compilato dai professori, Alessandro D'Ancona e Orazio Bacci, Vol. V | Firenze, G. Barbera, Editore: 1895. (Ab. A. D'A.)

Landau: La letterature italiana alla Corte d'Austria (trad. It) Aquila Grossi, 1880. (Ab. Landau)

G. Cugnoni: Pietro Metastasio e l'Arcadia, Roma, Forzani 1882.

Giosuè Carducci: Prose: Bologna, ditta Nicola Zanichelli, 1905. Page 887, Pietro Metastasio.

Oreste Tomassini, in Nuova Antologia: Pietro Metastasio e lo svolgimento del melodramma italiano, Vol. 33. An. 1882.

Davide Silvagni: La corte e la società romana nei xviii e xix secoli.

Letters from Italy, | by John Earl of Cork and Orrery | London 1773.

Emilio De Marchi: Letters e letterati italiani del secolo xviii, Milano, Briola 1882.

G. Guerzoni, | Il Teatro nel xviii secolo, | Milano, Treves, 1876.

Giosuè Carducci: Prefazione ai due volumi Lirici del secolo xviii, Firenze, Barbera, 1871.

(An account of the manners and customs of Italy, with observations on the mistakes of some travellers, with regard to that country, by Joseph Baretti, VOL. II, London, printed for T. Davies, in Russell Street, MDCCXVIII, page 175.)

1. Metastasio's life should be read in the anonymous *Vita di Pietro Metastasio, Poeta Cesareo,* from which all other biographers have

borrowed. This short narrative of an almost eventless life was not written with critical discrimination nor is it sufficiently documented. But it has the merit of actuality; it reveals the prudent reticence, the extreme courtesy of a contemporary who realized that Metastasio's friends could control his interpretation of facts and resent any indiscretion. The author says that he will simply tell "the history of this great man." This he could not do in a time when emphasis and flattery was expected from biographers. Simplicity was unknown to him, as it was to Metastasio. He has Metastasio's standards, and judges men according to the same criterion. Besides this almost contemporary narrative, C. Antonio Traversi, Giosuè Carducci, and others have published many of Metastasio's letters. Yet very little of the poet's inner life is revealed. Metastasio writes with the reticence of one who knows that his epistle will be handed around to friends, will be commented upon and admired, perhaps criticized, and probably be copied and preserved.

2. Felice Trapassi came from the city of Saint Francis, Assisi. His enlistment in the Papal Guard and his inscription in the roll of Assisi nobility indicate respectability. His wife, Francesca Galasti, was a Bolognese. To this cross of two races rich in vital stamina, Metastasio owed his healthy temperament. He was vicariously held at the baptismal font by Cardinal Pietro Ottoboni, nephew of the late Pope; a favor which Cardinals freely granted to anyone even slightly connected with the Papal court as was Trapassi, the former papal guard.

3. Children in those days were not much petted; very little cruelty existed even in the lower classes, but also very little care and tenderness. Wealthy and aristocratic families entrusted their numerous offspring to their valets, or to that humble domestic, the *abaté* of the house. Middle-class parents sent their children to priestly schools, colleges, and convents. The tradespeople sought easy ways for keeping children out of mischief. David Silvagni mentions little wooden

armchairs wherein children were solidly fastened for long hours every day. Elders must be obeyed and respected. Kissing the hand of parents and of aged relatives was enforced. Children addressed their parents in the third person or in the second plural, while they were spoken to in the more familiar "thou." Their amusements were few. Family portraits show the children in rigid composure and strict observance of decorum.

4. "Gravina gave his new pupil a room by himself, furnished with all requirements. He provided him with books such as suited his own ideas and fitted with his plan of education, and which might prove useful and appropriate." (V. P. M., p. 11.)

5. In a letter to Algarotti dated Vienna, August, 1750, when Metastasio was more than fifty years old, he describes the torments of these early years:

"I cannot deny that a natural disposition, a special aptitude for harmony and measure were noticed in me, at an earlier age than such gifts usually appear, that is between my tenth and eleventh year of age. This strange phenomenon so dazzled my great master, Gravina, that he considered me as a plant worthy of being cultivated. Hence, and until I was sixteen, I exhibited myself to speak in extempore verse on any subject, while Rolli, Vanni, and Cavalier Perfetto, all grown men, were my opponents. . . .

"Now this practice became for me both heavy and harmful; heavy because, in obedience to continual important demands, I was made to go about almost every day, sometimes twice in the day, either to gratify a great lady's whim, or to satisfy the curiosity of some illustrious blockhead, or to fill the gap in some solemn academy; thus losing the best of the time required for my studies; harmful, because it disagreed with my frail health. People noticed that in the excitement of this violent appeal to my brain, my head became heated, and my face red, while at the same time my hands and the rest of my body remained cold."

Giuseppe Baretti writes: "With regard to their *Improvvisazione* my English reader will not easily be made to conceive it as a thing which requires great poetical powers; nor is it possible to give a just idea of it to a stranger. Yet I can aver that it is a very great entertainment, and it excites great surprise, to hear two of their best *improvvisatori* 'et cantarepares et respondere parati,' and each eager to excel, expatiate in *ottava rima* upon any subject moderately susceptible of poetical amplification. I have been astonished at the rapidity of their expressions, the easiness of their rhymes, the justness of their numbers, the copiousness of their images, and the general warmth and impetuosity of their thoughts; and I have seen crowds of listeners hurried, as well as myself, into a vortex of delight whose emotion acquired more and more violence as the bards grew more and more inflamed by the repeated shoutings of the bystanders, and by the force of that opposition which each encountered from his antagonist." Baretti, *op. cit.,* p. 154.

Giuseppe Baretti (1719–1789) was born in Turin. He quarreled with his family in 1735, and left home to stay with his uncle in Guastalla. From Guastalla he wandered to Verona and other places, until he arrived in Venice where he made friends with the Gozzi brothers and was admitted into the academy of Granelleschi —the anti-Goldonian set. Thence he went to Milan and was admitted into the important academy, "I transformati," which met in the house of Count Imbonati.

In 1751 he went to England and remained nine years, teaching Italian and earning the good opinion of Johnson and his friends, and getting into mischief owing to his quarrelsomeness. On his return journey to Italy, he crossed through France, Spain, and Portugal; and afterwards made a very pleasant narrative of this travel in *Letters to his Brothers*. Failing to obtain a place in Milan, he returned to Venice and undertook the publication of the literary paper *La Frusta Letteraria*. His language was so severe and reckless that he got into trouble, was obliged to leave Venice, repaired to Ancona, and afterwards returned to London, where he died May 5, 1789.

In Mrs. Thrale's papers, this note was found for the *World:* "Mr. Conductor—Let not the death of Baretti pass unnoticed by *The World,* seeing that Baretti was a wit, if not a scholar; and had for five and thirty years lived in a foreign country, whose language he so completely mastered, that he could satirize its inhabitants in their own tongue, better than they knew how to defend themselves; and often pleased without ever praising man or woman, in book or conversation. Long supported by the private bounty of friends, he rather delighted to insult than flatter; he at length obtained competence from a public he esteemed not; and died, refusing that assistance he considered as useless—leaving no debts (but those of gratitude) undischarged, and expressing neither regret for the past, nor fear of the future, I believe. Strong in his prejudices, haughty and independent in his spirit, cruel in his anger—even when unprovoked; vindictive to excess, if he supposed himself even slightly injured; pertinacious in his attacks, invincible in his aversions. . . . " This judgment, considering that Baretti's whip had been laid heavily on Mrs. Thrale's shoulders, is not far from just.

For several years Baretti was a teacher in Mrs. Thrale's house. Though he lacked classical training and literary style, Baretti was an original and combative critic. The very violence of his attacks, and a certain amount of common sense and good judgment, gave authority to his essays. He fought the sentimentality of Arcadians; he fought for Tuscanism and purity of language, though his own Italian is not pure. He fought with Gozzi against Goldoni; and approved of some extraordinary attacks against Dante and other classic writers. He often presumed to explain etymology and the exact meaning of words, though with no real scholarship to back his amusing but unreliable opinions.

6. Cavalier Perfetti: "The subject we gave to Perfetti was 'Aurora Borealis.' He meditated, looking downwards, for at least half a quarter of an hour, to the sound of a harpsichord preluding *sotto voce.* Then he rose and began to declaim in rhymed octaves, softly,

and stanza by stanza. At first they succeeded each other slowly enough, but gradually the poet became more animated, and in proportion to his doing so, the harpsichord also played louder and louder, till at length this extraordinary man declaimed like a poet full of enthusiasm. The accompanier on the harpsichord and himself went on together in surprising rapidity, and perfect harmony between the music and the theme.

"When it was over, Perfetti seemed fatigued; he told us that he does not like to improvise often, as it exhausts his mind and body. His poem pleased me very much. In his rapid declamation it seemed to me sonorous, full of ideas and imagery. . . . You may be sure however, that it consisted in reality of much more sound than sense; it is impossible that the general construction should not be most often maimed and tortured, and that the filling up be not mere grandiloquent rubbish." (President des Brosses, *op. cit.*)

Bernardino Perfetti was of noble Siennese family, a Knight of the order of St. Stephen, and professor of jurisprudence in his native city. In 1725 he was in Rome as a protégé of Duchess Violante di Bavaria, Grand Duchess of Tuscany; he excited so much admiration by his improvisation at the Clementine College, and at the palace of the French Ambassador, Cardinal de Polignac, that Pope Benedict XIII approved of the improvisator's receiving the crown of the Capitol. The twelve members of Arcadia appointed to judge of his merits, after listening to him, awarded Perfetti the crown worn by Petrarch and proposed for Tasso. The annals of Arcadia and the official account in a decree of the Roman Senate record the granting of citizenship and of the title of Roman nobility to Cavalier Perfetti and his descendants.

7. Young men of honorable family frequently assumed the name and garb of *abati*. It was almost equivalent to a title; and it carried few restrictions. In every Italian city, and especially in Rome, there were *abati* of every sort and variety. There were *abati di diritto* and *abati di fatto;* and colleges, like Goldoni's Ghisleri, turned out

classes of *abati* every year. There were *abati* in almost every profession besides the legion that grazed on clerical benefits.

8. Gravina's death released Metastasio from strict bonds; but that he fell into dissipation is improbable. About his life in Rome, something can be gathered from his letters. Thus when he writes " . . . that, for not having acquired a sufficient knowledge of the human heart, he has been unable to avoid the thorny ways that forbid his settling quietly in his dear Patria," something may be guessed.

9. *Arcadia*—Christine of Sweden, daughter to Gustavus Adolphus, renounced the Swedish throne, abjured Lutheranism, and settled in Rome in 1655. Men of letters and science and persons of high rank used to meet at her Palazzo. After her death, fourteen of these continued these meetings and formed a sort of academy. In October, 1690, they obtained hospitality from the Fathers of San Pietro in Montorio, and finally settled in the *Bosco Parrasio* given them by King John V of Portugal. These academicians sought a regeneration of Italian poetry, by opposing bad taste, and by a reaction against the mannerism of *secento*. With all their pretentions to Christianity and their adoption of the *Bambino* as their patron, Arcadians were deeply imbued with paganism.

Arcadia grew; and extended its branches all over Italy. It became so important that almost every writer or otherwise notable man belonged to it. This wide expansion favored dilettantism; but it also spread the fashion for literary amusements, and popularized habits of courtesy, expressed in prose or verse on every possible occasion. It encouraged petty ambitions; but it also encouraged many writers; and it fostered a sense of Italianity through all the petty Italian States that then divided the Peninsula.

10. Giambattista Vico was born in Naples in 1668, and died there in 1737. In 1697 he taught rhetoric at the Naples University. Vico aimed to blend historical and philosophical doctrine in a grand

whole. He possessed intuition and the power of generalization. He divided human evolution into the three great epochs—of gods, of heroes, of men—which he imagined bound to return in regular cycles. This ponderous work he entitled *La Scienza Nuova*.

Vico was greater than any of his contemporaries or immediate successors. He investigated the origins of Roman laws and civilization, divining some of the conclusions that research has since proved true.

11. Vernon Lee gives this pleasing picture of Metastasio's life in Naples: "One day in the year 1722, a servant of Prince Borghese of Sulmona (Viceroy of Naples) announces that his most illustrious Excellency desires to speak with the *abaté*, Metastasio, Clerk of the Advocate Castagnola. Surprised and curious, Metastasio hurries to the Viceroy's palace and waits for the mysterious communication. The Viceroy appears, receives the young man in the most flattering manner, tells him that he has had the highest opinion of his poetical powers—probably from the Princess Belmonte and her family— and asks Metastasio whether he will undertake to write a short play to be performed on the birthday of the wife of the Emperor Charles VI, King of Naples and Sicily."

In a faithful translation from the original Italian "Life," she tells how Metastasio at first declined; how at last, on the Viceroy promising secrecy, he accepted the commission. The story is most improbable.

12. In the case of Romanina—as in every other love-affair of Metastasio —we have merely surmise or gossip. He burned all letters received; and he wrote his love-letters in the same sentimental, complimentary style as he used for occasional correspondence. Relations between the composer and the actors of a play are complex and intimate. Intellectual collaboration, communion of aims and ideals, and also participation in material interests and ambitions, are powerful bonds. When the collaborators are a famous singer, beautified

by the special halo which surrounds a much courted actress, and an author who is young, good-looking, inexperienced in love and in art; the natural conclusion of their mutual position is drawn. D'Ayala, the gossipy retailer of theatrical anecdotes, writes that "they lived in a very intimate and innocent friendship, whatever malign suspicion, supported by envy, may have thought or said, in its eagerness for slander." "This wise woman . . . had it in her mind to settle in Rome, her birthplace, and there to have her fixed residence. She talked the matter over with her husband, but did not mention it to Metastasio before the end of the season. Metastasio was greatly perplexed on listening to this idea and this plan of Romanina's, as he had not yet given up the idea of continuing his legal career. His affectionate friend endeavored to persuade him by all sorts of arguments. She promised that in Rome they would not only continue to live together, but that she would arrange to make of the two families one only, by dwelling all together. Besides the comfort of having his own people with him, he might hope to settle his position in Rome; that which he had not obtained formerly he might hope to obtain, now that his name was better known, and also that in Rome he could make much more out of his charge *Vacabile,* and make it more profitable." *Vita An.,* Vol. I, pp. 37–9.

13. A bull of Innocent XI had forbidden women actresses to appear on the stage, though it was not considered immoral to emasculate young boys, so as to obtain those beautiful soprano voices that sang in the Cappella Sistina and other churches. These interpreters of Metastasio's feminine rôles did not require Romanina's instruction; but she probably supervised the rehearsals and staging of his plays. Metastasio was paid 300 *scudi* for each play, and made something more out of the poems and cantatas he composed for patrons, especially for his godfather, Cardinal Pietro Ottoboni.

14. One can picture the group. Standing round the clavicembalo, the composer Sarro plays the opening chords of a recitative or the ritor-

nello of an air; Romanina sings the lines; and Metastasio, pencil in hand, corrects his work according to the suggestions of his friend. Thus Romanina and her galaxy of musicians trained Metastasio to his profession. What was the effect on his character is less easily discovered. That he lived on Romanina's bounty is improbable. He left the lawyer's studio after the success of *Gli Orti Esperidi,* after receiving 200 *scudi* from the Viceroy, and after receiving orders for poems from don Antonio Caracciola della Torella and others; and after he was sure that, through the patronage of Romanina and her musical friends, he could reckon on regular work and regular payment from the Teatro di San Bartolommeo. The protégé of several Princes and Dukes governed by traditions of Spanish munificence, need not depend upon an actress for his daily bread.

During this century, when Italians cared little for politics, and less for science, and did not indulge in sports, the hours spent in the theatre were of enormous importance. Well did the actors know how to make their profit out of this national craze. Goldoni tells an amusing story of his attempt to obtain favor for his *Amalasonta* from a group of singers, and how he was discouraged by the impudence of the soprano and the presumption of the other actors, who pretended to know more than the author.

Metastasio may have read in Benedetto Marcello's book how the poet never deemed it necessary to read the ancient writers since the ancient writers never deemed it necessary to read the modern. He must secure the assistance of some influential person, cook, or valet, agreeing to share all dedication fees with him, who will teach him all the names and titles to be put on the dedication. He must exalt the family and ancestors of his Mæcenas, and be profuse in such expressions as "munificence," "generous soul," etc.

15. Benedetto Marcello, the younger son of Senator Marcello of Venice, was born in 1686. He was a delicate and precocious child from whom his parents had to hide every book. He studied music, especially harmony, and wrote both prose and poetry. After receiving

his degree in law, he entered the service of the Republic as a judge of the Criminal Quaranzia. Marcello was sent to Pola as Provveditore of the Republic; but, as a result of the humidity and malaria, he died when fifty-three, in 1739. His little prose-work, *Il Teatro alla moda,* is a masterpiece of style. It purports to teach how best to suit the theatrical and musical taste of the day, recommending many absurdities. It gives a vivid representation of the theatrical life of his time.

For other description of theatrical life, see Goldoni's *L'Impresario delle Smirne, Il Teatro Comico,* and several passages of his *Memoirs.* Also Metastasio's *intermezzi* for the *Didone, L'Impresario delle Canarie.* Also Sografi, *Le Convenienze Teatrali.*

About the Venetian theatres, interesting information can be found in a book by Schneider describing Claudio Monteverde and the first melodramas. Even when Venice—end of seventeenth century—counted no more than 150,000 inhabitants, she had eight theatres. The oldest was the San Casciana; like most of these houses, this one belonged to a patrician family—the Trons. In early times admittance was free. The owners of the theatres offered this amusement to their friends and acquaintances. It was only after the performance of *Andromeda* by Monteverde, that tickets were sold, the Trons keeping a certain number for their friends. The price of a ticket was then fixed at four Venetian lire; the boxes being paid apart.

The theatre was illumined by a double row of lamps on each side of the scene. The spectators who liked to follow the recital in the book, carried a bit of candle in their pockets, holding it on or near the book that was often burnt or soiled with the drippings. There was a space some three yards wide between the orchestra and the first row of seats, in which people walked about. The audience was generally very noisy; it was considered fashionable to talk aloud even during the play. The box-holders behaved very impertinently towards the pit, and, it is said, would spit on the heads of those below them.

Ruzzante (1525)

Fiorinette (1533)

Coviello (1550)

Harlequino (1570)

Spavento (1577)

Isabella (1600)

Tabarin (1618)

Beltrame (1613)

The theatrical year was divided into three seasons. The first, also called the Carnival season, began on St. Stephen's night—the last of the year—and ended on the last Tuesday of Carnival. The second season began on the second Sunday after Easter and lasted till the 15th of June; the last one began on the 15th of September and lasted till the 30th of November. The actors largely depended on the success of the play. At first the poet got nothing more than his share of the applause; then, in some theatres, he was allowed to sell his book and keep the price. The composer was glad enough to take from the owner or manager the trifling sum of 100 ducats—about 150 gold francs.

16. The words, "taken a resolution" do not translate exactly the Italian "preso stato" which can mean either marriage or the convent. This mystery clouded Metastasio's spirit. The person for whose sake he entreated the protection of Cardinal Gentili and of another Cardinal, "protector of that pious house," probably belonged to some aristocratic family. Her sin was nothing worse than being in love with a man who was her social inferior. But such things were severely reproved by this Roman theocratic society, and while Metastasio was threatened with a lawsuit, the girl very likely accepted the convent as a release from a painful situation.

17. Vienna was then the Mecca of writers and adventurers. It was also the seat of the Holy Roman Empire, with its glamour of ancient traditions and associations. Moreover Austria had not yet become the arch-enemy of Italy. Austrian Viceroys in Naples and Sicily were generally Italians, who misruled no worse than the Medici or Farnesi or the Pope. Metastasio had already sung the birthdays, marriages, and other festivities in the Imperial family. His abstract patriotism was the traditional idea of Rome and Empire.

18. Bibliophile, philologist, collector of manuscripts and medals, editor of a literary review, *Il Giornale dei Letterati,* this poet who despised

his own poetry writes to Ludovico Antonio Muratori, "I am not surprised by your little esteem of melodrama. I feel in the same way, though I have written so many. By long experience I have learned that, unless one accepts many makeshifts, one misses the principal object of such things, which is to give pleasure. The more one sticks to rules, the more one displeases, and if the poem is praised, the theatre remains empty."

These rules which Zeno wished to observe were unity of action and respect for the two other unities, a dignified style, a grandeur of manners, and a better distribution of strophes and recitatives. But the rules of Aristotle, the example of Greek tragedy, were as uncongenial to the *settecento* audiences as the intellectual and moral atmosphere of ancient Greece was foreign to that century's interpretation of life. Italy was not centralized like France, but divided into independent states, each with its own fashion of poetical composition. Neither Gravina's teaching nor Zeno's scholarly melodrama could greatly influence such preferences.

Though imitating the Greeks, poets writing for Italian courts gave a large place to the conventional type of love which characterized Italian comedy. They disputed Aristotle's laws but infringed all of them. Pagan mythology and undigested Scripture, feeble attempts at symbolism, were mingled in melodrama; none of them was assimilated. The plot was termed "fable"; the number of episodes and of characters was limited only by the capacity of the stage. There were marvelous scenic effects, but little real literary production.

The most persistently disturbing element in the development of musical drama was the music. Woe to the poet who did not flatter the prima donna; woe to the poet who did not provide the *aria di bravura,* frequent sentimental couplets, and lilting strophes. Metastasio has given the formula. The first rôles must have at least two arias in each act, and one more for the prima donna; every act must close with a duet, a quartet, or at least with an aria of despair or wrath, exhibiting the most striking virtuosities of the singer. Thus while the melodrama wandered fancy-free, the limitations of human voices barred original creation.

Pursuing his plan of reform, Zeno laboriously produced more than sixty plays. He imitated good models. From Racine he borrowed the plots and the general construction of *Andromaque* and *Iphigenie*. He also borrowed from Ariosto's *Orlando Furioso*. *Achille in Sciro* is a dialogued idyll constructed with simplicity and some good character-study.

19. Some of Metastasio's biographers charge him with deserting his family; but Metastasio was a man of thirty-one, a bachelor; his only "family" was his father, a grown-up brother and sister—all of them quite able to provide for themselves, already having received from him good furniture, plate, and a house. In his progressive development in Naples, Metastasio had become still further estranged from that father who had so easily parted with him, from that lazy brother who had accepted without shame Metastasio's and Romanina's gifts. By leaving Rome, Metastasio did not desert Romanina, since she saw the advantage for him and urged him to go. Perhaps she hoped that a short absence might warm the tepid affection of her young lover.

20. His biographers have dwelt on his hand-kissing, his rapture at the slightest sign of Imperial favor; but servility is not the only interpretation of Metastasio's behaviour. Metastasio is a stickler for "duty"; but his sense of duty is limited. He ignores the great social or patriotic ideals, because such ideals were ignored by his contemporaries. When he engaged to serve the Imperial court, reverence and thankfulness were part of this obligation, as well as the hand-kissing and knee-bending that scandalized Alfieri and others. This strict interpretation of duty kept Metastasio at his desk, even when age and sickness made the effort painful.

As a conscientious employee he gives his best; he rewrites every line with care, even though he knows that presumptuous Charles

VI cares little for his art, and that the courtiers neither understand nor appreciate the drama which, in their eyes, is only a part of the official court ceremonies. It was not merely a courtier's adulation, when Metastasio transformed that Imperial and Royal fool, Charles VI, that Imperial and Royal housewife and matchmaker, Maria Theresa, into personages of Roman magnitude. It was the genuine exaltation of a poetical mind, roused by the pageantry of the court splendour, that concealed so much of the wickedness and coarseness that he ignored.

21. In a letter dated from Yoslowitz (October, 1749), he writes: "The river and also the lake . . . have suddenly frozen, and a biting breeze, blowing from the cold Trions, is paying us homage, even within the well-guarded rooms wherein we are fortified. In this sudden extravagant change of weather, I (born for the gentle quiet of Arcadia, rather than for the noisy magnificence of court) find, in spite of the attractions of city life, a great content; I am delighted with that uniform whiteness, stretching over such an extension of land.

"I like that concordant silence of all living creatures. I amuse myself with discovering well-known roads, trees, fields, pastoral huts, all objects to which the snow has given another colour without changing their shape. I consider with grateful feeling that the same friendly wood, that by its many leaves formerly sheltered me against the sun, now provides me with fuel to protect me from cold. . . . Like every other season, winter has its comforts and advantages." Thus if one Marianna initiated Metastasio to the joys and pains of theatrical life, another Marianna now brought him to the quieter delights of country life.

22. In this last period, Metastasio's life appears a strange mixture of sadness and glory. Although court favour and official praise, though every academy, every Arcadian Colony, repeated that he was the first poet of his time, though the theatres of almost all civilized

Europe still performed his plays, Metastasio knew that the times were changing around him and that the æsthetic and ethic worlds that had been his own were hastening to a speedy and inglorious setting.

All exiles lose contact with their own country and yet are rarely at home in their new environment. Had Metastasio been in closer connection with the Italian intellectual evolution, he might have followed the movement; and instead of his antiquated, sentimental, and pseudo-heroical ideals, he might have participated in the manlier and more realistic creations of Parini, of Alfieri. He might have shared in their struggle against prejudice, against outworn ideas. But he caught only a distant and distorted echo of the battle. Hence, that diffidence, that feeling of estrangement, of which the echo is found in his late letters. Reticent by nature, cautious by education, and by a long social intercourse with protectors and patrons, Metastasio conceals his inner feelings; and one must read his correspondence with sympathetic understanding to detect the growing sadness of his intellectual isolation.

Metastasio did not fully realize the greatness of this separation from his own people and from the reawakening world, though he realized some of its most superficial effects. In 1760 he writes to Count Florio: "Ever since I transplanted myself to this country, I perceived that our poetry is accepted here only so far as music seasons it, and representation interprets it; hence all beautiful images, choice of expression, elegance of style, all the charm of harmony in our verse, in one word, every lyrical beauty, is here habitually ignored and appreciated only because praised by foreign critics."

How bitterly depressing such misunderstanding must have been! His reasons for not returning to Italy were stronger than those mentioned in his letters. But such reasons did not assuage the bitterness of exile, did not compensate the poet for that vivifying communion with kindred spirits, participation in the emotions of his own people. To Neapolitan friends he writes that he speaks dialect as often as he can find the opportunity, that he remembers Naples as the place "wherein I was born to letters." That "stormy ocean of the Parthenopean forum, above whose troubled waters the most excellent and learned jurisconsul Castagnola taught me to swim," is remembered with tenderness and regret.

23. "Metastasio's spirit enjoyed perfect quiet in the exactness of his methodical life, and in the honest, noble, literary company of friends. Even in his old age he was full of life and animation, his memory good, his spirits cheerful, his talk witty and vivacious, abounding in pretty conceits; he was ever very accurate in his simple apparel, extremely polite and courteous towards every one. Till the very last days he could write and read without the help of glasses." (*V. M. P.,* II, 48.)

When the dangers that threatened her throne were dispelled, Maria Theresa wished to show her gratitude to those who had been most devoted and faithful, by granting them honors. Thus Metastasio, even when he was afraid of losing his charge, was the object of Royal favor and was offered titles. The Queen Empress wished him to become a Court Chancellor, a Baron or a Count of the Roman Empire. But he answered that he did not feel entitled to such honors, but merely wished to be allowed to serve her to the end of his days, with no other title than that of poet and historian of her court.

The Empress created the order of St. Stephen, first King and Apostle of Hungary, when she wished to show her gratitude to these subjects of hers. . . . On that occasion she also remembered Metastasio and wished to make him a Knight of that order. He was offered the little cross as a testimonial of his sovereign's favor, but he declined it on the plea that failing health and advanced age would not allow him to participate in official ceremonies, nor enjoy the privileges of the order. For this act of humility, Metastasio rose higher still in the eyes of all the court; and was held in as much consideration as if he were in fact a Knight of St. Stephen." (*V. M. P.,* II, 32 and 35.)

Count Perlas in a confidential letter to a friend, thus describes Metastasio's moral condition: "There is no real happiness in this world; that which appears to the public eye is not really possessed by the man we believe to be so fortunate. I am a friend of Metastasio's; he is reputed one of the happiest men alive, but in reality no man is more unhappy than he. Ever since the death of Countess d'Althan I have filled her place as his confidant. I am well informed of his sorrows, and if I could tell you how heavy they are, I might in some measure help you to bear your own burden."

24. To his sentimental experiences, his affectionate nature, and unusual intuition of the complex and often contradictory motives and expressions of woman's love, jealousy, and despair, Metastasio added a delicacy of interpretation, and an unequalled clearness of style that mirrored every shade of sentiment and allowed every intention, every shifting of emotion, to be adequately expressed and understood. He had also a vivid, if not a deep experience of woman's love. Stendhal wrote that Metastasio could not understand the fiercer and stronger passions. Stendhal failed to understand Metastasio's æsthetics, since neither he nor his audience could sympathize with these fiercer emotions. Unacquainted with the abysses of wickedness, the agonies of actual crime, Metastasio very finely describes the self-condemnation of one who had intended but not committed sin.

25. Metastasio spent his last years in serene, scholarly occupations, in the enjoyment of chosen friendships. When death released him from the "tedium vitae" which seems to have darkened his last moments, the outbreak of praise was universal, stormy, and transient, as such a tribute is apt to be, when a long-applauded and lately outgrown writer dies. It was then the fashion to lavish praise. Arcadians vied in official panegyrics. A list of those who celebrated the "Italian Sophocles" would embrace almost all contemporary European writers.

26. In the often quoted anonymous biography, there is this description of Metastasio's appearance (p. 67, Vol. II): "He was of middle height, tending rather to stoutness, but very well proportioned; his features were extremely fine and delicate; his black and penetrating eyes had a very sweet expression; his nose well cut, and his mouth rather large but adorned with a sweet smile and an air of composure; his cheeks full rounded and softly colored; his complexion clear with an additional bloom that added a finely finished charm to his physiognomy, which he preserved even to his advanced age. His portraits are not all lifelike; he used to call them satires, rather than likenesses."

CHAPTER II

METASTASIO: HIS TIME AND HIS WORK

Italian *Settecento* literature was first unduly condemned, and afterwards unduly praised: It is now time for an unprejudiced consideration: After the council of Trent, Italy was submerged in obscurantism: Literature was a pastime, religion was formality, and all social or political initiative was smothered: Arcadia, though justly ridiculed, had some merit: Metastasio selected the "canzonetta" form for his verse, which is the best Italian poetry of the period: The evolution of the Italian melodrama and opera: Metastasio's plays: *Dido* is the first truly Metastasian drama; the model is Virgilian: It is followed by *Siroe, Ezio,* and *Alessandro*: *Artaserse* shows Metastasio's progress: *Olimpiade* is most typical of Metastasio's first Viennese manner: *La Clemenza di Tito* is Metastasio's most admired drama, but *Temistocle* contains *Metastasio's* most complex and complete character, while *Attilio Regolo* is the unsurpassed blossom of this sort of tragedy. This greatest of Metastasio's works was first performed in Poland: Women's place in Italian Eighteenth Century society is mirrored in Metastasio's plays: The place and importance of the Italian highborn ladies, their influence through their *salotti,* and their emotions, are truthfully described: Metastasio's own career is an example of what feminine influence could accomplish: An analysis of Metastasio's feminine heroines: Metastasio has many qualities of a great tragic poet: The only rival to Tasso's *Gerusalemme Liberata* is Metastasio's verse.

M ANY historians consider the Italian *settecento* as devitalized, unheroic. Only a few philosophers, reformers, and writers have been excepted from this general condemnation. This error in literary criticism was a natural reaction after the great *Risorgimento* had ended. Whilst an Austrian Emperor was imprisoning Italian patriots, and condemning Italian martyrs to death or *carcere duro,* Italian critics could not appreciate the melodramas of Metastasio nor the *poeta cesareo* kissing the hand of another Austrian Emperor as a devotee kisses a relic.

Time, healer of national wounds, precursor of fair criticism, and the expansion of esthetic and ethic criterion has revised this judgment. *Settecento* art is now fashionable. The absurd draperies of Bernini's statues are praised. Tiepolo's loose drawing finds defenders. Justice towards early *settecento* literature is also *en marche.*

Italians are proud of Campanella, Giordano Bruno, Paolo Sarpi, who died for the truth; of Giambattista Vico's poverty and humiliation; of Muratori and Pietro Giannone. But the poets and *prosateurs* who merely voiced early *settecento* sentimentality have received scant approval. Yet some early *settecento* literature had merit.

After the Council of Trent, Italy was submerged in obscurantism. Jesuitism and the Inquisition fettered ideas, restrained philosophic speculation and scientific investigation. Most Italian writers feared persecution; their initiative was smothered by ecclesiastical restrictions. This repression began with the young child, and it released none but the dead. Priestly education may have had refined manners and encouraged a fastidious literary taste, but it enervated character. Literature was the pastime of polite society. Trade was degrading; political activity was forbidden; religion consisted of forms and appearances. The theatre, gambling, *conversazioni,* and literary assemblies absorbed the interest of a society that was hardly conscious of its emptiness. There was no revolt against sacerdotalism or existing political and social conditions, and little condemnation of the current decadent literature. Vague talk there was about literary "reform"; but normal literary expression implied a national conscience, and that was repressed by the Church.

Arcadia has been justly ridiculed; but it had the merit of creating intellectual unity out of the many Italian groups. It encouraged idyllic aspirations; and it fostered a fastidious literary taste. The idyll implies quiet and beauty. Metastasio's poetry is idyllic. Lyrical poems also poured from every *serbatoio,* or colony, of Arcadia. Every provincial town was a center of literary activity. These colonies corresponded with one another and with the Roman colony that still holds its solemn assemblies in the *Bosco Parrasio.*

This vacuity of spiritual content resulted in emphasis being given to the phrase, the word, the sound of the word, the musicality of the phrase. Poets wrote for the select few; elegant diction, musical verse, was their aim; the substance was unimportant. Prose words in their best order, poetry, "the best words in their best order" (Coleridge), was the Arcadian ideal. Their harmonious lines dripped caressing metres, daintily expressed similitudes, sentiments soothing sensitive nerves. Obvious wisdom, pragmatical advice flowed freely from Arcadian pens.

Settecento Italian morals were bad, but literary expression was good. These Arcadian singers were not hypocrites. Hypocrisy implies a desire to appear better than one really is. These amorous poets wandered chastely in paths of dalliance. They merely repeated, in more graceful, more elegant manner, the same things that others had said. Hence the charm of Rolli's, Frugoni's, and Metastasio's pastoral lyrics.

Metastasio's education was in accord with Gravina's literary ideal, imitation of Greece and Rome. This classical training imparted correctness and good taste to all Metastasio's poetic composition. Though never deeply imbued with philosophic method, nor able fully to grasp the grand "Cogito ergo sum," Metastasio imbibed something of philosophy from Caroprese. In later years, he happily expressed this manner of psychological introspection and questioning.

> Il dubbio, arduo in se stesso
> Vuol maturo pensier.
> —*Egeria*

Metastasio's lyrics are among the sweetest love-poems ever sung. Those dedicated to "Nice" and "Fille" have been termed "the love songs of a century." Italians have memorized the exultant cry in *Libertà,* of the lover who while conquering his passion, describes its bitter-sweet torment. Neapolitans demanding a constitution sang "Non sogno questa volta—Non sogno Liberta." These *can-*

zoni, serenate, and other Metastasian lyrics expressed the love Italians understood. Mild jealousy, melodious despair, shades of emotion, roused by passing incident or reminiscence, all daintily worded, were the ideal.

Metastasio selected the Italian *canzonetta.* It is not the French *chanson* with its humor and *gauloiserie* and a merry chorus. It is the Italian *canzone,* which *trovatori* had breathed in the *corti d'amore;* and free communes had sung in their popular festivals. In Metastasio's verse it outshines all the older forms of *Ballata, Ballatella,* and *similia.* It completed the evolution toward musical interpretation as the ultimate aim of Italian poetry. Fortunately for Metastasio, Romanina introduced him to great musical composers, to able singers, and to Porpora, the master who gave him sufficient musical science to develop his natural tendency.

At what early dawn, in what leafy forest of a twilight creation, in what lacustrine dwelling were words and music first blended for man's delight? David's singing to the harp accompaniment, Homer's chanting of his poem, are almost modern successors of still older traditions. Italian scholars and historians differed as to the relative importance of music or of words in operatic performances; but popular feeling clearly desired more music. The pastorals, the *serenate,* the interludes, developed variously in the different parts of Italy. From the first gropings of mimic, musical, and poetical arts, to the elaborate stagecraft of modern opera, the way is long; but it is uninterrupted.

Trovatori, mummers, pastoral fables, courtly pageants, all contributed to the formation of melodrama. The Metastasian drama differed from its predecessors in the relative position of music and poetry. The explanation of Metastasio's genius, of his triumph, and of his decline, is found in this concordance of words and harmony.

January 21, 1599, is a memorable date in both literature and music. On this day, in the Palazzo de Bardi in Florence, a poet, Rinuccini, and two composers, Jacopo Pieri and Caccini, revived the Greek drama and produced the first Italian melodrama, *Dafne*. They aimed at imitation; yet their achievement was an original episode in the history of arts and letters. They created the Opera.

Italian tragedies were never popular. They were written, performed, and applauded by court circles. From Musatto's *Ezzelino,* down to Maffei's *Merope,* neither beautiful verse nor the art of Poliziano nor the genius of Tasso nor lavish stagecraft could induce the large public to appreciate tragedies. Yet the nation thirsted for theatrical spectacles. Townsfolk had their mummeries and cavalcades; peasants their pastorals, their *maggi*. Itinerant players carried comedy into every corner of the country. The opera gathered something from all these forms of art. It was not the court pageant, though it preserved some of its splendour; it was not the pastoral, though it assimilated some of its artificial simplicity; it was not the carnival-festivity, though it borrowed some of its paraphernalia.

In France, under Mazarin and Maria de' Medici, the Italian opera, performed by Italian players, predominated every court festivity. At a later period, the French imitation of Italian opera assumed the magnificence and affected simplicity which it has retained. The English court of Charles the Second encouraged Davenant's efforts and assimilated as much of the Italian opera as was suited to so different a race and clime.

The evolution of melodrama in Italy followed a more natural course. The blending of music with poetry has always appealed to Italians. Even the darkest and most tormented ages have had their musical performances. To this racial inclination, the eighteenth century added its fad for harmonious phrasing and resounding words. Yet, even in this artificial age, Italian music possessed simplicity and pathos; witness the *Lamento di Ariana* in Monteverde's opera.

In the *canzoni* of Rolli, Frugoni, and other Arcadian poets, in the development of strophes are found the first efforts towards that reform of melodrama which Metastasio achieved. Metastasio succeeded because he aimed at possible things, easily understood by his contemporaries. He adopted part of the program traced by Apostolo Zeno,[1] but added geniality and the sense of harmony. Metastasio may have learned from Zeno respect for truth in the construction of such characters as Temistocle, Attilio Regolo, and Tito.

METASTASIO'S PLAYS

Thus equipped with a solid classical training, with some knowledge of philosophical doctrine, with considerable musical preparation and great natural aptitudes, Metastasio was well prepared for theatrical musical composition. Romanina's collaboration, the influence exerted by Sarro the composer, were his last limitations, soon to be discarded. *Gli Orti Esperidi,* though warmly applauded, were a promise rather than original achievements. *Dido* is the first truly Metastasian drama. It contains the germ, the characteristic elements of his later works.

In *Didone,* Metastasio adopts the Virgilian model with modifications. There is more Ovidian emphasis than Virgilian simplicity; yet there is a swiftness of action, a clearness of exposition, and a solid construction of a well-defined plot, that were new to the Italian stage. Tasso's characters were not more passionately feminine; the tender words of Marini's were not more exquisitely musical; nor did Ariosto's heroines express more frantic despair. No sweeter sounds had been heard since Aminta warbled her lamentations. Metastasio conquered his audience.

The plot has the inevitable second pair of lovers, and a spectacular ending: thunder and lightning, blending with the final conflagration and the suicide of Dido. This romantic *finale* is characteristic of Metastasio's manner. He copies Virgil, but he caters to his audience. Dido is not majestic. She does not advance towards her doom with Greek fatality; rather, she is Tasso's heroine, using every feminine art to detain her lover, stooping to every artifice. She has the weakness, the folly, of a lover, but has few queenly traits. She declaims like other passionate, distracted Italian lovers. Hence the popularity of a play, which has furnished many familiar quotations.

Aeneas is a *secento* lover. The model is Virgilian, but his character is as commonplace as Metastasio's times and genius could make him. This is no fated hero of ancient Greece, but a mere martyr to Dido's dominating will. The tragedy might easily be changed into comedy. Indeed the whole play suggests comedy. If only Aeneas would unbend at the last moment and remain with Dido! These comic traits in a tragedy did not offend a public taste which accepted as tragedy a conflict of events, a succession of startling incidents, and the ranting speeches of pseudo-heroes. The meaning of tragedy was not understood. To explore the human soul, to trace the strife between virtue and sin, between duty and desire—that is tragedy.

From *Didone* in 1724 to *Artaserse* in 1729, Metastasio gave a series of plays which, like Corneille's, are a crescendo of intrigue, of *imbroglio*. Metastasio does not soar so high as his French model. There is excess of intrigue, incidents, and episodes in these plays; but Metastasio returns to simplicity in *Achille in Sciro;* and, in *Temistocle* and *Attilio Regolo* of the next period, he retrieved his error. In *Catone in Utica,*[2] Metastasio realized the necessity of a tragic ending, and killed his hero in the last scene. But when actors and the public protested, the author changed his last act. Henceforth he always terminated his play with the forced finale of reconciliation, repentance, forgiveness, and general rejoicing, that suited the public taste.

Siroe, which followed *Didone,* was first performed in Venice, the

music being composed by Vinci. Rotrou, Corneille's great prede-
cessor, had already developed the subject; but Metastasio took no
more than a hint from Rotrou's *Cosroe*. Siroe is Cosroe's eldest son
and natural heir. He is deprived of his rights by the intrigues of
his younger brother, Medarse, and is accused of plotting murder.
Laodice, who loves Siroe, has stirred the senile passion of Cosroe;
while Siroe is enslaved to the charms of Emira, a distinguished
princess at Cosroe's court. This improbable intrigue and unlikely
dénouement is cleverly developed. Metastasio faithfully interprets
his people and the moral standards of his time. The wickedness is
only apparent; in the last scenes the villain repents and assures us
that honesty is the best policy.

Ezio in 1728 and *Alessandro* in 1730 were constructed on the
same plan as *Siroe*. They contain similar characters, similar incidents. *Artaserse* shows Metastasio's progress in stagecraft and in
verse-harmony. Arsace is accused of murdering Serse; appearances
are against him. Artabano, his father, has handed him the bloody
weapon that he himself had used. Artabano, a lump of wickedness,
with one noble passion, his love for his son, is the counsellor and
confidant of King Artaserse. The King, wishing to save Arsace,
asks Artabano to judge him. Artabano pronounces his son guilty,
but secretly hopes to save both himself and Arsace through a conspiracy against the king. In the last act, a splendid banquet is prepared; a sacred libation to the gods is to be offered by Artaserse.
The cup, poisoned by Artabano, passes from the King's hand to
Arsace, then to Artabano himself, as each one in succession pledges
his innocence. A wild mob breaks in, demanding Arsace's release.
But Arsace refuses to rebel, Artabano repents, and the lovers are
joined in happy wedlock. Thus all is well that ends well. *Artaserse*
marks a progress over *Siroe* and *Semiramide Riconosciuta*. The
plot is consistent, and the psychology of each personage is strongly
interpreted.

Olimpiade is typical of Metastasio's first Viennese manner. These characters throb with life, thrill with reality. The plot is compounded of classic and romantic reminiscences. The names are Greek; the manners and morals are of later ages. The friendship of Megacles and Lycidas suggests "Roland le preux" and "Olivier le sage" rather than anything classic. Lycidas is believed to be son and heir to the king of Crete. When Clistene, king of Siconis, proclaims that the hand of his fair daughter will be the prize of the forthcoming Olympic games, Lycidas entreats that great champion, Megacles, to assume his name, and win for him the prize. Megacles gladly accepts this chance to repay his debt to his friend. Then he learns that the woman whom he is expected to win for his friend, is his own passionate love, known under another name. He dissembles his longing to Aristea, but only provokes from her more ardent expressions.

In the second act, victorious Megacles is solemnly crowned by Clisthenes. The scene between Megacles and Aristea is beautiful; he telling her why he stands there, under an assumed name and in a false position, to win her for another man, although he adores her beyond everything save duty and honour. To Aristea's passionate "I know thee and adore thee," he replies that she would not love him were he proved faithless to his friend, perjured and ungrateful to the man who saved his life. This appeal does not quench the woman's love. Hence the famous aria "Se cerca se dici," with music by Pergolesi. Lycidas is revealed as the long lost brother of Aristea; every complication is solved. Megacles marries his princess, and Lycidas his patient lover.

Metastasio's admired drama, *La Clemenza di Tito,* was performed in 1734. Voltaire compared it to the best in Racine and Corneille. Suetonius furnished the subject and the historical outline. Around these are accumulated many episodes. The play is a masterpiece; the dénouement is logical. Impulsive, ardent, jealous

Vitellia is moved by remorse and sudden love for the man who adores her even to the point of death. Her confession accords with her character. Titus pardons Sesto, and forgives Vitellia's jealousy and passionate love for himself. He even consents to her marrying another. What sort of wife will Vitellia make, and what sort of submissive husband will Sesto become?[3]

The many plays that Metastasio gave to the Imperial Court Theatre, the many minor works that he wrote for the Imperial Princesses, all display a perfection of style and versification that his Imperial employers were unable to appreciate. His best works were written during the first ten years of his residence in Vienna; and the best of these are *La Clemenza di Tito, Temistocle,* and *Attilio Regolo.*[4]

TEMISTOCLE—ATTILIO REGOLO

Temistocle is Metastasio's most complex and complete character. Unfettered by historical exactness, he traced an imaginary portrait of the Athenian exile: a philosopher and hero. At the court of Serse, he relies on the generosity of his former enemy, since only the ungrateful can hate: "the ungrateful hates the burden of gratitude for the benefits received, whilst the benefactor must love him on whom he has bestowed favors." Farther on, he tells how "Virtue is purified by suffering and withers away in a life of ease." Serse refuses to surrender him to the Athenians. He even entrusts him with the command of his army. Temistocle accepts, but refuses to lead these forces against Athens (scenes 7 and 8 of Act II), and faces the awful consequences of the King's anger.

In the presence of the King, and of his court and army, and of the Athenian ambassador, and his own son and daughter, Temistocle proclaims that he who can without a blush consider all his past existence in the moment of leaving it, may die gloriously. Rather than fail in his duty towards his country, rather than fail in his duty towards King Serse, Temistocle will drink the poisoned cup. His hand is stopped as he lifts the cup to his lips; a general reconciliation sets everything right; and the curtain drops on the usual "Licenza" proclaiming the virtues of the Emperor Charles VI, "unequalled," says the poet, "by anything to be found in ancient Greece and Rome."

Attilio Regolo is the unsurpassed blossom of this sort of tragedy. Here Metastasio and the melodrama reach its highest plane. Romantic episodes complicate the plot; but the figure of Regolo stands out. Love, friendship, family ties, popular affection, accumulate obstacles to prevent the sublime sacrifice that he is resolved to make for his own glory and the safety of Rome. "These Barbarians deem me capable of felony . . . to avenge my death, you Romans must rise in arms and wrest from their fetters the captive eagles . . . gladly will I die if I can first see Africa shudder at the name of Rome." "Non va sino all' alma La mia servitu," he sings Romanly, and unafraid.

This greatest of Metastasio's tragedies was not performed in Vienna. It was several years later, in the boisterous court of Poland, that Regolo first uttered his martial speeches.

Woman's place in eighteenth century Italian society is mirrored in these plays: not the realistic painting of manners that is sometimes offered as truthful reconstruction, but an interpretation of the place and importance of the high-born lady. Metastasio's interpretation of Italian woman is a spiritual redintegration of the ideal that predominated in Italian society during the eighteenth century. Without profound knowledge of human hearts, without attempting abstruse analysis of human passion, Metastasio knew the power of jealousy—how the most devoted heart can feel the utmost resentment; and he could describe these emotions and make them articulate.

By their shrewdness, capacity, and intrigue, by the play of alliances and the peculiar talents that predominated in an emasculated society absorbed in æsthetic refinement and sentimental pleasure, Italian women influenced the political world of each petty State. They ruled by their *salotti* (termed in Venice *ridotti* or *casini*), the equivalent of the Parisian salons.

Metastasio was initiated in Romanina's drawing-room, where she ruled over a circle of great musicians, of celebrated actors. The praise there obtained was the key to wide renown. In Romanina's salon he may have seen some of the less refined manners proper to the green-room and the studio. But Metastasio was admitted to higher and more refined *salotti*. In Naples he visited those that retained much of the pomp and manners of late Spanish masters, and much of the magniloquent courtesy peculiar to Neapolitans. There he learned the value to a young man, of the patronage of noble-born ladies; there he followed the storms and turmoils of courts and drawing-rooms; and there he acquired his knowledge of expression, so measured, yet so forceful.

Later, in Vienna, in the Countess d'Althan's pseudo-princely society, and in his constant contact with the Imperial family, he saw the influence of women upon court manners, more supercilious but also more reticent. The grosser vices, the perversion that may have been underneath this magnificent surface, he ignored. His feminine characters gain in majesty after his settling in Vienna. The essential character is not modified. Metastasio's own career is a notable example of what feminine influence could accomplish in every social environment in the eighteenth century.

From Tasso and Ariosto, Metastasio accepted an outline of women, not merely in the theatrical contrivance of having them often appear in men's clothes, but in the more fundamental characteristic of masculine acting. It is the woman who stimulates man to heroic or criminal deeds; it is the woman who assumes the responsibility for crime and the sacrificial initiative. In *Artaserse*, Semira impersonates gentleness and devotion. She pleads eloquently for her brother Arsace. She accepts the unloved husband forced upon her, whom she must despise, after she has told him that he may obtain her hand but never her heart. Sabina, in *Adriano,* is also that complicated romantical character that Metastasio loved to trace. In the abnegation of her love for Adriano, she bids him marry her rival, if, by this alliance, he can secure his life and throne from Osroa's attacks. With few exceptions, such as Vitellia (*Clemenza di Tito*), Didone, and Semiramide, the Metastasian heroines are submissive to the law of love. Each of these women loves a hero-martyr, and each offers her own life for his, as Argene does in *Olimpiade,* or plots to release him. Always their amorous pains are expressed in sweet and pathetic strophes.

Metastasio's chief characters are often set in powerful relief, and show individuality, despite the similar situations and the monotony of development required by theatrical traditions. The secondary characters are sadly uniform, colorless. The inevitable *confidente,* the old servant that saves the baby he is commanded to destroy, the traitor who usually only suggests the necessary crime, the second pair of lovers who merely complicate affairs for their betters, these are generally vague phantoms. They sing beautiful verses, because Metastasio wrote no others, but they have no personality.

Metastasio has many of the qualities of a great tragic poet. His fame would have been greater if he had not squeezed plays out of those last weary years of his long life. But his devotion to the Imperial family held him fast to his task, even when inspiration failed. By the death of his first Imperial patron, Charles VI, the civilized world was threatened with the horrors of war. Metastasio's loving heart was dismayed by the disasters menacing the Imperial family whom he admired and loved, the young princesses he had taught, and the d'Althans whom he considered as his own family. His always delicate health yielded to some sort of moral and intellectual crisis which is vaguely mentioned in his letters, and clearly evidenced by his ensuing production. Except in *Attilio Regolo* his later manner is progressively oppressive.

Yet for every Imperial birthday, wedding, or other official event, Metastasio accomplished his task, laboriously producing some theatrical performance. Thrifty Maria Theresa's Imperial orders extended his labors even to the court of Madrid. The Empress paid some debt of gratitude to her Spanish ally by sending Metastasio's tragedy *Nitteti* to be performed at their court (1756). And so, on and on, even while he complained of failing health, of increasing difficulty in composing his plays—on and on, under the burden of that premature senility—Metastasio produced plays and sacred performances of scanty interest, until death released him from a life that seems to have been less pleasant in reality than it appeared to the onlooking world.

The theatres of great cities rarely performed his melodramas; the critics ignored him.[5] But in many a circle of quiet, intellectual men, often in the village *farmacia* that does duty for a club, wherever a few books are kept, and these few much read, one is sure to find some well-worn volume of Metastasio's plays. The only rival to Tasso's *Gerusalemme Liberata* is Metastasio's verse.

Thus it happens that—while Goldoni who loved the humble and painted their ways and manners with sincerity is now the delight of intellectual dilettanti who have learned to appreciate him—the two poets who yearned for the applause of Princes and relied on courts to preserve their fame are now beloved by the humble. Some of Metastasio's strophes, some of his proverbial lines, will long remain household words in the memory of Italians.[6]

NOTES

CHAPTER II

1. With the contrast between love and hate which was fundamental
to later *secento* dramas, the melodramatic poet also mingled romantic eccentricities and classical reminiscences. Historical truth
and simplicity were ignored. *Secentistic* musical drama was suffocated by absurd declamation, and the demands of *virtuosi*. This,
Apostolo Zeno and Pietro Metastasio tried to reform. In the composition of his applauded melodramas, Apostolo Zeno prefers classical subjects. *Andromaca* (Andromache), *Scipione* (Scipio), *Caio
Fabricio* (Caius Fabricius), were among his most successful.

He imitates both the ancient and the modern—but always with
a careful preparation, noteworthy in a time when historic subjects
were carelessly staged according to the caprices of the *virtuosi*. Zeno
composed more than sixty dramas. He has a fund of maxims and
opportune sayings. He developed the division between the *recitative* and the *aria,* and regularly added as a close to each scene the
final *strofetta* (short strophe). Thus he prepared the way for Metastasio. Zeno possesses another merit. The sacred drama had emerged
from that revolutionary *secento* with its symbolical personages
speaking a mannered language, and ingrafted with pagan and
Christian elements, far removed from the native purity of the *sacre
rappresentazioni*. Zeno, however, in the score of sacred Actions
which he published in 1735, brought to them the same serious exterior qualities as in the Drama.

After ten years of imperial service, he left the Viennese court;
and, in 1728, returned to his native Venice "without money and
exhausted by the journey." Here Zeno spent the last years of his
life in study, confident that the melodrama would now become a
noble plant. When Apostolo Zeno requested his dismissal, the Emperor Charles VI asked him to suggest a substitute. Zeno replied:
"The best poet whom Italy possesses, Metastasio."

2. Metastasio's *Catone in Utica* (1727) represents the hero dying in the last act. Traditions of happy endings, and the impropriety of representing death on the stage, aroused the Romans. A lampoon inviting *La compagnia della Morte* to come and fetch the corpses left at the Teatro Aliberti, caused Metastasio to rewrite his last act, and to give his drama a happy ending. To this prompt compliance with the wishes of his audience, which he considers competent to judge and appreciate his work, may be ascribed the continued progress of Metastasio's production, as long as he remained in Italy.

3. In the first act, Vitellia, descendant of Emperor Vitellius, and claimant to the throne, incites Sesto against Titus, whom she madly loves and whom Sesto loves with the gratitude of a devotee. Vitellia pleads so earnestly that Sesto has almost promised to murder Titus, when a messenger bringing news of Titus' purpose to discard Berenice, stirs such hopes of preference in Vitellia that she orders Sesto to stay his hand. Titus refuses the honours the Senate offers him and announces his intention of marrying Servilia, Sesto's sister, beloved by Annio. Servilia rejects the Imperial offer, protesting that she loves Annio. Titus praises her fidelity, leaves her free to follow her heart's desire. Vitellia knows of the offer and is ignorant of its rejection, so she again urges on Sesto to assassinate Titus. Sesto promises and departs. The minute he is gone a messenger comes from Titus, saying that the Emperor means Vitellia to become his wife.

Sesto wavers between duty towards his prince and love for Vitellia. By some equivocation, Sesto thinks that he has really seen Titus murdered in a public commotion; and he shows Vitellia the bloody weapon that was used. Vitellia's reproaches are a dramatical adaptation of Racine's Hermione's "Qui te l'a dit?" She pours on Sesto's head the maledictions of her passionate grief. Sesto laments in a grand musical theme, until he is comforted by the news that Titus is not dead. It is Lentulus dressed in Titus' robes who is killed. Sesto is persuaded to exchange cloaks with Annio who has provoked the popular revolt.

This exchange makes another dramatic complication: Servilia trembling for Annio; Vitellia afraid lest Sesto should denounce her; Annio fearing for himself and for Servilia. Lentulus, who has survived the wound, discovers Sesto's crime, reveals that the stab was intended for the Emperor. Sesto is condemned by the Senate, yet Titus cannot believe him guilty. His hesitation is expressed in a long recitative of great lyrical beauty. But the master-scene is the sixth, wherein Sesto as a condemned prisoner and Titus as a large-minded Emperor contend in generosity and heroism.

4. Metastasio's greatest activity was between 1730 and 1740, when, among others, he composed the *Adriano in Siria, Demetrio, Issi-pile, Olimpiade, Demofronte, Clemenza di Tito, Achille in Sciro, Ciro riconosciuto, Temistocle, Zenobia,* and the *Attilio* that was, however, performed for the first time in 1750 in Dresden. During the succeeding years his dramas followed one another at long intervals till the composition of *Ruggiero* in 1771. When death overtook the poet in 1782, a medal was struck in his honour bearing the words 'Sophocli italica.'

Metastasio's melodrama begins with the simple and passionate *Didone,* then becomes suddenly complex with artificial intricacies during the time that the poet remained in Italy, then again is gradually freed from this confusion, and rises to a more austere form and more solid structure, reaching its perfection in *Clemenza di Tito* (1734), *Temistocle* (1736), and *Attilio Regolo.*

Metastasio drew only the fundamental lines from Greek, Roman, and Oriental history and tradition, around which he grouped episodes and situations of his own invention. Love always plays an essential part, and gives rise to conflicts with other sentiments such as gratitude, patriotism, and paternal love. These conflicts, however, never rise to tragic heights; for emotions are calmed in a tranquil wave of *ariette* at the end of the scene; and all ends well in a happy climax. The poet avoids everything that could produce violent and unpleasant impressions. A few heroic personages such as Temistocle and Attilio Regolo are drawn with vigour; but they become typical personifications rather than real dramatic figures. On the other hand, when his personages tenderly pour forth their emotions, they live; but it is a superficial life.

In his best compositions he reproduces the simplicity of Greek tragedy, retaining the small number of personages, and observing unity of action. But Metastasio's *Didone* is simply a passionate, jealous woman madly in love, not Virgil's tragic queen. Alexander in love, and Achilles yearning for Deidanta are just eighteenth-century gallants, reflecting the society of the poet's times.

Hence Charles VI's "Cesarean Poet" is rather the forerunner of modern romantic drama than a continuer of Greek tragic literature. In the recitative, the dialogue has vivacity; real psychological and moral observation is expressed with a seeming spontaneity which is the result of finest art. Many of his lines have become proverbial. Metastasio's melodrama, as the last fruit of the Renaissance, presents once more that classicized idealization of modern sentiment, the tradition of which is to be traced to Boccaccio. It has its counterpart in the *opera bouffe* that, by joining music with comedy, represents actual plebeian life.

5. Deeper and more bitter than homesickness, must have been his moral isolation when Metastasio realized that his æsthetics were outgrown, that public taste was veering towards other horizons. His dream of writing dramas that could stand by themselves without the support of music was fast vanishing, because audiences clamoured for more music and less poetry. Metastasio wrote: "Our excellent singers ashamed of being men, strive only to vie with birds, flutes, and violins. When they do succeed in such efforts, they attract for a moment, rather as a marvel, than for the pleasure they give; they attract the ears, not the hearts, of their hearers, who endure the dullness of the play, or ignore it and talk. . . . I cannot waste my time in theatres, wherein for many years I have not set my foot." What a sad admission for a playwright! Indeed, for the poet who had aimed at Greek tragedy, for the musician that

had enjoyed the solemn pathos of ancient composers, the novelties that were leading up to Cimarosa and Rossini must have sounded as a very profanation.

His friend Rainieri de Calzabigi, in his *dissertazione sulla poesia drammatica di Metastasio,* insists "that the poems of Metastasio adorned with music" are indeed musical poetry; but yet "even without this musical adornment, they are real, perfect, precious tragedies." He adds that they "without any artifice penetrate the soul, awakening compassion and love, with the great aim, always in view, of correcting vice and enkindling the spirits to ever greater appreciation of virtue." This judgment expressed by one who might have rivaled Metastasio, since he produced many books for operas, was accepted by most contemporary critics; and modern critics echo this praise with limitations.

Metastasio realized that Italian *dilettanti* were turning to the *Opera Comica,* and deserting the serious tragical opera such as he conceived it. He aimed at the continuation of classic drama; but, *he actually introduced the later school of romantism,* though he refrained from the mixture of comic and tragic elements that was so soon to prevail. From the ancients he copied sustained grandeur and dignity; his tone is always elevated and often eloquent. He disdained realism and drollery.

The Italian public, who had hesitated to accept Goldoni's direct imitations of life, was now applauding realism and drollery when decorated by the light music of Piccini in the *Buona Figliuola;* and was soon to applaud the *brio* and light music of Lorenzini in *Il Socrate Imaginario.* Did Metastasio foresee how this hybrid of the melodrama would so completely supersede it, that even before Metastasio's death, the melodrama, as he had created it and carried it to perfection, was a dying form of art, a thing of the past? How many of us who enjoy the music of opera are interested in the words of the *libretti?* The nonsense which Donizetti accepted, Bellini tolerated, still fills the books of many immortal operas without destroying the enjoyment of the music. In this do we see the contrast. We speak of the melodrama of Metastasio, who wrote the words; we speak of the operas of Wagner or Verdi who composed the music.

Melodrama was a compound of many elements: music and poetry, choreography, stage-machinery and decoration. Owing to Metastasio's excellence, the poetical element was held supreme; but, after him, this form of poetry was considered so unimportant as not to deserve criticism. Any sort of verse was good enough, if it was adapted to the splendour of the melody. The silliest plot was accepted, if only it provided the opportunities required by the musician.

Metastasio witnessed the dawn of the *opera buffa* in Italy, and in France of the *opera comique,* which, with slight changes, still continues to fill the theatres of the world. In Naples, that had first applauded Metastasio's serious and poetical dramas, the *opera buffa* was cradled and fostered. What the melodrama is to tragedy, the *opera buffa* is to comedy—comedy such as Goldoni took from the *commedia dell'arte,* rippling with gaiety; or comedy such as the Neapolitan dialect-theatre provided, with all its wealth of farcical sallies, ready wit, and light-hearted humour. In the years which followed close upon the death of Metastasio, the *opera buffa* was sung in almost every Italian theatre.

At Naples, in the year 1709, there was represented the *Patro Callenno de la Costa,* in all probability the first *opera buffa;* though Signorelli believes the first to be *La fenzione abbenturate* (The fortunate pretences), performed in 1710; followed by the *Spellacchia finto Razzullo* by Carlo de Petris, with music by Tommaso Mauro. The new style found favor. At Naples the actors and singers represented contemporary plebeian life, showed the comicality, the gay carelessness of daily living in the streets and piazzas frequented by authors and spectators. The *Socrate immaginario* (Imaginary Socrates), performed in the year 1775, was written by Giovambattista Lorenzini. It remains the most vivacious production of the Italian musical comedy of the eighteenth century.

Casti devoted himself to musical comedy a little later. In 1784, Paisiello, who was returning from St. Petersburg by way of Vienna, was invited by the emperor to compose an opera for the court theatre. He consented, but manifested a desire to have a libretto by Casti, who then wrote the *Teodoro in Venezia,* a popular hero-comic drama in two acts.

Da Ponte competed with Casti for the position of court poet. He first wrote verses, and then composed the libretto of the *Nozze di Figaro,* set to music by Mozart, which soon silenced the *Teodoro* of Casti. Casti then composed the *La grotta di Trofonio,* in two acts, with music by Salieri. Fortune was not favorable to him. The Emperor Joseph II, one evening in the loggia of the theatre, made him a present of a hundred zecchini accompanied with the words: "These will be for the expenses of your journey." Da Ponte, now left without competitors, wrote *Don Giovanni,* also set to music by Mozart. In 1738 the Italian companies were dismissed from Vienna; but in Italy the comic dramas—*drammi buffi*—continued to delight the public for many years.

The century, which begins with the *Caduta dei decemviri* by Silvio Stampiglia, closes with the universal applause given to the *Serva padrone,* the *Matrimonio segreto,* and the *Socrate immaginario.* These are amorous sighs in minor key, whereon are woven *fioriture* of trills and runs, for the pleasure of a public which, amid balls, suppers, theatres, masks, and carnivals, was forgetting civic ideals and serious thinking. In *Fanfulla della Domenica anno IV; Il Metastasio: critico e prosatore,* Luigi Morandi analyses Metastasio's translations of Horace and Aristotle and his comments on classical writers. In a letter dated August, 1749, he praises Metastasio's description of a quarrel between a poet and Caffariello (the famous soprano) as a model of spirited and condensed narrative.

6. In spite of the monotony of his plots, the occasional incoherence of the characters, the abuse of the means for entangling the action and for leading it on to a precipitate *dénouement,* Metastasio remains

the most genial artist of his time. "Many," writes Goldoni, "have proved themselves after him both valorous and learned; but the ear accustomed to those sweet verses, to those gentle thoughts, to that brilliant manner of scenic-representation of the worthy poet, has not as yet found anything which is worth comparing with him." Abaté Golt remarks in a panegyric delivered at the Arcadian Colony:

> Diasi al greco coturno il primo onore.
> Ma il forte Shakespire e il dolce Artino
> Conobber piu di noi le vie del core.

("Let us give the first honour to Greek tragedy: Yet great Shakespeare and sweet Artino (Metastasio's name in Arcadia) knew better how to touch our hearts.")

Abaté Cordara di Calamandrana names Metastasio the "Italian Sophocles." The same epithet was engraved on a medal coined in his honour.

President Des Brosses (*Lettres Familieres,* etc., page 307): Pour les "tragedies en forme d'operas ils ont un excellent auteur: l'abbé Metastase, dont les pieces pleines d'ésprit, de situations, de coups de théatre et d'interet, feroient sans doute un grand effet si on les jouait en simples tragedies declamées, laissant a part tout le petit appareil d'ariettes et d'opera qu'il seroit facile de retrancher."

Goldsmith in *The Bee*: "Would it not surprise one, that when Metastasio is so well known in England, and so universally admired, the manager or the composer should have recourse to any other operas than those written by him? I might say that 'written by Metastasio,' put up in the bills of the day, would alone be sufficient to fill a house, since thus the admirers of sense as well as of sound might find entertainment!"

C. Burney (*Memoirs of the Life and Writings of the Abaté Metastasio,* three volumes. London, 1796): The frontispiece bears this inscription: "Omniaque ejus non solum facta, sed etiam dicta meminisset."

John Hoole translated two volumes of Metastasio's dramas. A letter of thanks by Metastasio is dated October 13th, 1768.

CHAPTER III

GOLDONI'S VENICE

The evolution of acting as a regular profession: Early professional comedians preferred improvisation to memorized recitation: Improvisations and masks are characteristic of the "Art Comedy": These comedians created a few personages, and made them famous: For more than two centuries Italian improvised comedy amused the courts of Europe: In the second half of the eighteenth century, this form of Italian drama had almost disappeared: The statue of Goldoni in the *Piazzette dei Mercanti* in Venice: Goldoni belongs to Venice: The spirit of revolt which swept through Europe found its echo in Venice: To measure the importance of Goldoni's theatre, one must understand the Venice of which his work is the reflection: Venice and the eighteenth century, is a fascinating theme with many variations: Underneath exterior magnificence there was senile decay: The great aristocracy was dissolved: Venice was the most orderly city in Europe: Many magnificent public festivals in which the entire populace participated: Chief among these was the festival *della Senza* (the Ascension), undoubtedly the most splendid spectacle performed in Europe: All Venetian life was theatrically inclined: Private entertainments almost rivalled the public festivals in magnificence: The Venetian lady of fashion: Gambling was the supreme vice of Venetian society. One gambled everywhere and at all hours of the day and night: All classes in Venice wore masks: The *cavalier servente* was a Venetian institution: The Venetian country "House party": The gondola played a very important part in the Venetian eighteenth century life: Goldoni ignored the Catholic Church in his plays: Worldliness of the nuns and priests: Prevalence in this Venetian society of Abbés of dubious charms and cunning ways.

IN the first half of the sixteenth century, dramatic compositions were recited in the courts of princes, in the palaces of lords, and in academic halls, by amateur actors who, after assisting in the entertainment, returned to their ordinary work. In course of time permanent theatres were built; and acting became a regular profession. In 1567 there was a permanent comedy company in Mantua.

These professional comedians preferred improvisation to memorized recitation; and, since similar parts were usually played by the same actor, the comic types of learned comedy became stabilized. Improvisation and masks characterize the "Art Comedy."

The stock themes of Art Comedy were love, quarrels, forced marriages, exchange of personages, disguises, and recognitions. They were taken from novels, or from the learned comedies, or were "lifted" from Latin and Greek plays. The scenic part, which indicated the argument and order of the scenes, was written. Guided by this outline, the actors memorized dialogues and monologues and a collection of sayings, descriptions, and ideas; and trusted to inspiration to give an unexpected turn to a dialogue of glittering metaphor and coarse buffoonery. As such plays could only be represented by professional actors, they were called "Art Comedies."

Thus the comedians created a few personages, who reappeared under the same name in all their plays. Sometimes this was the actor's Christian name, more often the name of the part which he had first made popular. Such impersonation sometimes acquired lasting popularity; and other actors assumed the name, dialect, manner of speaking, and dress of the actor who had made the part famous.

Thus, Flaminio Scala (1610), the author of many plays, was the Flavio of the Gelosi company; Isabella Andreini (1562–1604) was the Isabella, and her husband Francesco was the Captain Spavento; and Pier Maria Cecchini won great renown under the name of Frittellino; and Silvia Fiorello invented the multiform Pulcinella; and there flourished the fruitful race of Pantaloni, Graziana, Pedrolini, Brighella, and Arlecchini.

Moralists were scandalized by the scurrility of the actors; learned comedians despised them; but the common people crowded around their temporary booths; and Society delighted in these improvisations.

The comic companies were usually reformed each season, and they passed from town to town, and often crossed the Alps and seas. For more than two centuries, Italian improvised comedy amused the courts of Madrid, London, Munich, Vienna, and St.

Petersburg. The kings of France received these actors gladly, and loaded them with honours. Their recitations influenced the works of Lope de Vega and Shakespeare and especially Molière, who drew many arguments, personages, situations, and comic artifices from them.

Improvised comedy's heyday was reached about 1650. Invention was exhausted; the art had frozen into the traditional masks; and improvised comedy became a confused tangle of obsolete motives in which the wand of Arlecchino distributed blows; and little remained except loose gestures, indecent equivocation, and vulgar jokes. In the second half of the eighteenth century, this purely Italian drama almost disappeared, suffocated by its own degeneration and by the theatrical reform effected by Goldoni, the highest and most fertile dramatic genius Italy ever produced.

In the *Piazzette dei Mercanti* in Venice there is a statue of Goldoni. Half-way he stands between Rialto and la Mercaria, near the *riva* where the daily market was held; not distant is the Piazza San Marco and the bookshop where his friends and partisans met; and just beyond is the *Teatro San Luca*—now the *Teatro Goldoni*. He seems to be walking among his own people, slightly stooped, as if listening to the conversation in the crowds about him. Gossip murmurs around him now as then; now, as then, pigeons are cooing while the shop-keepers discuss the day's business or engage in wordy quarrel or banter. Step down from your pedestal Goldoni! You will find yourself at home in this twentieth century, and your comedies are still being performed in the Venetian theatres.

Goldoni belongs to these people. Like his own immortal "Pantalone," he was the synthesis of past centuries and the forerunner of a new age. That which he embodied, he understood; but that which he heralded, he did not clearly foresee, though now he is an essential part of it all.

Long before it was translated into acts, before it had even been formulated in theories, the spirit of revolt against accepted values had troubled Europe. When the hurricane burst, it came from all points of the intellectual horizon. The pyramid of classes and of castes in the different European civilizations was assaulted by many diverse and incongruous elements. Rhetoricians and idealists, artists and scholars, realized the truth of Vico's aphorism that "while men behave according to their inclinations, the result of their acts often exceeds their expectation."

Jonathan Swift and Daniel Defoe lashed accepted hypocrisies; Benjamin Franklin proclaimed anew the rights of men; Bayle protested against scientific dogmatism; Ludovico Muratori in patient analyses and Montesquieu in large syntheses demanded that history should consider the origins of power. Buffon, attempting to expunge the religious idea from creation; Jean Jacques Rousseau, exposing his social theories; deriding and gibing Voltaire—each believed that he alone had discovered the cause and the cure of social ills. Even more obscure workers, even those who merely listened, contributed to the great work of reform. Accepted moral laws and political organizations succumbed; new ideas and customs began to appear. One should not disparage the scepticism that challenges accepted standards and rejects those that are false. In cleaning up the earth, those who demolish assist the work of the architect. Though Italian scepticism despised the teaching of B. Vico, its curiosity was aroused by those intellectual currents which came from Germany—too different to be understood; from England—more admired than known; and from France—so eminently idealistic. These importations were not novelties. But their hypotheses influenced Italian literature, manners, and customs. And, since the theatre is in close contact with the society which it represents, with the social life which it expresses, in strictly governed Venice it was a most active vehicle for profound social transformation.

In order to measure the importance of Carlo Goldoni's theatre, one must understand the Venice of his time, of which his work is the reflection. Venice and the eighteenth century! What a theme with many variations! Although the treaties of Passarowitz, of Carlowitz, and of Utrecht greatly reduced the territory and the political influence of the Venetian Republic, nevertheless, one could still rest under an illusion. Venice still appeared like an oasis—splendid and tranquil. Everywhere else was the horror of war. Venice was the city of peace, luxury, refinement, and pleasure, to which came the worldlings of all countries. Venice was also the rendezvous of the intellectual, and it was the temple of art.

Nevertheless, under this exterior magnificence, and in spite of its solid government and the good order of its people, Venice carried in her side the same wound that threatened death to other ancient governments. This, the only independent Italian state, was ruled by an oligarchy. Democracy questioned the very reason for this government. Everywhere else in Europe, revolutionary ideas battled with the privileges of caste; even the broad sea could not defend England from the contagion; and her lagoons could not isolate Venice. No revolt, no declaration of rights, but inevitable destiny—the law which dominated the entire European evolution—sapped the foundation of this ancient power.

Long wars had exhausted the Venetian treasury. Disastrous treaties, the commercial competition of the English and the Dutch in the Orient, the rivalry of other Italian seaports, had sapped public and private wealth. The State acknowledged a deficit. Commerce was overwhelmed by competition. Recourse was had to expedients which hastened her ruin. One blow followed another. Now it was the reopening of the "Livre d'or"; next, a protective tariff embarrassed commerce; then harsh restrictions to industry. Then ships' cargoes were sold at auction in competition with merchandise purchased at higher prices. The great aristocracy dissolved like a worn-out organism.

The nobility called *Barnabotti* was recruited from among the failures of the great aristocracy or from those who had paid for admission to the Grand Council. These new nobles disturbed an organism already too complex. Holding a middle place between the commercial class and the ancient nobility, they had the faults of both without their virtues. Ignoring their patriotic duties, they insisted on their privileges, especially those of being maintained in the luxury and laziness of public sinecures.

Both these castes were dominated by a passion for display, pitiful reminder of past grandeur. Appearances replaced a vanished reality prolonged by mirage. Stately public pageants, sumptuous embassies, were parts of a deliberate system. Magnificent ceremonial surrounded the Grand Council; and the courts of justice were largely paid for by a government that was niggardly in regard to everything not seen. The salaries of all state employees were cut. Taxes were raised, and payments strictly enforced. The Government practiced every device for saving. The aristocracy economized on their real needs.

This Venetian aristocracy rarely had recourse to violence in order to make their privileges respected. Although duels were destroying the flower of European nobility, they were rare in Venice. The nobles had abandoned the institution of the "buli" or bodyguard, save for some poor country squires who wished to overawe their very pacific retainers. The aristocracy fought only for social preference, civic dignities, and public offices. Impudent bargaining, favoritism, corruption, and prodigality characterized the election of the doges and contests for government positions. And yet this government was less barbarous and less arbitrary than elsewhere in Europe. The honesty of the Venetian magistracy was proverbial.

The Princess of Ursins marvelled that "three policemen sufficed to maintain perfect order among the crowds of the most honest and good-natured people whom she had ever seen." Cardinal Bernis writes: "I have never ceased to admire and wonder that Venice, placed between ten other states, without gates, without walls, where one never sees either guardians or soldiers, which is the receptacle of all the evil characters from the neighboring countries, is nevertheless the Italian city in which there are the fewest thefts and assassinations." President Des Brosses writes that "one could not count more than four assassinations in a year," but this is probably less than the reality.

De La Lande (*Voyage in Italy*) writes: "these people are cheerful, gentle, quiet and easily satisfied. . . . In everything which does not interfere with the government, one enjoys in Venice the greatest liberty and foreigners are never troubled." The pages of Jean Jacques Rousseau, and many other memoirs written about Venice, give the same testimony. Cynical Casanova de Seingalt learned by experience the penalties of cheating in Venice, and that there was little profit in the profession of a spy.

Better even than the complimentary opinions of superficial travellers, the official documents prove the good order which reigned in Venice. The many decrees regulating business, instruction, and agriculture; the tariffs so often revised in the hope of restoring the commerce which had been turned toward other countries; the police regulation providing for lighting the streets and canals; hospital maintenance and quarantine at the slightest threatening of epidemic; the enlightened oversight restraining commercial bodies and trade corporations—all of which Pompeo Molmenti has faithfully recorded and explained—contradict the fables invented against the good reputation of that Venice which was still called *La Dominante.*

As for those famous *pozzi* prisons, when Napoleon's soldiers opened their doors, they only found four prisoners, common thieves. Indeed, how accept the impression of permanent carnival, which Venice gave to all foreigners, how conciliate this good nature, gaiety, and kindliness with the savage tales which flourished in the following century? On the slightest occasion the whole city made merry, welcoming some princely guest, celebrating some historic anniversary, or honouring one of the many saints of the national calendar.

The official documents have much to say about the festivals given in honour of foreign princes. Venetian rulers ingenuously believed in dazzling the great with pompous ceremonies. Patricians foolishly displayed their palaces, their riches, their collections of jewels, pictures and tapestries. What varied enchantments, miracles of luxury and elegance, were offered to royal and princely guests! Palaces were improvised and decorated with statues; and other palaces were joined together for magnificent balls. The square of St. Mark was changed into a basin in which floated fantastic boats. The lagoon of St. George was transformed into an ephemeral garden covered with palaces, towers, and forests—all created by the use of countless lanterns swinging from a thousand boats.

In 1709, during the war of the Spanish Succession, the Danish Frederic IV, traveling incognito, received more than royal gifts: twelve gondolas loaded with mirrors and the crystals of Murano, precious oriental commodities, magnificent cloth-of-gold textiles and beautiful embroideries, and three of the six cannon which were cast in his presence at the Venetian Arsenal. And how magnificent were the celebrations given in 1769 upon the visit of Joseph II, and in 1782 to welcome Pope Pius VI on his return from Vienna!

The many patriotic festivals to which the Venetians were passionately attached were equally magnificent. Chief among these was the festival *della Senza* (the Ascension). Along the entire length of the grand canal, that great golden and carved barque, the *Bucintoro,* like a shrine, glided majestically between triple rows of decorated gondolas and boats. All the actors of the apotheosis are in their places, clothed in brilliant robes, shining with glittering ornaments, and in the hieratic pose which had been consecrated by centuries of splendor. Europe is there in the person of its ambassadors; but they could not equal the ducal magnificence. The people of the Orient were there in their medley of costumes. Hastening crowds came from nearby *terra firma* or from the city's *calli* and *campielli*. The movements have the seriousness of a religious rite. With the high-sounding words "Disposamus te, mare, in signum veri perpetuique dominii," the Doge casts into the water the symbolic ring. Neither the senators who surrounded, nor the people who shouted, suspected the irony of that affirmation of perpetual rule made by the representative of an autocracy from which power had fled, and in the presence of an impoverished people.

Those Venetians also were on the way to being transformed. Around that oligarchy, which even in its decline possessed such prestige, pressed without hatred and without anger the crowd of common people who will so soon supplant them. The crisis which was upsetting the bourgeois class in the whole civilized world assumed in Venice a special character. The place in the sun, so violently demanded by the common-people elsewhere, "Pantalon" believed he would be able to obtain through the laws of his republic and by his commercial cleverness. Indifferent by tradition and by temperament to politics and other general ideals, he still applauded the magnificent festivals. In no place had the aristocracy been more powerful; and in no place in the hour of its fall did it find more appreciation and less reproach. Since they were collaborators, upon whom weighed great obligations, they deserved extensive privileges. The conflict of interests, the rivalry between the different social strata, were easily forgotten in the hours of pleasure.

In the Venetian festivals the spectators actually participated. Other Italian cities displayed magnificent spectacles. Those of Versailles unfolded an equal splendor and art; but in no other capital was there such a complete co-operation of all the people in the common entertainment. In Venice there was no hint of a merely curious public viewing some unusual spectacle. Upon this great stage of embellishment, the lagoons framed with magnificent palaces, churches and public buildings, the most important rôles were mingled with the choir of the people, all of them actors and artists by racial instinct. They crowded the great piazzas, gathered on bridges; or with joyful cries and eager faces, in gaily decorated gondolas, swarmed the canals. Every Venetian felt his participation in the picture and his contribution to the general effect by guarding his pose and his place. Courtesy marked the first motions in the duel between the enfeebled aristocracy and the people who were beginning to feel their power—a courtesy which was partly traditional and partly deliberate, of which the reasons were lost in the historic past.

The Goldonian comedy furnishes many episodes and characteristics; but, in order to connect these scenes with the universal Venetian life, it is necessary to know something of Venetian manners, habits, and customs. Venetian private life exhibited the same theatricality that characterized the public life of that period. The same egoism inspired the politics of the Senate and the conduct of the most insignificant *popolano*.

But as everything is not good in that which we call the best of worlds, so all is not bad in that which we call evil. That childish pride contained some virtue. To forget present distress by dwelling upon past grandeur brought a sentiment of commercial honesty and private honour— an idea of duty which had a real value and elevated social life.

The spectacularity of every form of Venetian Art at this moment, was a sincere expression of the Venetian desire to dazzle, to astonish. The exaggerations of Tiepolo and the mannerisms of Rosalba Carrera had replaced the grandeur of Veronese. In the enormous compositions of Tiepolo, the clouds are massed like the curtains of a theatre, the marble columns are bent and broken, and human bodies in disconcerting foreshortening rest upon marvelous unfolding of draperies. Venetian architecture manifested similar tendencies. Even the funereal monuments effected a shocking mannerism; this group of statues suggesting the final scene of an opera, or ballet, ornaments a tomb.

All Venetian life showed this same theatricality. Private entertainments almost rivalled the public festivals in magnificence. Political and business 'relations brought oriental ideas so near that Venetians rarely admitted strangers within the family circle. The foreigner only saw official functions and the public ceremonies which filled the days and nights of the Venetian world. Life was lived in the open; and the fashionable world was sure to be found in certain places at certain periods of the day and night. Even the private houses and their furnishings gave evidence of the lack of family life and of the passion for display. The palace, with its monumental marble columns and steps where the gondolas came alongside, its majestic stairway, its vast salons opening one into the other, reveals the temple dedicated to Vanity. The spacious rooms were paneled in tapestries decorated in gold, and lighted by many mirrors in splendid frames. Above the doors in scroll-carved brackets, shepherds and shepherdesses, in mannered graces, reflected the affected movements of the people who were strutting below them. Stiff-backed chairs with slender legs ranged along the walls, for it required space for the panniered lady advancing with mincing steps, resting the tips of her fingers on the arm of the cavalier in enormous wig and embroidered and brocaded cape who accompanied her. Space was needed for the low courtesies of the ladies and the salutations in which the long curls of the masculine perruque almost touched the ground. This entering a fashionable salon was an important ceremony. It was an art to place the chair exactly as required by the precedence of one lady, without offending the other grand ladies, each one intent on maintaining her rank. These social formalities of fashionable society began in the morning and continued until late at night.

Pietro Longhi, Goldoni's friend, has painted this fashionable woman at every stage of her daily routine: the morning at her toilet surrounded by her friends, the trades-people who tempt her extravagance, the little abbés, curled and perfumed, who regaled her with scandals while she drank her chocolate and read the billets-doux or the poetical verses which sang her beauty, but could not make her forget her pressing debts and the money lost last night in gambling. After the toilet and the Mass, came visits, excursions, shopping, lunch in the *parloir* of the convents where the nuns held their court, the visit to the fortune-teller, and then the "promenade." No lady of fashion could miss the promenade at the hour and at the place that fashion prescribed. For this stately daily parade was unique in its character. The *Liston* extended from San Geremia to the Riva de Schiavoni. There swarmed a motley crowd. Here the rich colors of the Orient mingled with the formal elegance of Senatorial robes; and the patrician's *tabarro* jostled with the *bautta*. The grand lady in finery rubbed against one in *zendado,* or disguised by a mask. Here were open stalls of every description. Mountebanks, exhibitors of tame birds, and fortune-tellers—a glittering ensemble in which each knew his own place.

One came to the theatre to continue the everlasting gossip. In the boxes society gambled, talked, and occasionally listened to a melodious soprano voice from a masculine throat. It was considered good breeding to judge the play by the opinion of those in the pit. After the theatre, the Ridotto, to gamble, to sup, and continue the everlasting talk. Gambling was the vice of this society which was more frivolous than wicked, more vain than luxurious. Gambling satisfied the instinct of the trader and the desire to splurge. Gambling might replace an income impaired by commercial speculations or wrecked by extravagances. One sometimes succeeded. For those who despised the modest gains of legitimate business, gambling offered an attractive profession. Ruined nobles, impoverished landowners, the new rich, and professional gamblers played faro, tresset, and bassette; dupes from every corner of the world came to Venice to be plucked. One gambled everywhere, and at all hours of the day and night. In the patrician's salons, the gambling-table was always prepared. Most men of fashion had some *casino* near Piazza San Marco, which served for business office and bachelor quarters. There they received merchants, usurers, others of uncertain character, and their most intimate friends of both sexes. Here one could freely sup or gamble or be otherwise amused.

Great ladies had similar "bachelor" quarters; some even received openly to avoid the formalism of official receptions. Others used these *casini* to encourage foreigners to gamble. Some owned them in partnership, forming societies, governed by rules similar to English clubs. The Counsel of Ten passed laws and fixed the principal charges of the Ridotto which was then situated in the Calle Valleressa. A pamphlet now preserved in the Museé Correr echoes the public indignation when a great Patrician was elected to preside over the ruin of fools.

One gambled in the barber-shops, rendezvous of the unemployed, and in the cafés which were never empty and never closed their doors. One gambled in the *malvasie,* where wine flowed for the gondoliers while waiting for their clients or masters, and also for the rich bourgeoisie and for the gentleman of fashion who entered stealthily, muffled in his cloak, when he wished to keep low company. Even the poorer women while working at their marvelous lace, in their doorways or on the low balconies, played their little games of chance, especially the *Venturina,* an exceedingly popular sort of lottery.

Common to all classes in Venice was the mask. Foreigners have always exaggerated or distorted this ancient and universal custom. It was not romantic as many seem to have supposed. In Venice the mask was not part of a special manner of dressing, or the obliging accomplice of shady intrigue. It was a necessity on certain occasions; it was the official incognito on others. Sometimes it indicated a partial relaxation of the laws of etiquette. The patrician who wished to go to Mass in his slippers, or to lounge in the *piazzetta* during business hours, threw a *tabarro* over his shoulders; the great lady put on a mask and a *bautta* to go shopping or to drink a cup of coffee in public. The *bautta,* a hooded cloak which hid the entire body as well as the head, and a mask, furnished with an ample frill, were a complete disguise. In most cases, as soon as the theatre or casino had been entered, the great lady and her cavalier freed themselves from their masks and heavy dominos. The mask was not only permitted for the carnival, the "Senza," and other occasions, but it was sometimes demanded by law, to restrict luxury in dress.

As for that characteristic Venetian institution, the *cavalier servente* or *sigisbée,* what an amount of virtuous indignation has been wasted in pious condemnation of the person who was "neither husband, lover nor friend." People intent on committing certain social sins do not confide in the public. In this Venetian world, saturated with Spanish formalism and Oriental jealousy, these *sigisbées* would not have been tolerated if their purpose had been questionable. There could be neither absurdity nor immorality in a custom saturated with the perfume of ancient gallantry, and the chivalric ideals of a very old aristocracy. The cavalier who agreed to serve a lady must protect her good name. If he abused his rights, he was despised. If he permitted another to supplant him, he became ridiculous. Neither high-born patricians nor their bourgeois imitators desired ridicule or dishonour.

The passing years have only slightly modified that other custom of Goldoni's Venetians, the Country House party. To go to the mainland, to see the trees, to walk over the greensward of the fields—what a joy for dwellers in a city rising from the sea, with narrow streets, few gardens, and many canals! This craving for *terra firma* had been most singularly transformed by fashion, vanity, and etiquette. The Venetian went into the country in order to continue his Venetian manner of living. In their princely villas on the mainland, the Venetian patricians offered a hospitality as lavish as that given by great English families in their country estates. This prodigality, however, was the only point of resemblance. For Venetians, *villeggiatura* meant the salon, conversation, the gambling tables, the garden walks for a short stroll, concerts, balls, theatrical performances; exactly as in the city. The bourgeois family, in leaving Venice for the mainland, sought the café on the village square and the street where he could strut with his companions. Not to be able to go to the country in the autumn, and be seen at one of the fashionable country resorts, would have been an acute humiliation.

Goldoni has also presented another peculiarly Venetian characteristic—the gondola. The gondola played a very important part in Venetian eighteenth century life. The severity of the sumptuary laws, even more than the learned Latin work of the Spanish Emanuele de Azevedo, testifies to the preference of the Venetian patricians for this luxurious but slow method of travel. A day in the pillory and three years in prison was the punishment for the gondolier guilty of wearing more than the permitted amount of silk. Severe laws forbade gondola proprietors from decorating them too gorgeously, and finally required their being painted black. The interior decorations of the gondola, however, were works of art. Bronze or brass marine monsters were shaped in many poses; there were mirrors, oriental carpets, and soft cushions. The gondola might become a love-nest, rocked by the quiet waters, and with a protecting and complaisant gondolier. Sometimes the gondola of the great lady became a jewel-casket in which to hide her beauty, to which the window of the *felze* with its dark interior made a most becoming frame. On entering or leaving the gondola, opportunities were presented for graceful gestures as the Venetian lady rested the tips of her fingers on the arm of her *cavalier servente,* when her foot left the edge of the boat and rested on the marble step of the palace.

The gondoliers formed almost a caste. Those employed by a private family were the confidants of family secrets. Of a fidelity that was traditional, they were also restrained by the professional honour. The gondolier of Madame would have been despised had he "talked" with her husband. Those in public service, all stationed in fixed places while waiting for their customers, were tenacious of their privileges, especially the right to a free place in the pit of all the theatres.

Goldoni, as an author, has deliberately ignored one entire side of Venetian life—the position of the Republic toward the Catholic Church. After centuries of combat and of resistance, the actual situation was one of ceremonious distrust. The Republic feared Papal encroachments upon its rights, and the frequent appeals to Rome of the Ecclesiastical courts. The Venetian judicial courts restricted the Inquisition. The Venetians were sceptical, light hearted, grown-up children; religion meant little more than a tradition, a question of propriety and good form, an excuse for public celebrations, a code of expediency respected by all social classes.

As for the convents and the abbés, they participated in all worldly pleasures. There is some exaggeration in the scenes described by Casanova, and also in the statements of President des Brosses that "the convents were the hotbed of gallantry," and that "three among them disputed for the privilege of furnishing a mistress to the Papal Nuncio." Nevertheless, intrigue flourished in the hot-house of convents. Their *parloirs* were more frequented than the salons of great ladies. The nuns received behind the lattice-work. President des Brosses describes them in the *parloirs* and at Mass, "talking and laughing together—they appeared to me to be very pretty and dressed in a manner to make their beauty most effective. They have a charming little coiffure, a simple but very effective costume, almost always white, with the shoulders and neck uncovered neither more nor less than the dresses in the Roman manner of our comedy actresses."

President des Brosses also speaks of the orphans trained by the nuns to perform those beautiful choruses which excited the admiration of Rousseau and other foreigners. Longhi's pictures show an elegant crowd pressing before the wire lattice-work of a *parloir,* bringing to the beautiful nuns the gossip of the world and its vanity, while they gave sweetmeats in exchange.

Scattered through all social ranks, petted in every circle, admitted into every lady's boudoir, the little abbés, of dubious charms and cunning ways, had a prominent place in this Venetian society where the feminine element predominated. It was a society of decadence and refined perversion in the highest spheres, which all the writers of the period have so often described.

Goldoni's Venice was like an old tree but with one of its branches—the middle class—still swelling with sap. Her wars were fought beyond the seas, mainly by mercenary troops, and Venice was sure to win; the Council was vigilant and wise—why borrow trouble?

Confidence in the ruling patriciate, long habit of avoidance of political discussion or religious argument, ignorance of distant danger, produced the atmosphere of tranquillity in which Goldoni's youth was cradled.

The romantic school has painted the Venetian government under dark colors, and claimed that Goldoni feared to reveal the sores.

Venice was not a hell of denunciations, secret judgments, darksome prisons, and horrors. But, about certain topics, Venetians talked in whispers. Life was pleasant; the government worked smoothly; there was little enticement to rebellion, even though the problems agitating the intellectual life of Europe found some echo in Venice.

Goldoni

CHAPTER IV

GOLDONI AND HIS PLAYS

Goldoni was a true Venetian, and this Venetian atmosphere furnishes the foundation of his plays: Goldoni's plays show that he was a marvelous observer but was unable to generalize: His satire is softened by his good nature: He vividly described the world in which he lived: His religious attitude is typically Italian: He respects appearances, but goes no farther: In his comedies, Goldoni severely judged the aristocracy, but regarded the bourgeois family with indulgence: He did not invent his types, which he completes by showing the same character in many plays: His Pantalone, the most ancient of the Masks, is Goldoni's favorite character: Goldoni's female characters are many and varied, and some of them are unsurpassed: Goldoni tried to reform the comedy, and partly succeeded: Goldoni hated militarism and loathed war: In Goldoni's social plan, the family is the nucleus of society: He admired the medical profession, and highly respected lawyers: He knows and loves the lower classes and asks for them fair play.

THIS special Venetian atmosphere furnishes the foundation of Goldoni's comedies and of his own life. In him the old time is summed up, and the new era begins. He was a Venetian of the ancient regime. His gentle manners, his gracious disposition, and his home environment harmonized with the world of which he was a part. That Italian word *simpatico* describes his charm. Education and environment can foster it; but they cannot create it. It is a gift of the gods. In Goldoni it gave sincerity to his compliments and seasoned his politeness. It was more than gallantry.

Goldoni never endured the isolation which crushes many loving natures. He paid the price. He was spared the struggle, but he lacked that strength which comes from battle; that hardihood which makes pioneers, he failed to develop. But there is value in obedience. There is power in repose. With Goldoni this obedience and repose was illumined by intellect and ennobled by human love. Goldoni followed the precepts of his time; he was in harmony with his environment.

In his memoirs Goldoni rejects any philosophical system other than "celui du Bon Sens." Considering his intimacy with Albergati Capacelli, his eagerness to secure Voltaire's approval, his long stay in Paris—then discussing Rousseau's Utopian dreams, Montesquieu's attacks on government, Beaumarchais' witty assaults, and all those excitements that prepared the upheaval of 1789—this reticence is remarkable.

In Goldoni's works there is unity, intent, and inspiration. He does not dictate the law nor condemn; but his common sense, experience, love and pity for his fellows, have given him a philosophy all his own. He has remarkable qualities as an observer; but is unable to generalize or to condense. An optimist, his satire is always softened by his good nature. He vividly describes the world in which he lived.

It is not just to speak of Goldoni's hypocrisy. In regard to the relation between the sexes, he deliberately passes over many things which were perfectly understood by his audiences. Goldoni's simple honesty wins us. As a lawyer, pleading with moderate success at the bar of Venice and of Pisa, he earned the esteem of colleagues and clients. He did his duty when he was a consul. As playwright and teacher of players, he was industrious and friendly. Goldoni's moral standard was in harmony with the Venice of his time. His religious attitude is typically Italian. He respects appearances; fears the Church's power; silently despises the dissolute clergy. In Paris he writes some almost atheistic sentences; in Venice he is more respectful. "He never could get to the end of a paternoster," and hopes that his wife's prayers will win for him a seat in Paradise; but he ventures no further.

From Rome, he writes Gabriel Cornet that he does not expose the clergy in his plays "because they are protected by their robes." The "robe" may refer to the patrician *velada* or the judge's *zimarra*, as truly as to the cloak of the priest. This is more probable, as the letter says that an author must "find his material in the Orient or

Occident, because some of the springs of inspiration are not available nearer home."

The Italian proverb *Roma veduta, fede perduta* applies to Goldoni. He knew cardinals and popes as they were. Pope Cardinal Rezzonico chatted confidentially with him about his own Venetians. When Cardinal Lambertini visited Albergati Capacelli, Goldoni learned many things which he could not represent upon the stage.

His pious mother had many friends among the nuns. These nuns flattered Goldoni's talent, patronized his youth, and proposed for him a brilliant marriage. Goldoni wrote verses for these pious patronesses; but he declined the wealthy bride of doubtful birth.

Yet he is no atheist. When Albergati Capacelli was sorrowing, Goldoni wrote him: "All of the amusements and all of the pleasures, all of the activity of the world cannot satisfy the human heart, which is made for love. Religion alone can satisfy this inclination. Then the heart cherishes an object superior to mankind, and judges worldly objects as unworthy of its attachment. I do not disapprove of devotion; but I have not as yet been graced with it. I do not know whether I can wish it to one whom I esteem and love; but I am persuaded that unless you become religious you will go on loving as you have ever loved." Religion is here suggested as a balm for sorrow, an equivalent of morphia to one in bodily pain. His friend had suffered from a series of conjugal and extra-conjugal mishaps; and Goldoni hints that a more noble affection might prove less deceitful. Goldoni composed a religious poem for Cardinal Portocarrero; but he humbly declares the *Incoronazione di Davide Re*, "fatta per ubbidienza." There is no religion in his plays, no appeal for divine guidance. Neither in himself nor in the world around him did Goldoni find the religious motive directing action.

Goldoni's is a real and typical expression of the intellectual and social and spiritual life of his Venice. Pursuing the way of least resistance, his character possessed sweetness and breadth of view, but lacked audacity and concentrated energy. Hence his excessive complaisance, his submission to men and to circumstances: but also his serenity, his indulgence to the foibles of others, and his good nature. His self-respect, his delicacy, and his feeling of personal dignity, were unusual; and his professional honesty was altogether greater than that of the world in which he lived. Goldoni was superior to the average man of his time. He was industrious, honest, steady, conscientious, faithful to his friends, and forgiving to his foes. In his love-affairs, he seems above the standard of his day. He dallied in several love-affairs before he married Nicoletta Connio; but his behaviour towards her won her devotion; his mistakes were forgiven; the dignity of the ménage was never imperilled.

As a writer, he had all of the natural gifts and few of those acquired from study. Sometimes his plays show haste and a poor choice of subjects. Sometimes he condescends to produce work unworthy of his talent. When he writes Italian, his language is defective. But his dialect is rich and elegant.

Goldoni composed nearly three hundred plays, though many of the plays so catalogued are duplicates, being played under one title in Paris, and under another title in Venice.

GOLDONI'S COMEDIES

It is difficult to classify material so vast and varied. The better comedies may be separated into those of intrigue and those of character. This arbitrary division was suggested by Goldoni himself.

These comedies of intrigue are pictures of Venetian society and family life; or rather of two classes—the aristocracy and the people. Goldoni severely judged the aristocracy; their gambling, debts, sexual immorality, discord, license, and, above all, their "serventisme."

Goldoni regarded the bourgeois family with indulgence. Here are living pictures. The scenes fascinate us; the episodes are never too many, never unimportant. Though truthful, the picture is tempered by a delicate sense of the proprieties. The comedy rarely becomes trivial.

Goldoni did not often invent his types, and these types were never completed in a single play but passed from comedy to comedy where the surroundings and the circumstances are so changed as to show each character under many aspects. La Cortesan is such a character. He is the courteous Venetian, the man of the world; but he is not dissolute. He is ardent in his love-making; but he is a man of honour. He makes many debts; but he pays them.

Goldoni's Pantalone is immortal. Pantalone is the most ancient of the Masks, the most Venetian, and the one most preferred by Goldoni. He is the clever but honest merchant; he is the father who exercises his authority but profoundly loves his children, especially his daughters. He personifies common sense and honest living, a member of the bourgeoisie—a bourgeois who respects the nobles, lends them money, and supplants them. Goldoni has individualized the character without detracting from its value as a type.

The Miser like the Prodigal, is a type characteristic of the decadent life of Venice, and made an excellent comic mask.

Goldoni's female characters are more numerous and more varied than those of his men. For Goldoni had loved much, and had associated with and understood the women of his time. He took those two types of Ancient comedy, the simple young girl in love, and the worldly-wise young woman, and gave them new significance.

Rosaura, in love, retains youthful innocence; but she has dignity and passion. In other plays, when wife or daughter, she is submissive and indulgent. Beatrice is her complement in the aristocratic world. Although very near to indiscretion, usually she does not sin. Goldoni treats his patrician ladies more kindly than their men. But his real greatness is shown in his portraits of middle and lower-class women. Mothers are tender or scolding; wives zealous or rebel; gossips' tongues are hung in the middle. But a solidity of character is common to them all. Goldoni loved his soubrette characters. Goldoni remembered the very good mother and wife that Providence granted to him. In almost every situation he shows the woman less wicked, less perverted than her masculine counterpart.

The modest, industrious, obedient young girl with some coquetry was a stage novelty. His Pamela was borrowed from sentimental romance; but dainty Lucietta, Mariana, Felicietta who come and go so trim and gay, playing their pretty pranks, pleading for their lovers, or plotting to captivate some grumbling old uncle, are truly Goldonian. Goldoni's Giannia, in the *Mercanti,* and the Dutch doctor's daughter in *Medico Olandese,* are more finished pictures.

In many plays the wife or the mother is protecting the family. In others, an honest wife patiently endures the petty tyranny of a jealous or miserly husband. Goldoni's highest ideal is the peace and honour of the family. Some of his women are bad; but their wickedness is an effect, not a cause. The coquettish wife is partner of a dissolute husband; the quarrelsome housewife is embittered by bullying. It is the suppressed woman who contrives and plots. Note that this thesis of the reform of society—through the family, and by the influence of women—is advanced in this Venetian society, and is unsupported by doctrinaire sermons.

The standard of morality in Venice was so unfair towards women that Goldoni is original in his subject and in his pleading. Feminine charms were fulsomly praised. There was much nonsense about the worship due the fair; bows and compliments were cheap. But that the woman was the man's equal, was not even discussed. In the scale of social reform, Goldoni sets feminine virtue and influence above masculine power. No preaching, no verbose arguments weaken his thesis. His picture is true; and its composition gives his full meaning.

His *servetta* is also a significant character. The servant, as nearest to the central group, must be an agent for good, strengthening family ties. Placed between the placid middle-class, in whose democratic bosom he was fostered, and the patricians who had opened their doors to his observations—between the declining old world and the dawn of a new era—Goldoni glimpsed every aspect of life; caught the spirit of every social rank. Sensing the changes that were to come, he made his own conclusions.

The censors were watchful; prudence was required; and Goldoni was prudent. Why should he offend either the patrician class or the clergy? The patriciate were the governing caste. Venice was well governed, protected against foes, feared abroad; and princes were sensitive and revengeful. He knew when and how to speak. Moreover his own ideas were too vague for strong expression or the declaration of a system of philosophy. He fenced rather than fought.

Goldoni promoted "reform." But this abstract, much abused noun had a vague meaning. It was like Hamlet's cloud, a fluid, shapeless meteor, the brighter for being so proteiform. When old-fashioned senators spoke of reform, they meant more severe laws. Carlo Gozzi's reformed comedy was padded with nonsense. Goldoni wanted to reform the comedy and partly succeeded. Why he partly failed is shown in his life and his work. He wanted to reform the language, to avoid both pedantry and triviality. In this, too, he obtained some success. He tried to promote social reform. He opposed tyranny, but bowed to law. He inherited that Romanity which holds that law is supreme. What the Torah was to Jews and the Koran to Moslems, the Roman Digest was for the descendants of Rome. A Venetian lawyer was not likely to break with that tradition. Goldoni does not even discuss the aristocratic government of Venice, sanctioned by centuries of glorious working. But he opposes the pretensions of a feudal aristocracy. The patrician landowners thought only to squeeze cash from their tenants; but the tenantry kept their masters in bounds by threatening the law and Venetian tribunals. As there was no oppression, there was no hatred. Between the tenants and the lord there was the steward, who made his profits out of both. In *Il Feudatario,* the situation is skilfully delineated.

Carlo Gozzi denounced Goldoni for over-praising the low-born and denigrating the aristocracy, in other words, for being a democrat. This is the tendency of all his plays. It first appears in the *Putta Onorata* and *La Buona Moglie;* and, after years of pleasant relations with patrons, and with larger comprehension, it is still found in those masterpieces describing the beauty of humble life: *La Barufe Chiozote, Rusteghi,* and *La Casa Nuova.* All Goldoni's plays show his love for the homely class, and his severe judgment of the aristocracy; sometimes the severity of these attacks is obscured by the episodes and amusing dialogue.

How bravely he starts on his quarry! First he assaults the duel, brutal inheritance from past ages, and practiced everywhere in Europe. It was still a privilege of the Venetian aristocracy. Yet Goldoni dared to denounce its cruelty. In the *Cavalier e la Dama,* one of his most honorable characters pleads against it. The sensation in Venice was great; the aristocracy were furious. In other plays, he renews the attack, and with his burlesque ridicules the duellists. With his dagger or with pointed sarcasm, Pantalone stops the would-be hero.

Goldoni unmasks the cowardice of the nobles. Most of his aristocrats, whether the dissipated husband, timid lover, spendthrift, gambler, *cavalier servente,* or the wit, are poltroons. Their vengeance is by treachery, frequently secured with the assistance of

Masked actors, Coviello and a Sicilian, from
Il carnevale Italiano Mascherato of Francesco Bertelli,
Venice, c. 1600

some armed lackey. It is middle-class *Pantalone* or the *Courtesan* or some *rustego* that openly faces his foes. Sometimes it is moral cowardice which he stigmatizes, as in the *Famiglia dell' Antiquario* and the *Donne Puntigliose*. Yet critics, who write that even a whisper was dangerous in Venice, have charged Goldoni with cowardice!

In contrast with Goldoni, Parini seems moderate and Alfieri respectful, though both came later when speech was freer, and Parini was protected by his cloth and Alfieri by his title.

Goldoni fustigates the higher class as gamblers associated with sharpers, borrowing money without intention to repay, trading on their names to gain the plebeian *dot* earned by industrious Pantalone, trading on their honour by winking at a powerful or wealthy *cavalier servente*. Goldoni knew camp life, and the effects of soldiering on his uncle Alberto Goldoni, and on his unlucky brother Giampaolo. He hated militarism and loathed war. *La Guerra* and *L'Amant Militare* are among the most significant of his plays. Swaggering officers, greedy speculating camp-followers, obedience enforced by threats and blows, are the things he represented.

In Goldoni's social plan, the family, the nucleus of society, must be controlled by the paterfamilias. Goldoni has analyzed this power of the patriarch, discussed and questioned it. He says: "Since Society is perverted by lax family ties, since the caprice and indulgence of women is the cause of so much harm, reform; but begin by tightening the family bonds, by correcting and ennobling the position of women." He shows the cause and the effect of a discredited marriage bond. The girl who has been forced to accept a high-born dissolute husband, selects some other man to whom she gives her affection. If the girl had chosen for herself, she would have remained faithful. He shows the middle class more delicate on the point of honor, wives more loyal, husbands more faithful. While the nobleman is flattered by his wife's conquests, or pleased to get rid of her so that he also may be free, Pantalone protests against such practices. Goldoni's plays are crowded with healthy suggestions about the reform and the greater influence of the family. His critics have denied him larger ideas of social reform, alleging that he avoided representations of the clergy, among whom the standard of morality was low. We have already shown that Goldoni felt the clergy were protected by their cloth. Because of the censors, he could not represent them as he saw them; so he did not represent them at all.

Goldoni did perceive the aspirations toward social justice, toward democracy and human solidarity that were then stirring the civilized world. Though he was not prepared by nature or education to give it philosophic or literary expression, his warm sympathy gave it echo.

If there is no violent language nor virulent apostrophe, there is suggestion. In a pastorale, *I Portenosi effetti della Madre Natura,* he writes: "Nature has made us all equals and Nature has taught us that we are all made of the same clay." The plot is contrived to show that the promptings of nature are virtuous; and Goldoni repeats and intensifies this primitive principle. Again in an adaptation of the old *farsa, Bertolde, Bertoldino e Cassas senno,* he writes: "My Lord, I will speak my mind. We all come naked into this world, and we must all die naked. Throw off that silver robe of yours and see whether our conditions are not the same." Again, *Bertoldo* proclaims that if "la belle Verita" is not admitted within the precincts of the court he the *villano* means to speak it, "even if by so doing he loses the chance of favor." Asserting that the lower born are highest in homely virtues, Goldoni also asserted that they are the more useful to society and ought to be held in greater esteem. There is loving understanding of the language, manners, feelings and rights of those simple-minded, loud-spoken, free and easy, but incorruptible gondoliers of *La Putta Onorata, La Buona Madre.*

He defends the actors, a class branded by public opinion. He shows them in true colors, praising those who tried to live right, and ridiculing those who did not: he castigates the individual; but pleads for the class. His *L'Impressario delle Smirne* gives a pretty picture of theatrical customs, and proposes a free association rather than any other form of contract—an intimation that he favored co-operative societies or some form of trade-unionism. Goldoni probably belonged to the order of Freemasons, so persecuted in Italy by the church. He accepted the dedication of one Francesco Grisellini, who signed himself "Fratello Operio" and gave the data according to the "restauration" of the Loggia. He did something even more dangerous, probably describing in his *Donne Curiose* the meetings of Masons, their fraternal *agapi*.

His *Filosofo Inglese* is a caricature of those who brag about philosophy. The cobbler who presumes to say "thou" to a great lady anticipates the sans culotte. He is skeptical when he hears big words applied to small things which are never translated into facts. He smiles at the bombast of the French pamphleteers.

The medical profession he represented *con amore*. His portrait of the physician who heals the spirit as well as the body, who feels tenderly for the weak and ministers to the ailing, is admirable; though often repeated, it has not been bettered. Lawyers he respected and admired. His *Avvocato Veneziano* is a hymn to this the noblest calling. In both of these professions he does not spare individual faults, thereby more truly showing his esteem for the professions. Most of his merchants are honest, respecting the tradition of integrity. He defends tradespeople of all sorts, even the humble *faccino di piazza,* the pawnbroker and money lender. Goldoni has enlarged the sphere of theatrical presentation; to his stage he admits many types. He is an adept of universality.

In his pleading for the lower classes, Goldoni does not exaggerate. He knows and loves them too well. He claims justice, and asks for fair play. With such a good-natured defender of human rights, a revolution could never overleap its aim and become a tyranny. He must have been dazed and horrified by the first results of the French Revolution. No violent upheaval but gradual progress was Goldoni's aim. This progress he foreshadowed and promoted.

In his life, and in every activity of his intellect, Goldoni earned the title of an enlightened worker for social and private justice. He never pretended to be more. He never failed to do that little share of the good work which he could achieve. Others have attempted to do more and have accomplished less.

CHRONOLOGICAL SUMMARY OF CARLO GOLDONI'S LIFE

Carlo Alessio Goldoni, his grandfather, dies in Venice, 1703.

Goldoni born in Venice, February 25, 1707.

Enters Jesuit college at Perugia, 1719.

Studies philosophy in Rimini under Candini, 1720.

Runs away from Rimini with company of actors, 1721.

Lives with his family in Chioggia, and accompanies his father on his medical visits, 1721 and 1722.

Studies law with his uncle Indric in Venice, 1722.

Admitted to the Ghislieri College in Pavia, 1723.

Expelled from college for a libellous writing, 1725.

Studies law in Modena, 1726.

Appointed clerk in the criminal chancellery of Chioggia, 1727.

Appointed to a similar position at Feltre, 1729.

Leaves Feltre (1730) and is with his father when he dies at Bagnacavallo, 1731.

Receives degree of Doctor of Law at Padua, 1732.

Mother leaves Venice for Modena, 1732.

Admitted to the Venetian bar, 1732.

Burns his tragedy *Amalasunta* at Milan, after it is refused, 1733.

Appointed secretary to the Venetian minister at Milan, 1733.

Goes with the Venetian minister to Crema when the French and Sardinians attack Milan, 1733.

Dismissed from his diplomatic position and leaves Crema, 1734.

Imer engages him to write plays for the San Samuele Theatre at Venice, 1734.

Has love-affair with an actress who deceives him, 1735.

Goes to Genoa and meets and marries Nicoletta Connio, with whom he returns to Venice, 1736.

Appointed Genoese consul in Venice, 1740.

This position he resigns in 1744.

Practices law in Pisa, 1744.

Writes a play for the Medebach players who are visiting Leghorn, 1745.

Agrees to write plays for Medebach, of Sant' Angelo Theatre, Venice, 1747.

Returns to Venice, 1748.

At close of his second season at Sant' Angelo Theatre, he announces that the next year he will present sixteen plays, 1750.

Contract with Medebach expires, 1753.

Signs contract with Vendramin brothers, proprietors of San Luca Theatre, Venice, 1753.

His mother dies, 1754.

Signs a second contract with Francesco Vendramin, whose brother Antonio has died, 1756.

Visits Parma and is appointed court poet with an annual pension of 3000 Parmesan lire, 1756.

Invited to write plays for the Tordinona Theatre at Rome, 1758.

Leaves Rome and, after three months in Bologna, returns to Venice, 1759.

Correspondence with the Italian Theatre in Paris, 1759.

Offered a two years' engagement at the Italian Theatre in Paris, and accepts same, 1761.

Signs a final contract with Vendramin, 1762.

With the play *Una delle ultime sere di Carnevale,* says farewell to Venice and leaves for Paris, 1762.

Il Figlio d'Arlecchino perduto e ritrovato is a failure when performed at Fontainebleau, 1762.

Appointed to teach Italian to Madame Adelaide, and is given an apartment at the palace at Versailles, 1765.

Receives from the French court an annual pension of 4000 livres, 1769.

His play *Le Bourru Bienfaisant* performed at Paris is a great success, 1771.

Teaches Italian to the sister of the King, who is engaged to marry the Prince of Piedmont, 1775.

Visits Voltaire in Paris, 1778.

Settles in Paris; the Italian Theatre there is closed, 1780.

Plans a magazine, writes plays, and tries various ways of making a living, but is troubled with partial blindness and poor health, 1781–1792.

Dies in Paris at the age of eighty-six, February 6, 1793.

CHAPTER V

CARLO GOZZI: HIS LIFE AND TIMES

Jealousy of Goldoni inspired Carlo Gozzi's plays: Gozzi and Goldoni contrasted: Gozzi begins writing poems when only nine years old: Is appointed a Government Secretary in Dalmatia: Writes a cynical description of his family's misfortune: The new Venetian Academy named "I Granelloni": Writes *La Tartana degli influssi,* a malicious attack on Goldoni: Composes an ignoble lampoon on Goldoni, *Il Teatro Comico*: Gozzi's first *fiaba* is performed (1760): Gozzi falls in love with the actress Teodora Ricci: Detail of quarrel between Gozzi and Gratarol: The *Memorie* describes Gozzi's increasing melancholia and misfortunes: Nievo's *Confessioni* describes this cruel moment in the history of Venice with the coming of the French: Sad end of Carlo Gozzi.

PATRIOTIC fervor, religious emotion, poetic imagination, delight in verbal harmonies, dramatic sensibilities, being in love, the need of money, the desire to impart information—are some of the reasons why men write. Ambition, vanity, malice and jealousy also seek expression through the printed page.

Jealousy of Goldoni inspired Carlo Gozzi's plays. Yet Carlo Gozzi's own personality and the merit in his writings entitled him to fame. He hated Goldoni; he loved all that Goldoni wished to destroy. An aristocrat, he raved against the son of a country physician, the petty lawyer who dared to pillory the vices and depravity of Gozzi's caste. A Venetian of the ancient pattern, he rebelled against the playwright who lovingly pictured the manners and revealed the souls of the humble. This hatred of Goldoni is Gozzi's master passion, the keynote of his character. It reveals the relative position of the two men.

Carlo Gozzi was descended from Pezolo de Gozzi, that warlike Lombard condottiere in the Milanese wars of the fourteenth century. Long established in Venice, his family had absorbed all the patrician prejudices and qualities. Moreover, his mother was a Tiepolo, of the family of the two great Venetian painters. Carlo,

Carlo Gozzi

Gozzi

the sixth child of the family, was born on the thirteenth of February, 1720. His family had fallen from its former splendour; the father, Jacopo Andrea, was helpless from apoplexy; and the mother, Angiola, was a poor housekeeper and an ineffective mother. Carlo calls his home a "hospital of poets." To escape from their creditors, the family left Venice for their villa and its absurd life of vanity and contrivances. The children, unprovided with teachers and with insufficient clothing and food, amused themselves with theatrical performances, satirizing their own and neighboring families—thus preparing for that life of idleness and hazard which then characterized the youth of the Venetian aristocracy.

Carlo was a leader and adept in this mimicry and improvisation. Encouraged by parental applause, he began writing poems when only nine years old. When twenty, he had written a treatise on philosophy. His brother Gaspare married Louisa Bergalli, well known under her Arcadian name of Irminda Partenide. When her husband gave Louisa Bergalli control of the house, she completed the wreck of the family fortune.

Carlo obtained a government secretariat in the Province of Dalmatia. Here, for three years, he shared in misgoverning that part of the Venetian State and pursued the idle but intellectual life habitual to Venetians. In his *Memorie Inutili Scritte per Umilta* Gozzi presents a vivid picture of Dalmatia. Carlo returned to Venice an accomplished cavalier, an adept in theatricals, dancing, and versifying, and with the swagger of a would-be military man. His home-coming aggravated the family disputes. The ancient palace in San Canziano was falling to pieces. The luxurious furniture, the historical portraits by Tiziano and Tintoretto, were in tatters. Mismanagement had dissipated the small patrimony. His brothers and sisters were estranged. The *Memorie Inutili* describes the Gozzi tribe trundling out of their villa: Gaspare, absent-minded; two sisters in their old-fashioned costumes; Almoro, the younger brother, weeping for his fowls and pups. "Altogether," says Gozzi, "something like the marching off of a troupe of comedians."

How this cynical description of his family's misfortunes, contrasts with Goldoni's conduct! Goldoni carried his wife on his back at a strait, and playfully shared the boat of itinerant players. Cheerful, sympathetic, he is sure of the good-will of others because he has kindness for everyone. Such is the contrast between the two antagonists.

After this family wreck, with painstaking honesty and talent, Gaspare pursued the career of letters. Carlo quarreled with him; the brothers drifted into lawsuits and an exchange of literary pamphlets more creditable to their wits than to their delicacy. Gaspare, manager of the Sant' Angelo Theatre, in his play *Esopo in Città,* parodied Carlo and his reputed mistress, Barbarigo-Balbi. Carlo retorted by litigation. He squeezed money out of the family estate, and lived in unprofitable activity. He composed many satirical poems and boasted that he did not write for money.

While thrones and empires were tottering, and society felt the impending catastrophe, Venetian titled fools played with airy bubbles. Literary groups multiplied and called themselves Academies. In 1740, Venetian wits established a new Academy called *I Granelloni.* They impudently imitated and plagiarized the language and style of the great literary masters of the thirteenth and fifteenth centuries. Their ceremonial meetings were grotesque. The *Granelloni* charged Goldoni and Bettinelli with offending literary traditions. Gaspare Gozzi wrote *La Difesa di Dante;* and Carlo, in 1747, wrote *La Tartana degli Influssi.*

This *Tartana* was a clever and malicious attack on Goldoni and Chiari. Goldoni was charged with plagiarism and with slovenly style. Because he painted the higher classes as vicious and cowardly, he was indicted as an enemy of established order—"which is necessary." In oligarchic Venice this charge was serious.

Fortunately Goldoni was protected by a powerful patron, and prudently pleaded his own cause.

In 1750 (the year which Goldoni calls "terrible" on account of his tremendous and glorious accomplishment of writing sixteen plays in as many months), Gozzi composed that most ignoble lampoon, *Il Teatro Comico all'osteria del Pellegrino*. Goldoni was described as a three-headed monster, a drunkard, and a buffoon. From each of his mouths poured parodies of his different manners of writing. This *Teatro Comico* is the first of the satires that Gozzi afterwards mixed in his *fiabe*. A satirical poem *La Marfisa Bizzarra* is another thrust in this duel.

While Goldoni in *Una delle Ultime Sere di Carnevale* bade a melancholy farewell to his long faithful Venetian audience, Gozzi was being loudly applauded for his first *fiaba*, *Gli Amori delle tre melarance* (1760). Such is the fickleness of public opinion; such was the perverted taste that attended the fall of a great nation. Venice, once the Queen of the Seas, the ruler of the East, the mistress of arts, preferred Gozzi's silly nursery tales and *lazzi* to the noble simplicity of Goldoni's plays. Stimulated by success and by jealousy, Gozzi soon produced the plays *Il Corvo, Il Re Cervo, La Turandot,* etc.

In that passionate, soured and grim soul, another antagonism had been stirred. With all the violence of an unbalanced temperament, Carlo Gozzi, the idler, surrendered to one of those disorderly affections that so often invade an empty soul. Sacchi was the best Truffaldino then playing. He and his troupe greatly contributed to the success of these *fiabe*. Gozzi gave the troupe immense care and affection, and to Teodora Ricci, the leading lady, a passionate devotion.

These senile amours are typical of Venetian customs. Count Carlo Gozzi is the official *cavalier servente* of the actress. He attends her everywhere; he directs her professional career; makes

of her a really good prima donna. Yet she flirts with several admirers and coquets with the man to whom she owes much, and
who loves her. In 1777, after many years of this attachment, happened the unlucky incident that ruined one of Teodora Ricci's
philanderers and disturbed Carlo Gozzi's amour.

To extenuate his responsibility, Gozzi composed his *Memorie
Inutili*. It is a human document. These memoirs are a picture of
eighteenth century Venetian customs, and are crushing evidence of
Gozzi's ungenerous, soured nature. They reveal him as an adven-
turer as skeptical as Casanova or Da Ponte. They also prove that
he is an able polemist. The memoirs contain the history of Gozzi's
entire life; and narrate his rivalry with Pietro Antonio Gratarol,
Secretary of the Senate, who presumed to flirt with Gozzi's pro-
tégée, Teodora Ricci. Gratarol was a beau; his elegance, his many
love-affairs, his wealth and prodigality, made him a dangerous rival
to surly, old-fashioned, gaunt, and impecunious Count Carlo Gozzi.
Both Teodora Ricci and Gratarol strove to conciliate him; he was
a valuable protector, a dangerous foe. Gratarol offers his rival the
directorship of a society of noblemen. He invites Gozzi and the
Sacchi troupe to his villa. Gozzi would not be bribed nor, as a
pseudo-husband, would he tolerate a rival. He sulked and nursed
his bitter feelings.

Meanwhile Sacchi was rehearsing Gozzi's play, *Le Droghe
d'Amore,* imitated from the Spanish of Molina. Gozzi pretended
that he wished to stop the rehearsals, but that Sacchi insisted on the
performance. Teodora Ricci thought that the character of Don
Adone resembled Gratarol. She whispered this to Gratarol, in-
tending that the Secretary of the Senate should quarrel with Gozzi.

Sacchi declared that the play was approved by Caterina Dolfin
Tron, wife of the Procurator Andrea Tron, known as "el Paron,"
the real master of Venice. El Paron dictated public affairs in Venice; but he could not control his wife's whims. Caterina Dolfin

Tron, central figure of one of those *salotti* that ruled Venetian public and private life, was offended with Gratarol for the same reason that Teodora Ricci was offended with Gozzi—desertion of their official attendance. Such a defection was serious in a society cognizant of every liaison and very curious about the behavior of *cavalieri serventi* and their ladies. Caterina Tron insisted that the play be performed. Gozzi hoped that the public would not notice the resemblance. Vain hope in Venice, where scandal was rampant, where feminine intrigues were seething, and where Sacchi was so eager to fill the theatre that he carefully imitated Gratarol's face, attitudes, and expressions. On the opening night, the theatre was crowded with all fashionable Venice. Teodora Ricci was elated; Caterina Tron was thrilled; Gratarol was inwardly raging. Storms of applause greeted Don Adone's appearance on the stage. His short rôle finished, the rest of the play was unheeded. When the last curtain fell, there were tumult, comment, quarrels.

Gratarol, the laughing stock of the city, resigned his position and left Venice forever. Then he published a pamphlet defaming unforgiving Gozzi, revengeful Caterina Tron, and many other patricians. He published this *Narrazione Apologetica* in Stockholm; and supposed he was safe from his enemies. But the arm of the Venetian *Serenissima* was long. The Senate confiscated all Gratarol's estates; and the poor man died obscurely.

Misfortune followed Carlo Gozzi until his death in 1806. His melancholia became a real mania. His nerves were shattered, and his imagination diseased. He had fits and hallucinations. The *Memorie* narrates this tormented existence up to the year 1795. How much more must he have suffered during the ensuing years until his death in 1806!

Everything in his world jarred with Gozzi's ideals and prejudices. What greater agony to such a nature than the revolutionary changes in every branch of thought? To the champion of absolute power, the admirer of the old social order constructed for the bene-fit and glory of the few and in disregard for the submerged masses, what a terrible cry was the "Liberté, Egalité et Fraternité" shouted by the French invaders! To an intense patriot, worshipping the splendour of Venice and relying on the wisdom of her leaders, what a heart-breaking experience to see this splendour bedraggled and this wisdom degraded as Venice sank into senility!

In Nievo's *Confessioni d'un Ottagenario,* we find a poignant description of this cruel moment that sounds like the echo of Gozzi's agony. The coming of the French was, "if not the biggest, certainly the most recent and imminent of their evils. Other mis-fortunes were forgotten; this one was the vivid and bleeding sore that spread over all the state. Every day brought news of some new treason, of some new defection. The *Doge* ruffled his cap on his head; the *Savi* were at their wits' end and ordered the ambas-sador in Paris to bribe some *concierge,* that they might know the secrets of the Directoire. They even tried to touch the heart of Bonaparte.

"One day we heard that the French had taken Verona: the armed peasantry was dispersed, the troops called to protect Ber-gamo and Brescia were in retreat on Padova and Vicenza. Then came the horror of the *Pasqua Veronese,* with all the frightful atrocities committed on the French garrison; Bonaparte's furious protestations, followed by a formal declaration of war. Venetians began to realize that things which had lasted so long might come to an end. They provided food for the *Serenissima Dominante;* but they gave no thought to prepare a defense; since, to speak the truth, no one believed in it.

"Because the *Maggior Consiglio* was not quick enough to sub-mit, they improvised a sort of funereal Magistrature, a board of grave-diggers for the dying Republic . . . some forty persons: Sen-ators, Counsellors, the three Magistrates of the Council of Ten, and as chairman, the Doge himself. This was known as the *Conferenza*. This *Conferenza* assembled on the night of April 30th in the Doge's apartment. Much nonsense was uttered. While they talked, the *Savio* received a despatch from Admiral Condulmer, stating that the French had already penetrated inside the laguna on floating casks. There was general dismay; some strove to get out of it all; others made proposals to surrender. The Serenissimo, Doge Lodovico Manin, walking up and down the room and pulling up his baggy trousers, uttered the memorable words: 'Tonight we are not safe, even in our beds.' A resolution was voted empowering deputies to negotiate with Bonaparte what changes were to be introduced in the form of government."

Nievo describes the solemn sittings of the *Maggior Consiglio*: "the old men pale with fright, the younger men affecting pride, though they knew that they were binding their own fetters. Bonaparte's demands grew more humiliating with the abject acquiescence of the Venetians, who seemed eager to cut off their own nails for fear of scratching those who were trying to smother them."

If such bitterness inspired the retrospective words of one writer some hundred years after these sad events, what must have been the feelings of Count Carlo Gozzi who participated in the awful fall of his beloved country, and could hope for no revival? It was more tragical than any drama he could have invented—this ending of his long life in solitude and depression after having outlived all his friends, and witnessing the crumbling of all that was dear to him. He who had gloried in the titles of "Cavalier" and "Conte," who was always addressed as "Eccellenza" and "Illustrissimo," signed his last will with the title of "citizen."

Perhaps in the melancholy of his declining years, in the dim consciousness of a mind tormented by incipient mania and fervid imagination, strained to breaking point by his ambition and jealousy, perhaps the son of Venice, the lover of all that was the greatness and splendour of his city, realized that in her hour of utmost need he had given his beloved Venice nothing better than foolish nursery tales and farcical representations of masks; then, indeed, the end of Carlo Gozzi was sad enough to cancel all the petty malice and venomous attacks of his jealous temper.

Mezzetin
After a painting by Watteau

CHAPTER VI

THE PLAYS OF CARLO GOZZI

Gozzi's plays secured the attention of his audience, but did not interest Italian readers: To German and English critics, Gozzi is the harbinger of Romanticism: To Italians, Gozzi's fantasy is the product of his surfeited memory: The *Masks* of Gozzi and Goldoni contrasted: In his *fiabe* Gozzi opened wide the doors of wonderland: The fickle Venetians were glad to see Goldoni parodied: Gozzi's Venetian plays made vulgar caricatures of real people: But they also contain some valuable motives: *The Pretty Green Bird* is the best of the *fiabe*: Though the story is complex, it is an interesting play: His comedy *Turandot,* written in verse and prose, has been widely praised: Gozzi failed to produce a true work of art. The invasion of foreign ideas distressed and distorted his mental balance. Gozzi presumed to oppose the the onward march of new ideas, and failed.

SOMETIMES an artist endeavors to make his work a finished picture; sometimes he aims at suggestion, trusting the onlookers' imagination to fill in the detail. In his great poem, Dante minutely describes the shapes and phantoms, and their environment. Milton merely suggests the vague greatness of Satan, the dazzling beauty of Gabriel. He relies on the imagination of his readers to complete the image. Each interpreted the inclinations and capacity of his own people. The Italian spirit is Greek and Roman. Classical training, communion with the masterpieces of antiquity, have made Italians artists and critics; but they are not an imaginative people. Gozzi failed to understand this. He secured the attention of his audience; but he could not rouse the sympathetic interest of his readers.

Italian critics scarcely afford him condescending benevolence; though in Germany, his *fiabe* were translated and welcomed as a splendid reaction from French pseudo-classicism. Hofmann and Goethe imitated them; Schiller translated *La Turandot.* To Northern critics his extravaganzas indicated genius, and Gozzi is the harbinger of Romanticism. As such he was praised by Madame de Staël, and by Paul de Musset. The English also have applauded

Gozzi. From Baretti to Symonds, they all approve of his un-Italian æsthetics.

Classically trained Italians abhor unlimited fantasy, monsters, giants, dragons, fairies, endless transformations; men turned to statues, statues that speak or laugh, waters that dance and ropes that sing, are absurd even to Italian children beyond the pinafore age.[1] "Fantasy" is a misnomer for these marvels selected from many sources and mixed without discernment. Imagination girdles the moon with pearly light; it mounts on the flaming plumes of glorious sunsets; it is the charm which adds a spiritual meaning to the landscape. It is the suavity which in every expression of art and literature suggests the infinite. Imagination is not parody and farce playing foolish pranks.

Gozzi's flights of imagination were the product of his surfeited memory—a formless mixture of such nursery tales as *Le Cunto delli Cunti* by the Neapolitan Basile,[2] or the many Italian translations and imitations of Eastern stories. These early recollections passed from Gozzi's pen unassimilated. In the first of his *Capricci scenici* or *fiabe,* the *Love of the Three Oranges,* he accumulated traditional childish nonsense in order that he might parody Goldoni's and Chiari's plays. Chiari's bombast was easily parodied; and Goldoni's style was sometimes slovenly. But Gozzi's style was not more correct. They all wrote incorrect Italian. They all used dialect and the Italian colloquialisms caused by political and geographical divisions and centuries of foreign oppression.

Though Gozzi and Goldoni championed purism, neither exemplified it. The Venetian dialect was a national tongue; and the study of Tuscan Italian, like the study of Greek and Latin, was a scholastic exercise. When Gozzi and Goldoni wrote Tuscan Italian, it was almost like translating into a foreign language. Hence the incorrectness of their Italian style. Gozzi corrected Goldoni; Baretti scolded them both.

Goldoni used some characteristic Venetian masks of the ancient *Commedia dell' Arte.* He adopted Pantalone, Arlecchino, Brighella, Il Dottore, Truffaldino; he accepted the traditional Leandro and Rosaura; he transformed them and gave them personality. His Pantalone was the typical *paterfamilias,* the honest merchant, the sensible citizen. He represented a whole class of Venetians. He was a living personality and no puppet. Brighella, the country lout from the north, became a devoted servant, a redresser of wrongs, a friend to his rakish young master. Sometimes he rose to the dignity of an innkeeper.

Arlecchino's irreducible pranks were confined to the background; and Rosaura assumed a matronly dignity unknown to Goldoni's predecessors. Even the *Servetta* grew into those delightful creatures *La Serva Amorosa,* that rival the best feminine characters in any theatre. Proud of this achievement, Goldoni was happy to see his fellow citizens adopting his ideas, and applauding his reform. Now Gozzi hated Goldoni; and he loved all the antiquated forms of Venetian government and art. Jealous and vindictive, he attacked Goldoni's reform. The babble, the practical jokes, the vulgar *lazzi* which Goldoni had minimized or omitted, Gozzi recalled to the stage.

This revival of the *Commedia dell' Arte* appealed to Gozzi's Venetian audience. Things that have but lately fallen from public favour are sure to find partisans. These masks, which had come from the antique Roman mimes, had lived across the darkest ages, had impersonated Italian regions and races, had amused so many generations, impersonated so many waves of ideas, should continue to live on the Italian stage.

On the 25th of January, 1761, Gozzi's first *fiaba, L'Amore delle tre Melarance,* was performed by the Sacchi troupe with enormous success. Goldoni heard the echo of this applause; and it confirmed his purpose of leaving Venice "To seek in new lands, and new experiences of manners, some better fruit. . . . Some day coming back to my beloved people, who perchance are now tired of me. . . . I may be then less old-fashioned and less unpleasant. . . . "

Such a gentle answer to Gozzi's rude attack! Such humility in an author of world-wide fame contrasts finely with the pompous prologue of the *fiabe* that sounds like the flourish of trumpets heralding the puppet-show of the mountebank. Here was no *cammino* or *calle,* no modest room with its balcony looking out on the quiet *canale* such as Goldoni preferred, and such as all immediately recognized as familiar and real.

Gozzi opened wide the doors of wonderland. A king of *coppe,* known only to cardplayers, has a son Tartaglia (the stammerer) afflicted with an extraordinary malady that can be cured only by laughter. When Fairy Morgana appears, Truffaldino, repeating a worn-out *lazzo,* trips her and sends her rolling head over heels. This clownish antic dispels the melancholy due to the *versi martelliani* which caused the prince's malady. Prince Tartaglia, personating the Neapolitan mask and stammering heroic verse, is thereupon condemned by Fairy Morgana to seek three beautiful oranges that are imprisoned in the fantastic castle of Creonta.

The first act represented a splendid court, with the knights and ladies portraying the phantom Kingdom of Playing Cards. In the second act, a fantastic castle is guarded by a rusty gate, a starving dog, a woman who sweeps her oven with her breasts, and a rotten rope. A devil-blown wind carries Tartaglia and Truffaldino into this castle; and they seize the three oranges. In parody of Goldoni and Chiari, the rope, the dog, the gate, all speak in *versi martelliani.*

In the third act, Morgana and Celio intervene. Tired and hungry, Truffaldino decides to eat the three oranges. When the first one is opened, a beautiful damsel steps out and cries: "For pity's sake give me some drink, or else I die," and drops dead. Truffaldino, having no water mimics prayer, dismay, hunger, cowardice; and finally decides to open the second orange.

In comes Tartaglia in pursuit of Truffaldino; and, when he has sufficiently amused the audience by his *lazzi,* he opens the third orange; and out of it steps a charming princess who cries for some drink or else she also must die. But this time, Tartaglia is there; he remembers that Celio Mago instructed him to open the oranges only where water was at hand; and, filling his iron shoe with water, he gives drink to the last surviving orange-princess.

Ninetta, the orange-princess, is envied by Smeraldina, the female counterpart of Arlecchino. Morgana has given her a magic pin which, on being stuck into the princess' head, changes her into a dove. This dove comes to the window of the kitchen where the King of Trumps is making magnificent preparations for the marriage of Tartaglia with Smeraldina. The roast is three times burned because of the magic sleep of Pantalone, the cook. He and Truffaldino seize the dove; and, stroking its head, discover and pull out the pin. The charm is broken; and the princess is restored to her own form. Smeraldina is punished; and the play ends in feasts and weddings.

This play obtained an astonishing success. The fickle Venetians were glad to see Goldoni and Chiari parodied. The representation of childhood stories, and the sumptuous staging, together with the extraordinary ability of Sacchi's Truffaldino and Darbes' Pantalone, won their applause; and the people asked for a second and third performance.

Carlo Gozzi knew that such puerile pageantry was short-lived. His aim was obtained by Goldoni's departure. With a theory of his art that was new in Italy, and partly original, he composed the second of his *fiabe, Il Corvo,* wherein an æsthetic thesis replaced the farcical parody. Here the *lazzi* and pranks of his beloved masks were reduced to the secondary rôle; and their parts were partly written by the author. He wished to show that Sacchi, Darbes, and the other actors were essential to Goldoni's success; but he proved that Sacchi, Darbes, and the other actors were essential to Carlo Gozzi.

In *Il Corvo* a magician is made the *deus ex machina* of extravagant, fantastic complications. This magical force, which torments and transforms, does not triumph to the end. Another magical power, a superior sort of justice, interferes with the cruel magician. This double current of mysterious forces originated in those Eastern tales which Gozzi imitated from the Neapolitan Basile. Gozzi reduced the Zoroastrian conception of the struggle between the spirits of light and darkness to this puerile antagonism of sorcerers and magicians.

Gozzi multiplies his personages, accumulates adventures, fills the scene with spectacular pageantry and with incredible apparitions. To Goldoni, painter of reality, chary of adornments, Gozzi opposed this revelry of colours, this swarming of figures and shapes, this mixture of comedy, tragedy, and farce. Gozzi is a harbinger of romanticism. In his *fiabe,* Gozzi gave his beloved comedians full opportunity for displaying their ability. Whether—like Goldoni—he could have persuaded his actors to drop their clownish pranks for a more restrained manner of recitation is questionable.

Within the circle of dreamland, his Venetian masks make vulgar caricatures of real people. Truffaldino and Brighella are transported to the courts of phantom kings, and clothed with gorgeous oriental garments; but their characters are not altered nor their speech or their morals corrected. They speak, play the traditional quips and pranks, and make the same grimaces as those used in plays that imitate the manners of their own people. The contrast was startling; it roused attention and provided matter of discussion.

The *Corvo* (Raven) contained all the discordant elements and perplexing æsthetic notions that we have indicated, but it also contained two valuable motives: the idea of punishment for needless cruelty, and strong brotherly affection. Both of these are powerfully expressed. As Millo, King of Frattaombrosa, reclined on his couch, Truffaldino informed the public how the King happened one day to kill a raven beloved by the wicked magician; how this magician sentenced the murderer to suffer until he should find a woman "with hair and eyebrows as black as the feathers of the fatal raven; and cheeks as red as was his blood, and skin as white as was the marble on which the bird fell and died."

In order to release the King, Millo's brother Jennaro has enticed Princess Armilla of Damascus on board his ship. She is as black-haired and as red and white as the oracle demands Millo's deliverer to be. Jennaro tells his brother's story and entreats Armilla to consent to marry him. The Princess replies that her father, Norando, is a magician who can "stop the sun, upset mountains, turn men into plants." Two doves are sent by the "Power-of-light," mysterious Ormuzd, to counteract the evils that wicked Arismane is preparing for Jennaro. These doves warn Jennaro that when Millo receives the hawk, it will pluck out his eyes. Woe to Jennaro if he warns Millo; he will be turned at once into a statue. The horse that Jennaro brings as a gift will kill Millo as soon as he touches the saddle. Woe to Jennaro if he betrays this secret; he will be turned at once into a statue. There is a third malediction with the same threat. A dragon will attack Millo on the night of his marriage with the Princess. Five long acts develop all this sorcery of witchcraft,[3] of transformations, and of the battle between the powers of Good and of Evil. On the same plan of spectacular staging and superfluous farce are constructed the other *fiabe:* the *Blue Monster,* the *Woman Snake,* and that jewel of the collection, the *Pretty Green Bird.*

In this last play, the buffoonery of Venetian masks, the stateliness of heroic verse, the unassimilated principles of a new philosophy, are mingled with something that is almost genial. Certainly Gozzi was unprepared to dispute the new philosophy. Yet his satire has a ring of bitter sincerity; and the broad humour, local allusions, traditions and proverbs, combine to make up an interesting play.

The story is complex. A wicked old Queen-mother has shut her daughter-in-law, Ninetta, in a dungeon. Ninetta had given birth to twins, Renzo and Barbarina. The wicked old queen, pretending that these are only two spaniel puppies, ordered Pantalone to drown them. The twins were not killed, but were brought up by the kind-hearted peasants, Smeraldina and her husband Truffaldino. Truffaldino, being a rough bully, has lately turned the children out of his pork shop; and they wander about in search of a home.

These children have been reading philosophy; and they prattle æsthetic principles and philosophical maxims with as little comprehension as did the Venetians of Gozzi's class. Renzo declares that orphans, ignorant of their parents, are released from obligations of obedience and respect; and that the death of their parents has destroyed the normal human longing for family ties. Barbarina confesses that she is courted by a pretty little green bird.

The scene shifts. In a dungeon, Ninetta is buried alive. The little green bird brings a bottle and a basket of food. He tells his own little story and the longer tale of Ninetta's woes. The shifting scene now shows Renzo and Barbarina wandering on a desert shore, and seeking distraction from their misery by talking of future good times. A speaking statue of Cadmon joins in the conversation, evidently presenting Gozzi's own philosophical viewpoint. He scolds Renzo for his distrust of human virtue, and for his doctrine that selfishness governs every action. Why suspect everyone? Supreme happiness comes from being as really good as you would like other people to believe you to be. "Love thyself by loving thy fellow creatures. . . . By thus doing, thou wilt become that which thou wishest to be."[4]

Tartaglia (1620)

La Cantatrice (1694)

Orazio (1645)

Narcisino (1650)

Biscegliese (1680)

Le Notaire (1725)

Polichinelle (1820)

Leandre (1850)

Gianduja (1858)

In the last act, everything comes right. Tartagliana is transformed into a frog, and Brighella into an ass. King Tartaglia learns that Barbarina, being his daughter, cannot be his wife. His Ninetta is restored to him after her long captivity under the sewer. The Little Green Bird becomes a royal Prince, and marries Barbarina. Barbarina promises that the nose of Cadmon's statue will be replaced, and the four statues of Moorish Kings will be mended with the profit made out of this performance.

Gozzi's *fiabe* amused the puerile and decadent Venetians. But the absurdities and impossibilties would surely weary us moderns. The acceptance by those Venetians of the misconstruction and misinterpretation of French philosophy which is found in these *fiabe,* gives pause for thought.

Though he had ridiculed versified plays and abused Goldoni's character studies, Gozzi now produced *I Pitocchi Fortunati* (the Lucky Beggars) and *Turandot.* "Fiabe tragicomiche," he called them, though they are merely ordinary comedies written partly in heroic verse, and partly in prose. *Turandot* has been praised by foreign critics.

The heroine, Turandot, daughter of Turan, is borrowed from an Eastern legend that was popular during the Middle Ages. Shakespeare did not ignore her when he traced the delicate picture of Portia and her three caskets. But Gozzi's heroine lacks the sweet Shakespearean maiden's charm. Turandot is a story-book character; her wicked pride requires that the successful suitor must solve three riddles of her invention or else lose his head. As a foil to her pride, her companion, Adelma, is sweetly loving. To this magnificently oriental court comes Prince Calaf, a "Prince Charmant" indeed, though disguised. Prince Calaf loves Turandot, faces the judges, and solves the three riddles.

The merit of the play is in the evolution of Turandot's character. When Calaf has won the prize, Turandot cries out that she hates him and will die rather than marry him. Chivalrous hero that he is, Calaf answers that he will give the Princess another chance. If she solves his riddle, his life will be forfeited. The riddle is to guess his own name. Adelma is in love with Calaf; and, in her eagerness to prevent the marriage, discovers the name and tells it to Turandot. Calaf, having lost, lifts his dagger to pay the penalty. Turandot's love conquers her pride. She entreats Calaf to take her for his wife and obedient slave.

Turandot has preserved the elaborate staging of the other *fiabe,* the display of oriental splendour, in the arrangement of scenes, the grouping of gaily dressed personages. There is also farcical by-play. Truffaldino, Brighella, and Pantalone do not change their manners although they are members of the "Divan." Sometimes they speak Venetian dialect, sometimes in verse, which, avoiding the cadence of the Martelliano line, has lost the harmonious flow of other Italian dramatists. *Turandot,* though the best of Gozzi's plays, is forgotten by Italians. Its length, the pretentious language, the turgid speeches, the puerile characters and situations, and the mixture of prosaic farce and heroic verse are in discord with Italian æsthetics.

Although Gozzi was a real poet, and his creative faculty equalled that of more famous writers, he failed to produce a true work of art. His unbridled nature and his jealousy of Goldoni's success prompted him to extravagant invention, to glaring contrasts. On and on, he urges his imagination; and is persuaded that there can never be too much of a good thing. He accumulates all possible material from ancient and foreign sources, and adds everything that his own imagination suggests. If Gozzi had curbed this indiscriminate appropriation of literary material, if he had made a scholarly study of modern Italian based on a solid knowledge of the classics, if he had not been intent on ruining a fellow worker, he might have been a foremost Italian poet.

Gozzi's failure resulted from the circumstances of his private life and the unwholesome atmosphere that then deadened intellectual activity in Venice. How terrible must have been the agony of the Venetians when they realized that around them was crumbling everything which they had been taught to consider most solid! Other Italian States hailed the French conquerors as liberators from foreign masters, as intellectual light-bearers; but Venice, after centuries of unequalled prosperity and undisputed freedom, now agonized with fear of bearing a yoke.

But sadder for Venetians than the loss of political power was the destruction of their faith in a social order that had proved itself so strong, that was reputed so just. It was not the invasion of soldiers, but the invasion of ideas which distressed and distorted Gozzi's mental balance. As a protest against impending evils, he conjured a fantastic world in which his ideals might shine brighter than reality: a puerile attempt, a pathetic instance of that suffering which attends all intellectual and social progress that is not willingly accepted.

A story told by Erckmann-Chatrian illustrates this inexorable law. In an Alpine village a group of men have sworn to prevent the advance of the first railway that is being constructed across their mountains. The dark gaping mouth of a tunnel has so excited their terror of the hellish machine which it is said will come out of it, that, after taking a solemn oath, they stand up in a row across the opening of the tunnel. Each stalwart mountaineer grasps an iron bar, all of them ready to oppose the expected monster. The train puffs out of the tunnel; it crushes, like broken twigs, the stalwart men and scatters their iron bars. Thus always will be crushed the units that strive to stop the onward progress of the many.

Thus Carlo Gozzi, tall and gaunt, stolid and prejudiced, a knight-errant fighting windmills, presumed to oppose the onward march of new ideas. Deeming Goldoni's realism vulgarity, he opposed to it the meaner vulgarity of masks uncurbed by any rule. When Truffaldino, Brighella, and others still more vulgar were let loose on the stage to improvise their *lazzi,* and were allowed to tickle the audience by their equivocations and vulgar pranks, they were certain to exceed the limit which Goldoni had traced for them.

Carlo Gozzi ridiculed Chiari's romances and plays for their superabundant episodes, adventures, and extravagances. Yet his own plays, stuffed with wonders and transformations, were worse examples of a decadent literature wandering in search of new aims.

The old world that was crumbling round him had expressed its own beautiful swan-song in Metastasio's melodrama. Its suave lyricism, its pseudo-heroical pathetic bombast, was dying. Goldoni was already pointing the way that the Italian Theatre was bound to follow. Had Gozzi adopted the temperate views and placid ideas of his brother Gaspare, he would have found in the *Difesa di Dante,* or in the periodicals *Osservatore* and *La Frusta Letteraria,* the signs of a radical reform that was sweeping away the ideals and principles he wished to consider unchangeable. Enlightened Italians were discarding the intellectual props and spiritual limitations that tradition had cherished. They accepted the motto, "cose e non parole" (things and not words).

Beccaria, Galiani, the brothers Verri, Parini, Alfieri: each of these names recalls some attempted reform—social, moral, or literary. Owing to the political divisions of Italy, and to the diversity of their aims and means, these attempts failed to secure any immediate success; but they show the intensity and extension of the intellectual movement in Italy. If Naples could produce such an apostle of free exchange and commercial legislation as the witty little abbot Galiani, while Milan listened to Parini's moral indictment, to Beccaria's thesis about the right of punishment, and to Verri's pamphlets; if the audiences of almost every Italian city were roused to patriotic delirium by Alfieri's tragedies; what chance was there for Gozzi to compel attention and influence by his puerile productions?

Moreover, Gozzi's plays lacked style. Assuming to stand out as a *Granellescho,* a champion of classical *Trecentism,* he uses absolute terms, faulty phrase-construction, and wanders from all approved form. Like Goldoni, like Alfieri and Manzoni in their younger days, he was handicapped by his use of dialect. But, unlike these really conscientious writers, he does not try to correct himself. Believing that the Venetian dialect ranked with national languages, even as the comedy of masks ranked with the more regular forms of the theatrical art, he supported the traditional masks and their questionable amenities, and did not banish the idioms or constructions that belong to dialect. The harshness and inharmoniousness of Gozzi's verse will explain the severity of the Italian critics and the forgetfulness of the Italian public.

NOTES

CHAPTER VI

1. In a conference by M. Serao, there is this analysis of Gozzi's plays: The laws of nature are all dissolved; time, space, is abolished; the three worlds are mixed up; the wild beasts speak; water sings and plays; dead people read out of books; women become men; and men are turned to statues. Thus also in the moral world of affections, everything is turned upside down: the most passionate lovers outrage their sweethearts; wives expel the husbands they adore; and mothers throw their children into the fire. Everything happens, everything that is strange, but, also, that which is impossible: travels of thousands of miles covered in a few hours; resurrection of the dead; old people growing young again; palaces built in one night and tumbling down in one moment; battles fought and won in less than one minute.

"And all through these extraordinary events, this crumbling of worlds, and these prodigies of unheard and unthinkable extravagance, these contradictory and maddening feelings, the heroes and heroines of Gozzi pursue their terrible ordeal of torments, facing all obstacles, enduring all pains, in an agony of suffering and grief, at times praying to heaven, at times challenging heavenly power, passing through every stage of despair; their life has nothing of the common life of mankind; they are impelled on and on by all powerful Fate, struggling against it in a struggle that is hopeless; this mysterious power being so strong and so far reaching."

Further on, the lecturer proceeds to tell why the fables of Gozzi have a charm. It is because they appeal to the memory of long past childhood. "Every one has a time of fable in one's memory, a time of simplicity, of innocence, of smiles; and it can be conjured for an instant, a flitting but always bright instant." The world created by the imagination of Gozzi is—according to M. Serao—"alive, though made up of borrowed elements." (In *La Vita Italiana nel Settecento,* Fratelli Treves, Editore, Milano.)

Tasso and Ariosto have created similar types of hardy heroines. It is a fantastic type for the Italian stage during those most unheroic centuries, when convent education, sedentary habits, and the fetters of public opinion and fashion condemned the Italian woman to a life of futile pleasure. The audience that applauded the courageous deeds of one of Metastasio's or of Gozzi's heroines, would have been shocked if any women of their own world had spoken with the slightest independence. In Gozzi's plays, Zobeide is the most complete embodiment of these virtues; Angela in *King Stag,* and Armilla in *The Raven* (*Il Corvo*) add some other traits of womanly heroism.

Carlo Gozzi has adapted several plays from the Spanish theatre. Besides the too famous *Droghe d'Amore,* he imitated Calderon, Tirso de Molina, Moreto, and Roxas.

A recent play entitled *Carlo Gozzi,* by Renato Simoni, gives a vivid comment and illustration of his life. It might almost be called: "The rise, splendour, and decline of C. Gozzi." The plan of the play follows the *Memorie Inutili,* and adopts the author's viewpoint. After showing Gozzi as a young man, ill-treated by his mother and suspected by all the family because he alone tried to check the general extravagance and disorganization, Gozzi is shown in full activity and full triumph, already tormented by his sour temper, by his jealous disposition, and falling a facile prey to the intrigues of Sacchi-Truffaldino and his pupil Teodora Ricci.

The character of this prima donna is cleverly traced, and is an illuminating instance of Italian manners. She is a typical Venetian actress, puerile and fickle rather than wicked, who manages to love Sacchi, Gozzi, and Gratarol at the same time—each with a different sort of affection. If the cards get mixed and trouble comes, she is surprised and startled like a baby who has caused more mischief than he realizes. In the last act, Gozzi is a lonely old man. His elderly housekeeper, and several old-fashioned servants make a comfortless home for the man who has outlived his fame. In comes Sacchi, as broken down as his former protector and patron. He has come to say goodbye; and their meeting is pathetic. Sacchi would cheer his lonesome friend with an amusing performance: Is he not still the Sacchi that could set an audience roaring with laughter?

Gozzi sits surrounded by his servants, and Sacchi, straightening his stooping form and forcing his aged limbs to assume the attitudes of his rôle, commences one of his traditional scenes. But his jokes fall flat, his *lazzi* fail to stir even a smile, and when the worn-out actor, throwing down his cap, breaks into sobs, he finds an echo of the same despair embittered by conscious failure, in his aged and forlorn patron. They fall into each other's arms for a last farewell and Gozzi's parting word is a name that has been all the time in his mind, in his heart, but which now trembles on his lips: "Teodora?" The scene shows Gozzi's housekeeper robbing him, and he ignoring this larceny, because this woman's tenderness is the last ray of sunshine that warms his lonely and disconsolate existence.

2. D. Ciampoli, an able critic, prefacing a recent edition of C. Gozzi's plays, suggests that the idea of borrowing from Basile's *Cunto delli Cunti* came to him through the more famous poem of Lorenzo Lippi, *Il Malmantile,* and that Gozzi tried to disguise this suggestion. Another book, the *Gabinetto delle Fate,* contains the story of Prince Fadhallah, which is the story of *King Stag.* Gozzi added an interesting silhouette of Cigalotti, a well known public crier and story-teller, which he imitated from life.

Carlo Gozzi explains in his *Memorie* that he discontinued writing *fiabe* because every sort of literary composition is liable to decline after reaching a certain point of perfection.

Concari, in *Il Settecento,* sums up the divergent opinions of many critics, from Luigi Settembrim, who declares *L'Amore delle tre Melarance* "a unique masterpiece," to the attenuated blame mixed with some praise of Zanella, Graf, De Sanctis, etc. Cf. *Storia Letteraria d'Italia, scritta da una Societa di professori,* Edit. Francesco Vallardi, Milano.

3. Jennaro gives the hawk and the horse; but stabs each in its turn. Millo's jealousy and suspicion are stirred by this strange behaviour; he imprisons Jennaro. Jennaro escapes. When the dragon is touched by Jennaro's sword, he vanishes into thin air; and Jennaro is discovered with a drawn sword at the door of his brother's bedroom. The case is discussed by an assembly of elders; by Pantalone, Tartaglia, Truffaldino, Norando. The wicked magician reminds Jennaro that if he speaks, he will be turned to a statue. But Jennaro speaks out, and is turned into a statue that will return to life only if Armilla's blood is shed over it. Armilla stabs herself and sets Jennaro free. Before the curtain falls, Armilla is magically recalled to life.

In *Il Re Cervo* (the King Stag), Gozzi has introduced the fable, dear to Eastern story-tellers, of men transformed into animals or into other men. King Deramo, having imprudently confided the secret of this sorcery to his faithless minister, Truffaldino, is first transformed into a stag, then into an old man. After the traitor has usurped the throne, he attempts to seduce Angela, the young Queen. Under Gozzi's management, the tragic situation becomes a matter for stage tricks and transformations. Yet when Deramo—now a dirty decrepit beggar—entreats Angela to believe his incredible story and beware of the man who has robbed him of his own body in order to seduce her, there are elements of real beauty.

Angela is modest and shy; yet when stirred by love she acts with courage and prudence. She is the first pencil of a character Gozzi will develop in other plays. Such a feminine hero was familiar to Italian poets; but Gozzi adds traits that give this figure a new charm. The same character is shown in *Zobeide,* the principal personage of the play of that name. Zobeide's adventures are appalling. She sees her sister and sister-in-law transformed into beastly forms. She is threatened with transformation into a cow, by the magic and cruelty of King Sinadab. Yet she loves him so, that she will not believe in his wickedness. The good sorcerer leads her to the very brink of destruction before he can persuade her to turn Bluebeard-Sinadab into a monstrous animal, thus rescuing all his innocent victims.

4. "Man is but a part of supreme Love; by loving himself he loves his Creator." "No man so well loves himself, as he whose every deed is of charity, piety, virtue." "Lift thy snout from the ground, Renzo, look on the stars and sky; and never bind thy thoughts to the senses and to nothingness." Cadmon explains that he is the "King of Simulacres," with power over all the statues "that are so much better than men." He owes a debt of gratitude to the ancestors of Renzo and Barbarina and he will protect them during their terrible ordeals. He bids the children pick up a stone, and carry it to the King's door; then to fling it on the ground.

In the second act, King Tartaglia weeps bitter tears on the death of his beloved Ninetta. He remembers how Ninetta came to him out of an orange; how eighteen years ago she was a dove; and how she was restored to her beautiful form and married to him. Truffaldino, who breaks in on this soliloquy, pretends that he comes in pure friendship for the King. Then he begs for assistance because he is ruined by Smeraldina's extravagance and foolish kindness to strangers. Yes, he did go to the *osteria;* but only twice every day. Yes, he gambled; but that was only to get back that which his wife gave away. Yes, he visited harlots; but he always preferred those of the lowest sort. With such foolish speech Truffaldino amuses the audience.

Comes the queen-mother, "Tartagliona," who stammers like her son. Her quarrel soon degenerates into very vulgar language. Her son complains of her cruel treatment of Ninetta; she retorts that she had borne him for nine months, that she had given him milk: he peevishly answers that he will pay an ass to bear her for as many months, and a she-ass to give her milk. Brighella, as an impromptu poet, declaims humorous compliments to the queen-mother. Then, opposite the royal palace, is discovered a magnificent building that has developed out of the stone that Renzo and Barbarina had received from Cadmon.

The third act shows alternately both these palaces. Philosophical, hard-hearted Barbarina permits Smeraldina to enter, on condition that she never mentions their past and consents to be treated as a servant. From his balcony, King Tartaglia sees Barbarina standing at her window, and makes love to her; she laughs at him. But jealous Tartagliona, following Brighella's advice, cries: "Beautiful you are, but ten times more would be, if in your hand you held one of the singing apples. Beautiful you are, but might be ten times more, if the water that plays and dances, you held in your other hand."

Barbarina urges her brother to start on the quest for the magic apple and the wonderful water; Renzo consents because the little green bird has promised the revelation of great secrets, the accomplishment of great marvels, if he succeeds. Then occurs a whirlwind of wonders and transformations. The magic wind that urged Tartaglia and Truffaldino on other journeys, carries them to the mountain where dwells the little green bird. There statues come to life, and men are turned into statues; there the fated dagger drops blood to warn Barbarina of Renzo's danger.

For Carlo Gozzi, *see*: Vittorio Malamani, *Saggio bibliografico degli Scritti di C. G.,* ed. Zanichelli.

Le Fiabe riprodotte per cura di Ernesto Masi, Zanichelli, Bologna, 1885.

Le Memorie Inutili della sua vita scritte da lui medesimo e publicate per umilta. Also in a free translation by Paul de Musset: Paris, Charpentier, 1848. And in English by J. Addington Symonds, London, Nimmo, 1890. His *fiabe* in German translations: Wertes, Bern, 1777–9.

Gli Amore delle tre Melarance, was only partly written: the rôles of the masks, a mere sketch, in 1761.

Il Corvo, in October of the same year.

Il Re Cervo, January, 1762.

Turandot, a few days later.

La Donna Serpente, October, 1762.

Zobeide, November, 1763.

I Pitocchi Fortunati, November, 1764.

Il Mostro Turchino, 1764.

L'Augellin Belverde, 1765.

Zeim Re de' Geni, the same year.

CHAPTER VII

THE SETTECENTO BEFORE ALFIERI

Influence of the French classical tragedy during the eighteenth century in Italy: Maffei's *Merope,* the only successful tragedy before Alfieri: The tragedies of Conti, Verris, Landi, and Gozzi: The work of Ringhieri and Varano: Ducal patronage of the theatre: Gigli's *Don Piloni:* Nelli: Types of Italian comedy of the eighteenth century: The Lachrymose Drama, importation of French and English sentimentality: Life and works of De Gamerra: Influence of this type of drama on later forms.

ITALIAN preference for the French tragic theatre increased during the eighteenth century. The Bolognese Pier Jacopo Martello writes that he "burned with shame to see the Italian Theatre occupied by a foreign and haughty nation." This antagonism was the reverse of contempt. Martello declared that, though Italy possessed tragic poets, she lacked the tragic verse that was indispensable; and that such verse must be very simple and analogous to that used by the French.

Martello and Scipione Maffei were not widely apart. Maffei insisted on simplicity in tragedy, but he wished to retain the scenic ability of French drama. Italian tragedy must abandon the classic traditions of prologues, long monologues, nuncios, messengers, nurses, oracles, intervention of the supernatural chorus, and variety of metre. His *Merope,* composed according to the Italian tradition and the French influence, was the only successful Italian tragedy before Alfieri.

The action begins with a dispute between Polifonte and Merope; Polifonte has taken husband, children and throne from her, and he now wishes to marry Merope. Adraste arrives and announces the capture of a "Youth of lofty mien in low estate, of noble face, though in plebeian garb," who is a murderer. The murderer enters (Sc. 3) and the amazed Merope pleads for him.

At the beginning of the second act, her messenger, Arbante, returns with tidings that her son Cresfonte, has fled. Undoubtedly he has been slain by Egisto and Polifonte. Egisto is bound to a column and Merope tries to extort a confession of participation in the murder. As the spear is about to pierce him, Egisto cries out: "O dear mother, if in this moment thou shouldst see me!" "Hast thou a mother?" exclaims Merope; and the poignancy of the whole scene consists in her repetition of that name. "Tell me, boy, what name has . . ." Polifonte enters and promises Egisto protection. "Since Polifonte protects this youth, certainly he must be the slayer of Cresfonte."

Night falls. Egisto sleeps; Merope, raising the axe, cries: "Dear shade of my slain son, accept this holocaust, and take this blood which now on earth I spill." Polidoro rushes in and arrests her arm: "Hold, Queen, I tell thee, hold!" Polidoro confesses that Egisto is her son Cresfonte.

Merope consents to marry Polifonte.

To prevent "a ferocious massacre" of all those she loves, she is dragged to the nuptial altar: Egisto, that is Cresfonte, rushes in and slays Polifonte.

Although *Merope* was an immense success, it is no marvel. But it is better than any previous Italian tragedy. There was the happy ending dear to the public. Evil is punished and the innocent are consoled.

Antonio Conti's four tragedies, *Giulio Cesare, Marco Bruto, Giunio Bruto,* and *Druso,* are strictly classical. Conti prefers Roman subjects because they contain lofty and useful teachings. The poet adapts actual events to the exigencies of his art, and is not particular about historic accuracy. But he tried to give his audience a true picture of Roman life.

Alessandro Verri's two tragedies (1779) disregarded the classic unities. *Pantea* is sentimental and melancholy; the *Congiura di Milano* shows Shakespeare's influence. Verri was a precursor of the romantics; but he was not the first to disregard the Greek and Roman traditions.

Very many Italian tragedies of the first half of the eighteenth century show much reasoning, much philosophy, much humanity, and little political significance. Several Italian *settecentisti* had already drawn subjects from the national history. The Marquis Ubertinio Landi of Piacenza composed *Alessandro Farnese* and *Corradino;* and Gaspare Gozzi with his *Isaccio* and his *Marco Polo* (1755) gave examples that found Venetian imitators. The Jesuits Roberti and Bettinelli also preferred national subjects for tragedies. Indeed the Jesuitical theatre of the eighteenth century differed little from the lay theatre.

Ringhieri (1721–1781), a Bolognese, was a most heretical *frate* tragedian. His popularity came through censure. Ringhieri used melodrama, choral songs, fantastic spectacles, celestial prodigies, and infernal enchantments which appealed to the eye rather than to the ear, and he often introduced inappropriate love-scenes. Alfonso Varano deserves mention for the remarkable *Giovanni di Gascala* (1754). The pious Ferrarese has made of Giovanni, "the perverse one," a hero of some grandeur and moral vigour. Varano's tragedy is original and uninfluenced by the French theatre.

In 1770 there appeared the *Programma offerto alle Musa Italiano* by "a glorious prince." This prince was the Infante Don Ferdinando di Borbone, Duke of Parma, Piacenza, and Guastalla. Inspired by his French minister, Du Tillot, and his Piedmontese librarian, padre Pacciandi, he offered a hundred and fifty *zecchini* each year to endow Italy with good tragedies. The *Programma* stimulated many ambitions. The *Auge* of Filippo Trenta (1774) received the second prize, while the first fell to the *Valsei ossia l'Eroe Scozzese* by Antonio Perabò. Conte Orazio Calini won a prize with his *Zelinda,* a copy of the *Blanche et Guiscard* of Saurin, with some added passages from the *Zaire* of Voltaire.

The Italian comedy of the eighteenth century means Goldoni.

Girolamo Gigli of Sienna wrote *Il Don Pilone ovvero il Bacchettone falso* (Lucca, 1711), adapted from Molière's *Tartuffe*. Though an imitation, "Don Pilone" represents the wisdom and wit of peasant society under Cosimo III, when priests and friars ruled the family, and regulated all social life by rigorous custom. Don Pilone is an apostate Jew who had become Catholic after having married two wives in Portugal and three in Catalonia, after having falsified the coinage in Holland, violated four nunneries in Brittany, and carried off many girls. This Sienese hypocrite churchman Don Pilone has something of the *Fra Timoteo* of the Mandragola and of the *Ipocrito* of Aretino; he is a vile weed which prospered all through the eighteenth century.

With Jacopo Nelli (1676–1770) we return to the action in the *piazza,* to intrigues, to disguises of names and persons. Other comedies are pictures of domestic life. Among the most praised is *La Serva Padrona*. Love plays a notable part in the comedy of Battista Fagiuoli (1660–1742). Sometimes he depicts manners, censures vices, and draws a moral as in the *Cicisbeo sconsolato*. Written about 1708, it became popular in Florence. Though the play has witty scenes, it is mere dilettantism, with few ideas.

The literary and regular comedy, without intrigue, without masks; and the ridiculous comedy with its complications, recognitions, and disguises, formed the repertory of the lordly and academic theatres; the general public preferred the popular and improvised comedy with the traditional masks, the miming, the *lazzi*.

The Lachrymose Drama, or bourgeois tragedy, was a rebellion against the classical tragedy of the French school of the seventeenth century. Also it was "the law of nature in contrast to the written law, the proclamation under all forms of the rights of man in respect to the society which violated them" *De Sanctis*. The French poet, Nivelle de la Chaussée, invented "Quel la Societé, telle la littérature." The true polemics about the bourgeois drama began in 1757 when Diderot published the *Fils Naturel* and the *Dialogues Critiques*. No more Greek and Roman heroes, who do not nearly touch us; no more lyric and epic on the stage. Instead we shall have facts, personages, customs, images of contemporary life. Wherever man is, there is passion, vice, very often crime. Almost every family has its little tragedy of faults, imprudences, prejudices, which can furnish material for tragedies. Superlative characters, heroic virtues, bestial vices, extraordinary dramatic developments appeal to a morbid public sensibility.

The bourgeois tragedy, or lachrymose drama, was the last importation of French philosophical literature into Italy.

The dramas of Diderot and his followers were received in Italy as a foreign novelty; and translators and imitators multiplied. Giovanni De Gamerra in his *Piano,* presented in 1786 to the King of Naples, repeats the arguments of Diderot. The passions, the sentimentality, the rain of tears, in the new dramas proved a relief from satiety. It dominated the Italian Theatre at the close of the eighteenth century.

In Italy this bourgeois tragedy had precursors. The sentimental romance of Richardson is reflected in the Goldonian *Pamela,* and in the *Putta onorata.*

Giovanni De Gamerra began as an *abaté* (abbot). In 1767 he was a sub-lieutenant in the Clerici regiment in the service of Austria. In the year 1770 he quit the military service. In 1773 he was present in Vienna at a recital of his *Maria Stuarda*. De Gamerra did not find at Vienna the fortune or happiness for which he hoped; he left there between 1776 and 1777 and returned to Tuscany ill and very poor. His father was dead, his relations refused help, and his fellow citizens were not friendly.

Horribly loaded with so many ills
What yet remained there for me to endure?
'Twas then that my misfortune to complete
Tyrannic Love, from Erseta's bright rays,
Sent forth the dart. . . .

De Gamerra now fell madly in love with Teresa Calamai (Erseta) of Livorno. After a most bitter contest with her relations, on the morning of August 28th, the two lovers renewed their oaths of eternal fidelity and De Gamerra embarked at Leghorn for Naples. The battle between love and duty had shattered Teresa's delicate nerves. In August, 1781 De Gamerra arrived in Pisa only to bid her a last farewell. Hardly a year after Teresa's death, he married in order to meet with his wife's dowry the expenses of printing a poem on conjugal infidelity! "Here, speaking to you in friendly confidence, is one of the strongest motives which led me to matrimony, to be able with the *dot* to assist myself and to diminish the debt contracted towards the publishers." Towards the end of 1785, he began to consider the Neapolitan enterprise. He had been preceded at Naples by his *Piano* (Plan) for a new theatre, of which De Gamerra was to be poet, director, and administrator; and he brought with him twelve plays all written in conformity with his "Plan." Had the king approved it, the new theatre was to be opened the first of Easter week, 1787. But something went wrong and nothing more was done. De Gamerra turned from the dramatic to the lyric theatre. In January, 1787, his *Pirro* was performed at the San Carlo. He was assailed even here "by indecent cabals," and the *Pirro* was suspended until after the Easter holidays.

In 1788 he returned to Pisa to a life of bitterness and poverty. Between the vicissitudes of De Gamerra's life and his theatrical poesy and lachrymose dramas, there is an immediate relationship. In this consists its importance, its defence, and its originality.

Even after the French revolution De Gamerra remained conservative and a faithful servant of the House of Austria; and in 1793 he was recalled to Vienna.

In 1797 Casti left Vienna. De Gamerra, "poet of the Imperial theatre," sought the post of "Cesarean poet" but was refused. He was poor, ill, aged before his time, father of two daughters, unhappy in his family, separated from his wife, yet always industrious. Between 1794 and 1801 he published ten new lyrical dramas as well as many reproductions and rearrangements of his previous dramas. About 1803 he returned to Italy and settled at Vicenza where he died on August 29th, 1803.

As Goldoni in Paris had had to return to the *Commedia dell' Arte,* so De Gamerra at Vienna had to return to writing lyrical dramas in which the music outweighed the poetry. De Gamerra was the most accomplished Italian representative of the new school. The principal English and French exemplars of the lachrymose drama reappear in his plays. In the *Madre Colpevole* (the guilty Mother), De Gamerra, to strengthen the horror, has made his characters related by blood; and in the *Solitari* (Solitaries), he has represented a sect of sanguinary misanthropes who condemn the woman who for love introduced herself among them, and is killed by the man who loves her.

The misfortunes which befall the personages of these dramas are expressed in gasps, sobs, and interjections.

The lachrymose drama or domestic tragedy is the origin of the modern drama and comedy. It represents a profound mutation in the sentiment and forms of literature. The intellectual movement of the eighteenth century gives us the naturalism of the Goldonian Comedy. But had we not also received the sentimentalism of Richardson and Rousseau, and the heat of the lachrymose drama, we should not have arrived at the modern romance and drama.

CHAPTER VIII

LIFE OF VITTORIO ALFIERI

Political importance of Alfieri's tragedies: Alfieri was a neglected child, a lonely boy: Through fault of his tutor Alfieri hated study: Read little except French novels, and admired French plays: Obtained commission in the army, and during next six years was restless, vain, and idle: Traveled almost everywhere in Europe: In the Netherlands, falls in love with a married woman: In Turin, he begins an intense system of reading: In London, becomes entangled in a love-affair, and fights a duel with the husband: In Madrid, has a fight with his valet, Elia: After much wandering, returns to Turin, and becomes *cavalier servente* to the beautiful wife of the Marquis of Priero: In 1775, his tragedy *Cleopatra* is performed in Turin: In 1777 he begins his life-long attachment to Countess d'Albany, wife of the Young Pretender, who was a brute and a drunkard: The story of Alfieri's semi-royal amours: Countess d'Albany leaves her husband and lives with Alfieri until his death: Her meanness of character contrasts strangely with Alfieri's extravagant praise of her: Her *salon* in Paris was the resort of many famous men and women: Alfieri fiercely loves liberty, yet could not comprehend the French Revolution: Though a military officer, he never fought for his own country: Has several love-affairs, and ignores the love made to Countess d'Albany by the painter François Xavier Fabre: She wept when Alfieri died, and married Fabre: The rhetorical eloquence of Alfieri's tragedies entitles him to be ranked among the great Italian writers.

ALFIERI was an apostle who through his passionate tragedies directed a political movement that lasted long after his death. His ancestry was notable. In 1276, Tommaso Alfieri signed his name to a peace treaty between the free City of Asti and the neighboring City of Alba. At about the same time, Ogerio Alfieri was *balia* in important transactions and the author of a *Cronaca* that narrates the history of his city. Many other Alfieris are mentioned in the history of Piedmont; chiefly they were warriors, though some were prominent churchmen. All were devoted to the house of Savoy; all shared in the vicissitudes of their country.

On the 17th of January, 1749, Vittorio Amedeo Alfieri was born in Asti. His father died soon after his birth; and his mother accepted a third husband, Count Giacinto di Magliano. In his autobiography, Alfieri idealizes his mother as prudent and loving. Yet

Alfieri was a neglected child in his stepfather's house. The lonely boy was overwhelmed with grief when his sister Giulia was sent to a convent school.

At an early age he was entrusted to one of those family abbots who was something between servant and tutor. Father Ivaldi made Alfieri hate study. The reading of the usual "Lives" and "Fables" from Latin schoolbooks was unrelieved by association with other boys. In 1758, when nine years old, Alfieri entered the "Accademia," a famous military college in Turin which provided superficial classical instruction; but neither trained the character nor directed the youthful conscience.

When his uncle and guardian returned from Cuneo, where he had been governor, Alfieri was allowed a few privileges, given some books, taken to a theatre, read law, took dancing and fencing lessons, and was permitted to meet his sister who, because of a juvenile love-affair, was now in a Turin convent. Soon after she married Count Cumiana.

Upon the death of his guardian, Alfieri, though only fourteen, was declared of age. He now indulged his passion for riding; and his health improved. He read little except French novels. The future champion of Italianism spoke, wrote, and read in French; as did his friends and companions. At sixteen Alfieri experienced a boyish romance that was quickly forgotten. He obtained a commission in the army, and the King reluctantly granted him leave to travel; but Alfieri was unfitted for military discipline. He was restless and vain, and became dissipated and idle. This lasted six years.

Alfieri cared only for riding or driving fiercely. He threw aside a precious manuscript of Petrarch, made no attempt to speak Tuscan, and was wearied by the monuments of Florence, Sienna, and Pisa. Rome did not impress him, but Naples and the boisterous gaieties of its Carnival proved attractive. He returned to Rome, and, with his faithful valet Elia, settled in furnished rooms near Trinita dei Monti. When the aged and deaf scholar Count della Riviera, Ambassador of Piedmont, read to him some lines of Virgil, Alfieri confessed that he did not understand. He was granted an audience by Pope Clement XIII, "an old man with an air of natural grandeur enhanced by his magnificent surroundings, so that I was not much disgusted by having to kiss his foot and perform the usual knee-bending."

Alfieri hastened through Marseilles, Aix, and Lyons, eager to reach Paris. His first impression was unpleasant. He disliked the miserly magnificence of its buildings, the dirt and "gothicism" of the churches, the vandalic structure of theatres, and the rouged and painted faces of the ladies. The façade of the Louvre, and French plays pleased him. This admiration for French plays and French actors influenced his future career.

Alfieri has traced an amusing picture of the Royal Court of Versailles, of Louis XV's supercilious acknowledgment of the homages of his courtiers. His being overlooked when presented to the King wounded his vanity. He had avoided Parisian salons, but in London he was introduced to several important personages and frequented drawing-rooms. He soon tired of these mild diversions, and again found amusement in fast riding and driving.

Alfieri visited the Netherlands and there fell passionately in love. The lady was sweet; she gave him as much of herself and of her time as her accommodating husband would allow. Then she wrote Alfieri a nice little letter saying that they must part because she must protect her reputation. Alfieri was furious. He pretended illness; a doctor bled him; and he unwrapped the bandage and tried to bleed to death. Watchful Elia saved his master's life. Alfieri's passion soon cooled.[1]

Shortly afterwards, traveling through Switzerland, he reached Turin and there visited his sister, Countess Cumiana. Here Alfieri

Alfieri

began reading, but without method. Rousseau's *Nouvelle Heloise,* *L'Esprit* of Helvetius, Voltaire's *Henriade* and his *Pucelle,* were devoured but not digested. Plutarch's *Lives,* however, fired his imagination. Alfieri says that when reading it he would shout with admiration for the *Life* of Caesar, Brutus, or Cato, while the consciousness of living under a tyrannical government made him weep.

His relatives urged him to marry and settle down. But Alfieri hated monotony and obtained another leave of absence. In the year 1769 he visited Vienna and saw Metastasio kissing Maria Theresa's hand. After Vienna, he passed to Berlin. He considered the Prussian King a mere crowned corporal, and military force the instrument of tyranny. He spent the winter in Norway, driving swiftly in a sledge as often as his delicate health permitted him to face the cold. He read much, especially Montaigne's *Essays,* although unable to understand the Latin and Greek quotations. He crossed Sweden and Finland into Russia which bitterly disappointed him. Alfieri avoided the Russians, and refused to see Catherine "the autocrat."

Again in London, Alfieri became entangled in an affair even more discreditable than the usual triangle, since a fourth personage, a groom or a jockey, partook in the adventure. The husband of this lady, Ligonnier, suspected, scolded, and fought a duel with Alfieri who was wounded in the arm. His rival, the groom, played the spy, and provided necessary witnesses for the divorce. Yet Alfieri remained with this woman for several months. Years later he met her and realized that she had found compensation for the loss of rank and reputation.

On he traveled, restless, unsatisfied. In Paris he refused to meet Rousseau whom he admired. One evening, while in Madrid, Elia, the faithful valet, was curling his master's hair and pulled it. Alfieri struck him with a heavy candlestick, cutting his brow. Elia hit back. Alfieri drew his sword; servants interfered; explanations and peace followed. Elia kept a handkerchief, soaked in his own blood, which he would pull from his pocket and show his master whenever Alfieri became angry. In Lisbon he met Abbot Tommaso di Caluso, a man of great learning, who directed his mind towards the intellectual food he really wanted. Alfieri writes that the Abbot was a Montaigne in the flesh, as saturated with antique learning as was his favorite author.

Alfieri pretends to give a true account of his amorous adventures in Spain. But critics find omissions and untrue interpretations.[2] His autobiography describes the sort of man and poet he wanted to be. This literary masterpiece is definite, aesthetic, with well-balanced contrasts, vivid coloring and good drawing; but its errors are revealed by comparison with Alfieri's private *Giornali*.

When, after much wandering, Alfieri returned to Turin, he refused to enter the diplomatic service and became *cavalier servente* to beautiful Gabriella Falletti di Villa-falletto, wife of the Marquis of Priero—or, as the Piedmontese dialect would have it, "di Prie." In his *Life*, Alfieri narrates that one morning when the marchioness was in bed and he was performing his duty of *cavalier servente*, inspired by a series of *arrazi* representing the amours of Antony and Cleopatra, he composed the first scenes of his tragedy *Cleopatra*. The critics—and especially Signor Bertana—allege that Alfieri slightly arranged his story. It is certain that in 1775 Alfieri turned to intellectual pursuits. On June 16th, 1775, Alfieri's *Cleopatra* was performed in Turin, and was warmly applauded.

Alfieri now began the most intense study. He resolved never again to speak or read French. He retired to Cezannes, an Alpine village. There and in Pisa he studied pure Italian, and worked at his first plays and at translations from the Latin. In order to avoid a young woman who was in love with him, Alfieri moved from Pisa to Sienna; and here met another precious friend, Francesco

Gori Gandellini, an ardent republican. Under his influence Alfieri wrote *La Tirannide,* a political pamphlet which expresses his hatred of Princes. In 1777 Alfieri met the woman who was to fix his lifelong affection, whom he has idealized in imitation of Petrarch's Laura or Dante's Beatrice, although she was wanting every virtue and quality that deserve immortality.

Louise Caroline Emanuelle de Stolberg-Gedern's father, Prince Gustav Adolphus, had served and died in the armies of Maria Theresa. Her mother claimed direct descent from Robert Bruce. Her husband Charles Edward Stuart, Count of Albany, the "Young Pretender," had fallen very low since his bright day at Preston Pans. He had lost all interest in his own cause and was a drunkard.

Educated in the monastery of Sainte Vandren, and already entitled "chanoiesse," she was flattered with the idea of becoming a Queen—*"in partibus."* For the sake of her royal title she overlooked her bridegroom's faults. On Good Friday, April 17th, 1772, they were married in Loreto: the bridegroom displaying the full title of King Charles III with all its prefixes. The pseudo-royal pair settled in Rome with as much pomp as they could, though the Pope refused to recognize their title. "Her Majesty" could not fill her salons because of Charles Edward's bad manners and wearisome babble about Preston Pans and Culloden. In 1774, when the "Jubilee" was filling Rome with authentic Kings and Princes, the Albany—or "Albanie," as the Pretender spelled his name—left for Florence.

Grand Duke Peter Leopold refused to recognize the Pretender's claim; but Florentine society accepted his wife's invitations; and even many English addressed her as "Her Majesty." Countess d'Albany had the art of presiding over a salon. Her beauty, a certain air of grandeur, her wonderful dark eyes, a sort of halo due to the bad reputation of her husband, some whispered scandal,[3] some exotic charm in this pseudo-Queen, roused Alfieri to lavish praise and tender expressions.[4] Alfieri's feelings were further stirred by a natural pity for the wife of a sodden brute.[5] Even in her servants' hearing there were coarse reproaches; and worse things were whispered. When Charles Edward's jealousy became justified, he dared not affront Alfieri, though he bravely struck his wife in the privacy of their apartment.

Countess d'Albany had friends, and she knew how to obtain ecclesiastical support. At luncheon one day, when a Countess Orlandini and a Mr. Gehegan were the guests of the d'Albanys, there was mention of certain embroideries on exhibition at the convent of the *Bianchette* in via del Mandorlo. All four drive to the door of the convent. It opens for the Countess to enter. When her husband reaches the threshold, the heavy door is closed. He knocks and swears; and Mr. Gehegan tries to soothe him. The Abbess declares that "superior commands" have ordered her to keep the Countess of Albany in the convent so long as it pleases her to stay.

After her husband has departed, the Countess and her maid leave the convent in a carriage with Alfieri in disguise, pistols in his pockets, sitting by the driver. Having escorted her to the Tuscan frontier, Alfieri returned to Florence, while the lady went on to Rome. In Rome the fugitive wife of one princely brother found hospitality with his other princely brother, the Cardinal of York— a striking commentary on contemporary manners and morals. The Cardinal of York supported his sister-in-law either because he disapproved of his brother's behaviour, or because Countess d'Albany was as charming as she was shrewd. There, in the palatial residence of a cardinal, Alfieri freely visited his lady-love.

Even before joining Countess d'Albany in Rome, Alfieri had made that much discussed settlement of his financial affairs. He gave his whole fortune to his sister, Countess Cumiana, in exchange for a fixed revenue. The annuity and cash he received did not amount to his entire revenue; but it offered the advantage of security. Alfieri's estate was under the perpetual menace of confiscation. By the laws of Piedmont, prolonged absence entailed this possible peril. There was even more probability of a confiscation as punishment for expressing opinions offensive to the sovereigns. Under the circumstances, Alfieri's character appears not quite as impulsive as he pretends. Nor was Countess d'Albany less worldwise. Marie Antoinette of France promised her protection; and a son of Maria Theresa, the Grand Duke of Tuscany, granted other favors. Perhaps these patrons meant to reward the daughter of one of Austria's greatest generals.[6]

The story of Alfieri's semi-royal amours has been often told.[7] How the pair wandered in France and in England, after keeping apart in Italy; how they secured untrammeled liberty and yet retained high social standing, reveals the moral standard of the times.

Through all her divers avatars Countess d'Albany appears a typical *grande dame* who expects to retain the privileges of rank, even when indulging in an irregular life. Her liaison with a famous poet became a bright feather on her cap; she must be addressed as "Her Majesty." When Charles Edward died, she refused to marry Alfieri and thus lose her royal title. Such meanness of character, such lack of spiritual elevation, contrasts strangely with Alfieri's extravagant praise. How could the king-hater, the poet who raves against tyrants, who despised Metastasio for kissing the hand of a queen, approve of Countess d'Albany? In the pseudo-matrimonial quiet of later years, did he not realize the lady's open infatuation for their friend and guest, the painter Fabre?

To investigate the moral worth of such a woman may be unimportant; but to understand the soul of a great poet is interesting. One of Alfieri's latest biographers has undertaken this analysis. Comparison of dates and letters, the "Life" Alfieri meant to publish, and the diaries he wrote for his private use, shows that Alfieri and the Countess, after a first period of real affection, continued to play a *rôle*. It was partly blindness, partly reticence, and chiefly through Alfieri's infatuation for the great Italian poets. Because Dante sang of Beatrice and Petrarch of Laure de Sade, Alfieri also must worship at a shrine and adorn it with flowers of rhetoric and garlands of poetry.

Although Countess d'Albany lacked many qualities, she was a perfect hostess. The ruling fad was for a salon. Every contemporary writer mentions his own triumphs, or other people's discomfiture, in these salons. Countess d'Albany could preside over a salon. She had a majestic figure in white flowing robes and ample "fichus Marie Antoinette," a great name, large experience, and an acquaintance or relationship with great personages. Her drawing-room was almost continuously open. Sir William Wraxall describes her apartment in rue de Boulogne, Paris; the throne under a dais, the emblazoned plate and other paraphernalia of the would-be royal lady.

Among her visitors in Paris: Necker, Montmorin, Malesherbes, the Papal Legate, Mercy d'Argenton, represent statesmanship; Beaumarchais and Madame de Staël represent letters. In London, after being presented at Court, she might have basked in the sun of social splendour; but she disliked English ways.[8] This would-be Queen of England wrote that "in England everyone can be bought for money." Countess d'Albany is cosmopolitan; any people, any place will do, provided she can find a stage for her little personage. She preferred Paris, in order that she might shine in the reflected light of Josephine Beauharnais or Madame de Staël. Indeed the Alfieri and d'Albany ménage delayed so long in Paris[9] that they were all but stopped by a group of *sans culottes* who took them for "ci-devants" on their way to emigration.

This false idealization of his lady-love is not the only equivocation in Alfieri's autobiography. He proclaims his hatred for France, yet continues to live in Paris. For a writer whose Italian was deficient, for one who wished to *disfrancezarsi* (to unfrench himself), Paris was not the best place wherein to revise and correct his plays. Alfieri fiercely proclaims his passion for liberty, yet could not comprehend the French Revolution. From Paris, August 14th, 1792, he wrote that the "Constitution is still-born, ready for the tomb." He seemed indifferent when Piedmont and other Italian States were threatened by French invasion; yet he was an officer in the Piedmontese army.

Restless wandering and aimless agitation characterized Alfieri's youth, followed by eager study when ambition pointed the way to glory. When, in 1793, he settled in Florence, he was very tired. He complains of prolonged attacks of gout. His condition was aggravated by worry. Both the Countess's and Alfieri's money was chiefly invested in France. The French Revolution restricted their income. His home life was dignified, if not as serene as he pretended. He flirted with a lady whom he visited almost every evening. He wrote her sonnets almost as impassionate as the more famous ones in praise of his pseudo-legitimate lady. There was another love-affair with a Siennese noblewoman,[10] while in his own home, in the Palazzo Gianfigliazzi on Lung Arno Corsini, the painter François Xavier Fabre made love to Countess d'Albany.

In that delightful collection of anecdotes and reminiscences which Massimo D'Azeglio entitled *I Miei Ricordi,* there is a pen-picture of the triumvirate; D'Azeglio himself playing the rôle of a *bambino* to be painted on the lady's lap, so as to represent in a village parish church a most sanctimonious "Santa Famiglia." D'Azeglio, like most Italian and foreign writers, shows little reverence for the woman who proved herself unworthy of a poet's affection.

Italian writers all condemn Alfieri's pseudo-widow who hastily married Fabre. They deplore her inconsiderate treatment of Alfieri's legacy. She bequeathed Alfieri's manuscripts and books to Fabre, enabling him legally to carry them out of Italy and give them to Montpellier University.

She shed easy tears for the death of Charles Edward;[11] she wept easily for Alfieri. A few days after his death (December 9th, 1803), she wrote to her friend D'Anse de Villiers: "J'ai tout perdu! C'est comme si on m'avait arrache le coeur . . . depuis dix ans je ne l'avais jamais plus quitté: que nous passions nos journées ensemble, j'était [sic] a côté de lui quand il travaillait . . ." and so on. But what about her lover and prospective husband, Fabre?

Both Fabre and Countess d'Albany published their common grief in the magnificent marble monument which Canova raised for Alfieri in "Santa Croce"—a theatrical and academic piece of sculpture. For the poet, and for his right to be numbered among the great Italians, his works speak. Though his rhetorical eloquence is somewhat obsolete, his works have left in Italy an influence which pleads his claim to a glorious remembrance.

NOTES

CHAPTER VIII

Carlo Emanuele III reigned from 1730 to 1773, a better and wiser king than Alfieri shows. He tried to reform the antiquated laws of his country; issued a code which was an indication of excellent purpose. The King opposed foreign travel and especially prolonged sojourn abroad by his subjects; and greatly interfered in family affairs.

He enticed Pietro Giannone (1676–1748) from Switzerland, and imprisoned him and his son. For thirteen years Giannone was prisoner in the fortresses of Miolans and Turin, was forced to write an "Abiura," and only released by death in 1748. Giannone's crime was his *Storia civile del regno di Napoli,* and other historical essays, wherein he discussed the origin and limits of civil and religious "jus"; for which he was persecuted by the Roman Catholic Church. Carlo Emanuele III is also blamed for the harsh treatment inflicted on his own father, who abdicated the throne, and afterwards intrigued to recover it.

King Vittorio Amedeo III, 1773, fought French invasions, and attempted a coalition of Italian States. In 1796, Bonaparte forced him to sign the treaty of Cherasco, by which Nice and Savoy were annexed to France, and by which French troops might pass through Piedmont to Lombardy. Alfieri, although he had been educated in a military academy, and wore a Piedmontese officer's uniform because it enhanced his personal charms, never fought for his country —not even when, in 1794, the French invaded the neutral Genoese Commonwealth to enter Piedmont.

King Carlo Emanuele IV, in 1796, courted the protection of the French Directoire. He adopted reforms in order to conciliate those among his subjects who favoured the French Revolutionary opinions. His soldiers even fought with those of Bonaparte; but Bona-

parte wanted Piedmont; he charged the king with imaginary trea-
sons and forced him to exchange prosperous Piedmont for the
barren, uncivilized kingdom of Sardinia. King Carlo Emanuele IV,
on his way towards exile, stopped in Florence and was comforted
by another illustrious exile, Pope Pius VI, and was visited by Alfieri. For this visit of Alfieri to King Carlo Emanuele, for all events
during these last years of the century in Florence, *see* Pierfilippo
Covoni's *Cronachette Storiche Fiorentine,—negli ultimi due anni
del secolo de corso.* Firenze, M. Cellini, 1894.

1. This Dutch Romance is to be found in *Vita, Epoca Terza,* Chapter
   VI. It begins like one of Goldoni's anecdotes invented to entertain
   his readers; then it suddenly becomes dramatic when the poet describes his attempted suicide. In the absence of names and dates it
   sounds apocryphal.

   Alfieri confesses that his ignorance of mathematics made futile
   his study of astronomy, although he exclaims that such studies
   would have ravished his spirit. (*Vita, Epoca Terza,* Chapter VII.)

2. For his travel in Spain, *see* in *La Revue de Paris,* December, 1921,
   an essay on "Les Grandes Routes d'Espagne." Alfieri is not mentioned; but contemporary French visitors of Spain describe the
   roads.

3. From a letter of Countess d'Albany to Bonstetten, one of her most
   faithful admirers, we can select this evidence of a flirtation which
   may have been perfectly innocent. "La tendre Ratznau (femme de
   chambre et confidante) m'a dit souvent: M. de Bonstetten était le
   seul homme qui aurait été dangereux pour moi . . . et je le crois,
   car vous êtes gai, aimable, et sensé, par caprice: voila comme je
   désire un amant et qu'il n'ait l'air de l'être que seul avec moi. Je
   ne peux pas souffrir la maniere de faire l'amour a l'Italiene; on le
   chanté sur les toits."

4. Among the less known of Alfieri's poetical trifles, let us quote this
picture of his love-making at that time: Charles Edward napping
by the fireside, the two lovers exchanging glances:

> Felice me, propizio
> Par che m'ascolti il Nume,
> Vacilla il capo debile,
> Reggersi in van presume,
> Sul petto il mento labile,
> Ecco cade, e ricade;
> In braccio al sonno giacesi
> La gia canuta etade,
> Gia dai begli occhi fulgidi,
> Negri, amorosi, ardenti,
> Bere il velen piacevole
> Io posso a sorai lenti;
> E gia sento che tacito
> Serpeggia in ogni vena;
> Ne il labbro oso disciogliere
> Cotanto l'alma ho piena . . .
> Ma, ahime! che veggo svegliasi!
> Appena era sopito,
> E a terra io deggio affiggere
> L'occhio che sol fu ardito.

Which was tolerable for Alfieri as an Arcadian and *cavalier servente,* but unworthy of the great tragic poet.

5. About Alfieri and Countess d'Albany many books have been written. One of the less prejudiced is by Emilio del Cerro: *Vittorio
Alfieri e la Contessa d'Albany—Storia di una grande passione—*
Roux e Viarengo, 1905. Also Emilio Bertana: *Vittorio Alfieri
studiato nella Vitá, nel Pensiero e nell'Arte, con Lettere e documenti inediti.* Torino, Loescher 1903. This volume of 547 pages
seems to be the definitive analysis of Alfieri's works and life. It is
pervaded by a spirit of acute criticism and diffidence against Alfieri's interpretation of his own character.

6. About Countess d'Albany's financial arrangements much has been written. She knew how to attract sympathy and secure assistance. Gustav III of Sweden tried to arrange matters with her husband; Louis XVI interfered in this important affair; yet it ended in a separation "a mensa et thoro" pronounced by Pope Pius VI on March, 1784. For the sake of conciliating the King of France and getting a pension from him, the Countess surrendered some of her jewels and some of the money she might have obtained.

7. Saint René Taillandier, *La Comtesse d'Albany,* Paris, Levy, 1862. Vernon Lee, *The Countess of Albany,* London, Allen and Co., 1884. G. Pélissier, *Le Portefeuille de la Comtesse d'Albany,* Paris, 1902. Pélisson, *Lettres inédites de la Comtesse d'Albany à ses amies de Sienne.* Paris, Fontmongt, 1904.

Ferrero, "Gli Ultimi Stuardi," in *Rivista Europea,* 1881, page 683. *Nuova Antologia,* Marzo 16, 1903, Sassi, "La Comtessa d'Albany."

A very complete study by Baron Alfred de Reumont: "Die Grafin von Albany, Berlin, 1860, 2 vol.

8. Even skeptical Horace Walpole is scandalized when he hears of her presentation at the English Court. In May 1791 he writes to his friend and gossip Marquis Du Deffand: "La Comtesse d'Albany n'est pas seulement à Londres, il est probable qu'en ce moment même elle est au palais de St. James. Ce n'est pas une révolution à la manière française qui l'a restaurée, c'est le sens dessus dessous si caractéristique de notre époque. On a vu dans ces derniers mois le pape brûlé en effigie à Paris, Madame Du Barry invitée à diner chez le lord Maire de Londres, et la veuve du Prétendant, présentée à la cour de la Grande Bretagne. . . . La veuve a été annoncée sous le titre de Princesse de Stolberg. Elle était vêtue fort élégamment, et ne parut pas embarrassée le moins du monde."

If the ambiguity of such a situation shocked the worldly-wise Walpole, how can we accept the interpretation of her behaviour offered or suggested by Alfieri's eulogies. Chateaubriand was asked by Fabre to say nothing that could ruffle the feelings of Countess d'Albany, but later—in 1822—he wrote of her: "un visage sans expression, une taille épaisse . . . si les femmes de Rubens vieillissaient elles ressembleraient celle là."

9. Saint René Taillandier says: "n'osant pas braver l'opinion publique au point de se retrouver en une ville d'Italie, elle lui donna rendezvous en Alsace." But the *Life and Letters* show that the Countess resided with Alfieri in Paris longer than in Alsace. When Alfieri's health failed, in a letter to E. Bianchi, Alfieri mentions twenty days in bed and talks of dying, assured that his lover will take due care of the edition then preparing of his plays by Didot, Paris.

10. Alfieri was made love to by a Venetian lady of noble birth: Alba Corner Vendramin. There are several letters in *Lettere Inedite,* etc.

11. Charles Edward had been living some time with his illegitimate daughter (by Miss Walkinshaw) when he died on the 7th of January, 1788. On his tombstone his name is inscribed as Carolus III. The monument by Canova raised to him and to his brother (under the name of Enricus IV), is in St. Peter's, Rome.

CHAPTER IX

ALFIERI'S TRAGEDIES

Alfieri lacked poetical discernment, but his patriotic emotion burned fiercely: His tragedies answered to Italian aspirations for freedom: Alfieri aspired to rank among the greatest Italian poets: Alfieri's passionate patriotism was limited to his writings; he never drew his sword: More than he loved liberty, Alfieri hated tyranny: In his first tragedy, *Filippo*, tyranny is personified: In all his tragedies, Alfieri paints his personages with the color of his own soul: His plays follow classical models: *Saul* is Alfieri's masterpiece: Saul is torn by contrary passions. He struggles with God, he struggles also with himself: Saul is mad, but he possesses a majesty that inspires compassion and admiration: *Mirra* is Alfieri's final masterpiece: The drama lies in the horrified struggle of a chaste soul with an unclean obsession: It is a horrible yet pitiful picture: Alfieri's theatre had a political importance which surpassed its artistic worth: His appeals are trumpet calls: Alfieri is greater than his work; his own people understood him and magnified merits.

"POETA Nascitur"; yet Alfieri insists upon early dislike for all literature, especially poetry. In order to prove his will-power, he constantly repeats: "Volli, Volli Fortissimamente Volli." Alfieri's poetical work resulted from intense application.[1]

He lacked poetical discernment. With equal fervor he praises Homer and Ossian, Seneca and Crebillon. When he was more than fifty years old, he started to read ravenously. He studied Italian grammar and the Latin classics in order to create an Italian tragedy fashioned after the antique. He asserts that he did not read French plays. His borrowings from them are many; but they are charged with a fervor that was his own message, and answered to Italian aspirations for freedom.[2]

Alfieri's nature was violent; his affections were passionate; everything became for him a devouring flame; and his patriotic emotion burned fiercely.

> Venne quel grande, come il grande augello
> onde ebbe nome, e all'umil paese
> sopra volando, fulvo, irrequieto,
> Italia, Italia,

Egli gridava a dessueti orecchi
ai pigri cuori, a gli animi giacenti;
Italia, Italia rispondeano l'urne
d'Arqua e di Ravenna.[3]

Thus grandly Carducci has summarized Alfieri's apostolate. To slumbering souls and deaf ears he cried the magic word "Italia." The tombs of Petrarch and Dante answered to Alfieri because they had uttered the same cry centuries before. This tradition of Italian unity was almost realized under the Longobards. Though seemingly destroyed by the "Holy Roman Empire," by the establishment of Catholic temporal power, by many invasions, dissensions, and civil wars, this tradition forever reasserts itself. Sometimes the standard is raised by those who fought for limited and selfish aims. Cola di Rienzi, Crescenzo, Cesare Borgia, Guilio II, rallied hearts and seduced intellects because they preached the idea of a united Italy built out of many feeble states.

Alfieri appealed to emotions that were already seething in the intellectual and moral atmosphere around him. His tragedies expressed the aspirations of a people that realized their bondage but saw no way of release. Through his French education, his many travels, his reading of Rousseau and Montesquieu, Alfieri was awakened to an appreciation of the great Italian poets; and he aspired to rank among the greatest.[4]

Even his passionate patriotism was limited to his writings. Alfieri, descendant of warriors and diplomats, officer in the national army of Piedmont, wrote fiercely against Austria, yet never drew his sword. Alfieri's patriotism was a mental effort to emulate Dante and Petrarch. When French Revolutionaries dismantled the Bastille, Alfieri sang the glory of "Parigi Sbastigliato"; but when they seized his income and threatened his liberty, then these revolutionaries were wicked.

He distinguishes between good and bad kings: the good kings are those whose power is limited by law. Alfieri is not explicit as to the basis of this law. He scorns the "rabble." His scorn for "The Few, the Many" is a complement of his hatred of tyranny. Alfieri hates his own King, foreign invaders, the French, and militarism. His violent love is for an idealized Italy that did not exist. Gioberti dreams of a federation of States under the supremacy of the Church; Verri, Cesare Beccaria, Antonio Genovesi, and other patriots write and toil for the advancement of science, and for the solution of Italian social problems; but Alfieri's ideal is vague.

Giovanni Fantoni wrote that in Alfieri the man and the thinker were first to be studied, and then the tragic author. By adopting this plan, Alfieri's biographers have emphasized the influence of his plays in the Italian political movement, rather than weighed their literary value. Alfieri writes of the indisputable, certain, and inviolable rules of art followed by him in the selection of his subjects in the weaving of his plots; yet Alfieri's own sentiments and his own temperament are the very essence of his tragedies. His historical characters are puppets expressing his own ideas. Hence there is no real psychoanalysis. Those conflicts of human passions that are the very essence of tragedy are never attempted. His ideals of liberty dominate his theatre.

More than he loved liberty, however, Alfieri hated tyranny. In his first tragedy there is nought but Filippo (Philip), tyranny personified. Saturated with French ideas, Alfieri first wrote the plan of this play and most of its dialogue in French prose. After his conversion to liberalism, Alfieri wrote in Italian. *Filippo* was rewritten several times. Many of its well-known lines are contemporary with the passionate outburst, *La Tirannide*. Philip's cruel and perverse character expresses Alfieri's hatred of all crowned despots. Unprepared for historical documentation, Alfieri presents events and characters which he does not comprehend. These contrasting characters and opposing passions are forerunners of the romantic school. Yet he slavishly follows those limitations which the French classics dictated.

Imitating Corneille, Alfieri's preface explains his motives and tries to forestall criticism. He confesses that Filippo's jealousy is not "fiery" enough for a tragedy. This oft-repeated adjective *calda* discloses his weakness. Since Philip of Spain cannot stride the stage in a storm of volcanic passion, the poet makes him a complex tragical personage. A monstrous being with insatiable pride of power, void of affection, scruple, compassion, generosity, or joy, his mind becomes soaked with suspicion and consumed with hate.

This darksome tyrant, cruel father, steals his son Carlo's fiancée, to secure for himself a wife and slave. Isabella is the sweet dove that flies with the strongest wind. She submits to a hateful marriage; yet she listens to Carlo's tender words. Carlo is passionate yet wise, lachrymose yet brave. His speeches about justice and freedom arouse his father's wrath and increase his jealousy. There are the necessary confidantes and agents. Gomez, the traitor, urges Filippo to commit the murder; Perez and Leonardo also discuss the matter. Futile argument! Filippo has already decided Carlo's fate.

Alfieri writes to Calsabigi, Sept. 6, 1783, that he paints his personages with the colors of his own soul, moulds their characters in resemblance of his own, but strives to make his personages such as he imagines them. Hence the sameness of situations and of characters in all his plays. Hence also contradictions which are the necessary result of trying to fit stock characters within different plots.[5]

The plot, the characters, the events of Alfieri's classical plays were fixed for him by classical models. Thus guided and restrained, Alfieri wrote *Agamemnon* and *Oreste*. In the first, Clytemnestra murders her husband. In the second, Oreste comes, fifteen years later, to wreak vengeance. Clytemnestra's remorse, her terror of Oreste, yet her love for him, her torment under the perpetual reproaches of Elettra, her love for Egisto embittered by his ingratitude, present a magnificent situation which Alfieri has made the most of.

He shows Clytemnestra, torn by desire and terror, repulsed by her son Oreste whom she would save at every cost, insulted by Egisto who fears that she may have learnt too well the lesson of murder he has taught her. Oreste, the classical impulsive hero, is contrasted with his devoted friend Pilade. There is a combat of heroism between them. Both claim to be Oreste, the victim of Egisto's hatred. The plot is brisk. Oreste is seized by Egisto, released by Elettra; and the people rise against the tyrant. Oreste pursues Egisto, but stabs his own mother and becomes insane with grief. This is in accordance with the classical model; but he is not pursued by the Eumenides; not even seeing them in his delirium, as Racine shows him.[6]

In 1782 he undertook to measure himself with Scipione Maffei and with Voltaire selecting the same subject, *Merope*. It was an enterprise greatly to tempt the pride of Alfieri. Maffei's was the best play yet produced in Italy. Voltaire praised, imitated, and vilified it. Alfieri could not compete with Maffei, the patrician, of noble life, devoted to intellectual pursuits and public charges, with literary training and fastidious taste. Maffei scorned to court public favour, after giving one recognized masterpiece.[7]

Alfieri lacked the character, temperament, and experience needed successfully to delineate maternal love. He held no tender memories of childhood; since his unnatural mother disposed of him when he was barely nine. Nor had he such experience in his attachment to childless Countess d'Albany, and there was no feminine tenderness in his own character. Yet Alfieri frequently represents a mother's tragedy. Alfieri wished to make Merope the "Mother queen in tragedy," and to interpret the anxieties, doubts, agonies, terrors, hallucinations of a mother trembling for an only son of whose fate she is ignorant. The play was very successful in Italy and in France because of Ristori's thrilling impersonation of Merope—a mother sentencing her own son to death, thinking that he is a stranger, the murderer of her real son. When the equivocation is cleared, then Merope fights for the life of her son Egisto. How, in order to pacify Polifonte, the usurper of her throne, she consents to marry him, how he deceives her, and how Egisto kills Polifonte, make up the Alfierian rendering of the classic theme.

Saul is Alfieri's masterpiece. No other tragedy has been so often performed in Italy. Here is emotion, pathos, and a religious spirit which might have developed in more congenial atmosphere. It is the stern Jewish interpretation of divinity, rather than the more benign Gospel teaching.

Saul knows that he has sinned and that he deserves divine punishment. Saul is tormented by remorse, even to madness. He fears and hates his rival and destined successor, David. Then he becomes gentle and reasonable under the softening influence of song and of paternal love. No other play of Alfieri's possesses these psychological contrasts. Saul's terrors, like Lear's sufferings, appeal to the most sensitive chords of the human heart.

David is rather a symbolic impersonation of every virtue than a normal man. Michal is the Biblical woman, utterly devoted, loving blindly both husband and father. Alfieri could not adequately represent both Saul and Jonathan in one play. The action of the play is complicated; yet all the events are necessary for the development of the characters.

Especially admirable is the lyrical chant which David improvises to soothe the tortured soul of Saul with its beautiful strophes, each one a picture of glory, of rejoicing, or of quiet; each one suggestive of some passing emotion in the soul of Saul. This much-praised passage, however, is closely imitated from Dryden's *Alexander's Feast*. It has the same plan, the same series of images and the same emotions in a royal listener. Other passages in Saul are paraphrases of Psalms, as, for instance, David's prayer; and they too are very beautiful.

In what does the remarkable beauty of *Saul* consist? Saul is torn by contrary passions. He struggles with God; he struggles also with himself. The old warrior king, intoxicated by many victories, feels the crown oscillating upon his head, the sceptre trembling in his hand; his radiant star is setting and that of David, friend of his son Jonathan, and beloved husband of his daughter Michal, is rising. And the old warrior King loves David and fears him.

While Saul, alone and undefended, slept in the cave of Engadden, David, instead of slaying him, has merely cut off a piece of his cloak. "Now," exclaims David, "the evident sign hast thou, Saul, of my heart, my innocence, and my good faith." Saul is moved, and cries: "My son, thou hast conquered . . . thou hast conquered." (Act II, sc. 3.) But where the reason vacillates, calm cannot long endure; and Saul is mentally diseased. Fury is succeeded by prostration. He is aware of his impotence. He is tormented with the thought that "perhaps" Samuel may have anointed David as King—"perhaps" Jonathan knows it! Jonathan, who trusts David, forgets that for a throne "the brother slays the brother; the mother, her sons; the wife, her husband; the son, his father." Here, and in the following scene in which Saul condemns Achimelech to death, his passions and his cruelties, his reasonings and his aberrations are wholly regal.

His last delirium is a form of hallucination not new to the tragic theatre. Saul rushes upon the stage terrified, suppliant, imagining himself pursued by the shade of Samuel. The hands of Michal restrain him, and the horrid vision vanishes. He exclaims: "What sound do I hear? Ah! it seems to me of battle! My helmet, shield, spear, now quickly bring me; now quick the arms, the king's arms. Die would I, but in the field!" The vacillating, tottering old man becomes once more hero and king. He hastens where "lodges Death whom he seeks." As the victorious Philistines rush on with torches and swords, Saul proudly regards his sword. "But thou remain'st to me, sword, faithful minister to the final need; now come . . . impious Philistria. Thou wilt find me, but at least as King, here . . . dead."

A madman, yes, but in his madness a majesty that inspires compassion and admiration. In Saul, Alfieri has interpreted the passion which he best understood—a life of clamors and battlings and deliriums for the conquest of glory. It also proves what he could do when he adopts a Biblical subject and forgets political propaganda. Saul and Merope are the only tragedies that Alfieri elaborated and achieved quickly and without effort.

When, however, he again searched the Bible for inspiration, he was unfortunate in his subject and in his treatment of it. Abel is not a personage adaptable to the modern stage. Impersonations of Sin and Death can hardly stir the interest of modern audiences. Not all the beauty and harmony of Milton's lines could fix the attention of an audience or awaken a responsive echo. Alfieri's efforts to build up a grand spectacle—*tramelogedia* he named it; to direct a phantasmagoria of optical illusion, apparitions and musical interludes; failed.

Mirra is Alfieri's final masterpiece. It is Mirra, the chaste, struggling against her incestuous love for her father Ciniro. Her world is idyllic; King Ciniro is happy in his kingdom and loves his wife. Cecri is the sweetest mother and the worthy wife of Ciniro. The faithful nurse Euricles is a second mother. Young Prince Pereo, ingenuous, tender, devoted, is the pearl of lovers. And the drama lies precisely in this terrified, horrified flight of the soul from an unclean obsession; from a destiny which, at every fresh effort to break its bonds, closes in around the horrified victim of unnatural passion. To eliminate the moral ugliness of Mirra's passion, it was necessary to create between passion and conscience a mortal dissension, a naturally pure mind struggling against an irresistible fate. But, in this dualizing of the personality of Mirra and the dark mystery of her shameful obsession, it was necessary gradually to raise the veils of that soul, and sometimes even to tear them with swift audacity as in the powerful scene 7 of Act IV, where the brutality of the overwhelming passion betrays itself in the cry of the jealous woman against her rival, that rival being Cecri, her own mother, a horrible yet pitiful figure!

Between 1775 and 1779, twelve works were conceived; then the production slackened as the strife for excellence became more intense. In 1782 the *Merope* and the *Saul* were finished. In 1784 he conceived the *Agide,* the *Sofonisba*[8] and the *Mirra;* and, in 1786, the two *Bruti* (Brutuses). Finally, in 1789, at Paris, all the tragedies saw the light in their definitive form.[9]

Alfieri's theatre opens with the dark figure of a bloody tyrant, and closes with that of a magnanimous tyrant slain. Alfieri's theatre has a political aim, content, and value which surpass its artistic worth. It contains fine traits and many fine details, but only two great creations: *Saul* and *Mirra*.

In all his plays, Alfieri's object is to rouse his countrymen to action. He cries that men must not be slaves; that there is a force stronger than tyranny and gold, stronger than that abstract power —"the thing that is." How and when this rebellion is to be enacted, he does not say. His utterings are a trumpet call; they did not summon a host, but they breathed hope; they appealed to future generations. Such appeals uttered on the stage by actors trained to emphasize every line of their rôle, produced immediate effect.

The importance of the Alfierian theatre in the history of Italian literature is great; and many were the early *ottocento* Italian tragedies that it inspired. Alfieri is greater than his work because he aimed at grandeur and strove towards high ideals. His own people realized the beauty of his unrealized dream. They understood him and loved him and magnified his merits.

NOTES

CHAPTER IX

1. Many books and essays have been published about Alfieri; his plays have been frequently translated. Ernesto Masi, Emilio Bertana, Del Cerro, Guido Mazzoni, De Sanctis, and Carducci are amongst the best critics.

2. In his *Life,* Alfieri relates how, when 54 years old, he learned Greek "so that he could read Pindar and the tragic poets and the divine Homer, translating them into Latin or Italian." To celebrate this achievement, he wore a collar bearing the names of 23 ancient and modern poets, and supporting a cameo representing Homer, on the back of which was inscribed a Greek distich that Alfieri "invented this order to proclaim himself a Knight of Homer."

   See a Lecture of Isidoro Del Luugo's in *Vita Italiana del Settecento.* Firenze. Barbiera.

3. "He came, the great One, like the bird whose name he bore, and to the humbled country, overhead flying, brawny and restless. 'Italy, Italy,' he cried; and to deaf ears, to slothful hearts, to dormant souls, 'Italy, Italy,' answered the graves of Arqua and Ravenna."

4. Ernesto Masi, *Nell 'Ottocento—Idee e Figure del Secolo XIX,* says that Alfieri's mind was fashioned by the writings of Rousseau and Montesquieu, though by instinct and by hereditary conscience he is a direct descendant of Dante and Petrarch.

5. Of Alfieri's inability to realize the meaning and the drift of historical events, and his tendency to transform events and characters according to his own preconceived ideas, an instance is to be found in *Etruria Vendicata,* a poem wherein he narrates the murder of Alessandro de' Medici by his cousin Lorenzo. Although a poet may have

the right to alter the order of events—as, for instance, to show Lorenzo himself stabbing the tyrant, instead of using the arm of his paid accomplice, Scoroconcolo—it is not permitted to transform and misinterpret the whole subject in hand. Lorenzo could not represent a hero and a patriot; Florence could not look like Sparta; Lorenzo's supposed speeches would have been absurd to the Florentines; Scoroconcolo's ghost delivering sentences worthy of Cato was ridiculous.

Alfred De Musset enriched the French stage with a little masterpiece on the same subject, *Lorenzaccio*. It has lately inspired Sem Benelli's *La Maschera di Bruto*.

6. A comparison of Alfieri's and Racine's *Oreste* measures the distance between the two writers, and also the difference between two historical and national epochs. Racine portrays the hero as the Hotel de Rambouillet and the Court of Versailles imagined him, lovelorn and romantic, full of the honeyed sentimentalism of that epoch; Alfieri's hero is an imaginary figure which he presents as an ideal for his own and for future generations. The nobility of Alfieri's intent excuses his faulty versification and clumsy conclusion.

Agamemnon is Alfieri's first tragedy in which a good king appears; he is one of Alfieri's most human characters. He is disturbed by Clytemnestra's coldness and Egisto's presence. Egisto, the son of Tieste in Argo, under the roof of the son of Atreo (Atreus), is "a strange thing." What does he want? What does he meditate or plan? Agamemnon is suspicious, because he knows of the sad doom which weighs upon his line. Since a liaison between Clytemnestra and Egisto is for him a moral impossibility, he is not suspicious when, in trembling and confused words, Electra, who knows all, warns him against Egisto. (Act IV. sc. 3.) What a dilemma is hers, torn between the affection which she still has for her mother, and her deep respect and affection for her father!

The true protagonists of the tragedy are Clytemnestra and Egisto. The woman is slowly perverted by guilty love, and prepared for the final crime. At first, Egisto, son of Tieste, is an instrument of fate, controlled by a ferocious heredity of revenge and blood. He, then, becomes the conscious evil-doer, loving baseness and cunning. Through Clytemnestra's crime he will destroy the son of Atreus, and also gain a throne. And Electra well knows "he will be a wicked tyrant."

In the *Agamemnon,* Egisto is a potential tyrant; in the *Oreste,* Egisto is faintly defined, a personage *di ruolo,* probably because Alfieri wishes to concentrate attention upon Oreste. And yet Clytemnestra's emotions are more vivid and more human than the exaggerated furies of Oreste. She is always a mother suffering the scorn of Electra and fearing vengeance of her son. She knows Oreste to be weak, hesitant, pursued by the implacable hatred of that Egisto to whom she is indissolubly joined by complicity in crime, and by guilty passion.

The abstract idea of tyranny that produces the gloomy figure of Filippo, reappears in the successive tragedies. In *Polinice,* the mad desire to reign overpowers every other instinct; Eteocle is another Cain. He thirsts for his brother's blood even more than he desires the kingdom. The same demon drags Polinice to fratricide. "I am forced to be deaf to pity: I hasten. . . ." (Act IV, sc. 3.) Between the two madmen is their anguished mother Giocasta, a dramatic figure because of her "maternal, immense, impartial love."

The *Antigone* is perhaps the weakest of Alfieri's plays. At the beginning, Antigone is dominated by the pious duty of giving burial to the dead Polinice; but later (Act III, sc. 3), in defying the inhuman decree of Creonte, she thinks more of his son Emone than of the unburied Polinice. She says to her lover, "I cannot ever be thine; what boots it that I live? Oh heaven, of all my desperate grief, the reason true I do not even know." This is no longer Antigone; but one of the many tragic maidens for whom a hopeless illicit love renders life insupportable.

Alfieri's boiling, "ardent characters" frequently appear in the tragedies; and often approach the "sublime degree" of "heat" that burns in poor Oreste. "Sublimity" or "heat of soul" Alfieri noted with satisfaction in the Raimondo of the *Congiura dei Pazzi* (The Conspiracy of the Pazzi), conceived in 1777 after the *Oreste*. Raimondo, "blind through too great rage" (Act V, sc. 5), wounds himself while beating the tyrant.

Rage darkens Oreste's reason; hate deadens Raimondo's conscience. His is a moral madness, a bloody obsession. "No tie remains there for me in the world, saving the solemn inexorable oath of extirpating tyranny and tyrants." (Act III, sc. 2.) Stage figures are the tyrants in the *Congiura*. Astute Giuliano is despicable; Lorenzo is fantastical, a tyrant ennobled by sincerity and courage. The whole tragedy is a dialogue about tyranny. In the *Congiura,* the hatred is between tyrants and rebels against tyranny; in the *Don Garzia,* hatred rends the tyrant's family. Cosimo, of the wicked race of the Medici, has two sons worthy of himself: Diego, the image of violence, Piero, the prototype of duplicity and baseness. The third son Garzia, is nobly proud, humane, generous, and liberal.

Don Garzia has Alfieri's most complicated plot. Salviati, the victim of Cosimo's ferocity, and Giulia, Salviati's daughter, beloved by Garzia, do not appear upon the scenes. Garzia confesses to Cosimo his friendship for Salviati, and his love for Giulia. Garzia must kill Salviati, or the enraged Cosimo will torture Giulia. Love prevails. Garzia enters the dark grotto to slay Salviati (Act IV, sc. 4), but kills Diego, whom the fiend Piero has persuaded to hide there (Act IV, sc. 1). Cosimo stabs Garzia in his mother's arms; and the tragedy ends in a last crime.

Maria Stuarda, Rosmunda, Ottavia, Timoleone, the four tragedies composed after *Don Garzia,* are unimportant. In his preface to *Timoleone,* "una tragedia di liberta," Alfieri boasts of its simplified action, and of having idealized the magic words "Liberté, Fraternité, Egalité." Timoleone and Timofane, sons of Demarista, dispute for supreme power in Corinth. Timofane is the hero-warrior and autocrat. He has promised to yield the supreme power to his brother Timoleone; but now calls him a rebel. Timoleone pleads the stock arguments of democracy. Nothing happens, but much is discussed. Timofane, the dying tyrant, pardons his foes; Timoleone weeps over the corpse, and the curtain drops.

7. Scipione Maffei was a remarkable man. Besides his participation in State affairs with Apostolo Zeno and other writers, he founded and edited the *Giornale de Letterati*. His composition of *Merope* was due to chance. One day he said to some friends that, if ever he wrote a tragedy, he knew no better subject than Merope. He was challenged to try; and in a few days wrote the play that was long considered as the best in the Italian Theatre. Alfieri tried to surpass him, with doubtful success.

Voltaire first praised Maffei's play, then satirized it. Yet his own tragedy *Merope* has borrowed much from his Italian rival.

8. Alfieri's best plays were modeled on those already composed by others. He did not servilely imitate; but he needed the suggestion of a simple and grand model. Among Alfieri's innovations are the displacement of pronouns, the shortening of sentences, and other changes sometimes borrowed from the classics. He had no ear for music; his prosody is harsh. He cut off all ornaments of style as hindering the tragic effect.

The subject of Alfieri's tragedy, *Sofonisba,* was dear to Italian tradition. At the very dawn of the Italian tragic theatre, Trissino had developed this history of Sophonisba and her two husbands. In Livy and in Appian the story of Sophonisba is thus told. Hannibal threatens Rome; in Africa Scipio is warring against Syphax and Massinissa. Syphax defeats Massinissa, and then, with Scipio, marches against the Carthaginians, who are defeated. Massinissa enters the city, rushes into the palace, where Sophonisba falls at his feet, pleading for his protection.

Alfieri's plot observes the unities. All the action is in Scipio's camp. Sophonisba marries Massinissa believing her husband Syphax dead. Syphax did not die as he should have done, so he makes the extraordinary sacrifice described in the fourth scene of the fourth act.

Sophonisba exhorts Massinissa to exhibit equal magnanimity, and show the world that theirs is not a "vulgar love." But Massinissa cries: "Ah, with quite other flame than thine does my heart burn. May my kingdom perish; may the whole world perish; thou shalt be mine. Nor perils nor dangers do I know, nor fear. Ready for all am I, save but for losing thee." Sophonisba, however, follows Syphax's example and kills herself. These characters are hot enough outside, but icy cold within. Even in the supreme moments they calculate the effect of every act, and sermonize.

In the Roman tragedy of *Virginia,* Alfieri introduced a novel personage, "The People"; but it is Alfieri and not the gathered Romans that speak. Appio desires Virginia, who loves Icilio; Appio bids Marco claim Virginia, as being born of his slave. The Romans insist that the sentence be suspended until the return of Virginia's father. Alfieri expressed his own democratic ideas through the speeches of Icilio and of Virginio, who exclaim (Act III, sc. 3): "passionate words cannot rouse a people oppressed in chains . . . but blood, and blood alone can do so." Virginio, stabbing his daughter to keep her from Appio's hands; Icilio, stabbing himself to avoid murder by the tyrant's satellites; Icilio's ranting; the lamentations of Numitoria, Virginia's mother, expressed national feelings. Icilio is a verbose "Roman and lover"; Virginia is Roman more than she is lover and maiden; Virginio, "father and Roman"; Numitoria, "mother and Roman"; and Appio, "vicious, but Roman." The love of Appio is a sensual caprice. He is amorous only so long as that desire serves his political interest. As the French Revolution was dominated by classical reminiscences, so these ideas recalled to the Italians their own glorious past. *Virginia* had a clamorous success.

In the spring of 1786 Alfieri wrote the two *Bruti.* In Voltaire's tragedy of Brutus, the action develops around the soul of Tito (Titus), tortured by many conflicting passions. Alfieri restricted the field of the passions; but greatly extended the general design. The first act presents the ideal upon which the republic is founded. That ideal is a sublime rivalry in hatred of kings; but the upper class must remain distinct from the plebeians; the Great will exhibit fortitude, dignity, patriotism; the plebeians will have a minor part in the republic; concord, yes; fusion of classes, no; and one is to have always "the more eminent place." (Act II, sc. 3.)

Ambassador Mimilio persuades Brutus' simple sons that the monarchy is to be restored. They must save their father by winning the favor of the king, by joining the conspiracy. The poor youths obey. (Sc. 2.) Brutus returns victorious from his battle with the Tarquins. "Littori, hulloa there, let Titus and Tiberius be straightway brought before me," commands Brutus. The enormous crime against the republic is expiated. "Joyously for Rome we shall die." Brutus, making "of his mantle for his eyes a veil," so as not to see the blood of his sons, replies to those who proclaim him, "God! I am the most unhappy man that ever lived." Alfieri and Voltaire represent the conflict between the citizen, the magistrate, the patriot, and the father. Alfieri has given a more inexorable, yet more suffering Brutus than Voltaire; and has lightened the guilt of his sons.

Bruto Secondo (the Second Brutus) reproduces the plan, movements, concepts of Voltaire's *Mort de Cesar*—a Brutus who admires Caesar's genius, and who struggles between patriotism and love. The Countess d'Albany wrote from Paris to Alfieri that she had seen Voltaire's *Mort de Cesar*. Alfieri replied that Voltaire could not impersonate Brutus; yet, although ignorant of historical documents, Alfieri presumed to write a tragedy with this Brutus as a protagonist.

9. A list of Alfieri's plays: *Filippo, Polinice, Antigone, Virginia, Agamemnon, Oreste, Rosmunda, Ottavia, Timoleone, Merope, Maria Stuarda, La Congiura de Pazzi, Don Garzia, Saul, Agide, Sofonisba, Bruto Primo, Mirra, Bruto Secondo, Antonio e Cleopatra, Abele, Alceste Seconda.*

The six comedies that Alfieri hastily wrote in 1800 add little to his glory. Nothing but their titles is remembered: *L'Uno, I Pocchi, I Troppi, l'Antidote, la Finestrina, il Divorzio.* The three first satirized the despotism of "one ruler," the confusion of power subdivided among the "few," and the anarchy of a democratic regimen of "too many." He was working at the last-mentioned play when he died—"comme un oiseau, sans agonie, sans le savoir," as Countess d'Albany wrote to François Xavier Fabre.

CHAPTER X

GIOVANNI BATESTA NICCOLINI

The contrast between Niccolini's frail body and the great work he accomplished is almost unparalleled in literary history: When he was graduated from the University of Pisa, he was penniless: In 1807, he became professor of history at the *Accademia* in Florence: In fifteen years, Florence saw many changes in government under foreign rulers: But Niccolini was always writing and plotting for the freedom of his country: His great hatred was for the political power of the Church of Rome: His intellectual combat preserved him from other desires: His lifelong attachment to the actress Maddalena Pelzet: When old and sad he settled at the house of Carlotta Cortellini: Niccolini did not trust the promises of political liberty of Pope Pius IX: He was not in sympathy with Cavour, Mazzini, or Garibaldi: He died in 1860, and was buried at Santa Croce.

A NOTED Italian statesman was asked: "Eccellenza, what was the most decisive event of the Risorgimento?" He replied: "Why! Of course the *Arnaldo da Brescia!* That was the flourish of trumpets: the alarum which stirred us all to arms." Then, after a pause, while memory flamed and his eye sparkled: "I saw Niccolini in Florence, in 1857, at the theatre which now bears his name. The performance was his *Medea*. But who listened? Mad with enthusiasm, we pressed into his box; we fought in the passage for one glance at him, for a chance of kissing his hand or his coat. A little, shrunken, stooping old man, a sallow, wizened face; he looked dazed and kept repeating, 'that will do boys! Basta! Basta!' When he rose, tottering and bent, we crowded round his carriage, unhorsed it, and dragged it to his lodgings in Via Larga."

The contrast was striking. A timid, pallid man, a student unfit for contest, his small delicate hand scarce strong enough to hold the pen, his voice almost a whisper—yet what vital literary production; what intensity of purpose; what power he exerted over a whole generation! What a conflict between the body and the spirit! The simplicity and grandeur of his career has scarcely a parallel in any literary history.

Niccolini

Niccolini was not a great poet, nor was he a hero. He was something rare in any country, something unique in his Tuscany: he was a strong character. When contrary winds and conflicting events shook the firmest souls, uprooted principles, and made men doubtful of their creeds, Niccolini stood firm. Unmoved by the vagaries of popular opinion, he kept repeating his motto: "Viva l'Italia! War against the Church of Rome!" And when at last the United Kingdom of Italy was proclaimed, and Papal temporal power was apparently abolished, Niccolini the prophet was exalted by those who had despaired of success. "A stopped clock comes right twice every day." Niccolini, like the clock, was right at last. Niccolini's uneventful life must be interpreted in its actual surroundings; his poetical work must be considered by the light of contemporary agitations.

Ippolito Niccolini, his father, belonged to the ancient Tuscan nobility, poor in money, rich in traditions, high breeding, and intellectual culture. Settimia Filicaia, his wife, was descended from Vincenzo Filicaia, the poet who celebrated Italy's weakness and beauty in one immortal sonnet.[1] Ippolito Niccolini was appointed *Commissario Regio* over the fashionable summer resort of San Giuliano near Pisa. Niccolini was born in October, 1782. When his father died, the little family lacked money to prosecute a lawsuit against the city of Florence; and the paternal estate was confiscated. His mother's friends sent Niccolini to the Friars' school where he received a sort of education. At an early age, he entered the University of Pisa and studied law. He wrote Latin and Italian epigrams, gained the favour of the poet Fantoni, and applauded the French Revolution. In 1802, in Florence, he received the degree of Doctor. He was penniless.[2]

Florence was bleeding under the flail of the "Spedizione Aretina." Under the leadership of a woman, "Sandrina Mari," and the pretence of nationalism and religion, these fanatics were scourging

Tuscany, killing, imprisoning, wasting, and shouting "Viva Maria." The bloody Aretini were quieted by the news that the Grand Duke was returning, and by the organization of a regular government, "Il Buon Governo," to rule over Tuscany in the Grand Duke's name. But Bonaparte chose to place the half-witted Prince Louis of Parma and his Spanish wife on the throne of Etruria. Tuscany could not resist. Niccolini bowed his head and was employed first in the *Archivio delle Riformazioni,* then (1807) given a chair of history and mythology in the Accademia delle Belle Arti.

When Bonaparte transformed the Kingdom of Etruria into three departments (de L'Arno, de l'Ombrone, de la Méditerranée), and his sister, Elisa Bacciocchi, ruled with the title of "Grande Duchesse de Toscane," Niccolini was appointed "Bibliotecario Palatino." But he soon realized that he could not accept servitude. He refused all offers of other employment than his chair at the *Accademia.* In less than fifteen years, Florence saw more changes in government, more pompous progresses, and also more quiet departures, than any other European nation has witnessed in as many centuries. The arrival or the departure of an exiled King of Savoy or of an exiled Pope scarcely roused a comment. But when, in 1814, Grand Duke Ferdinand came back to his Tuscany, there was great rejoicing.[3]

Though the Grand Duke had Austrian bayonets for his escort, the Florentines trusted him to rule mildly and to keep the Austrians away. And so he did. And so, for some thirty quiet eventless years, did his son and successor, Leopold II. Florence adopted the motto of the Minister Fossombroni, "Il mondo va da se." But sullen resentment smouldered in Niccolini's heart, and was always felt in his lessons at the *Accademia,* and in his lectures at *la Crusca.*

Marchese Gino Capponi, son of a grand-ducal *ciambellano,* petted by Archduchesses, showed a strange disposition for a nobleman. His liberal opinions were strengthened by his frequent and prolonged travels. From his English friends he acquired a certain reserved attitude, and a manner of dressing that was imitated by Florentine men of fashion.[4] In Capponi's Florentine residence and in his villa of Varramisto, the traditional hospitality of Tuscan aristocracy was expressed. Every Italian writer whose name has survived was his guest. Each received the meed of support or comfort that he deserved. Niccolini and Capponi had been fellow-pupils; and their friendship was intensified by mutual comprehension and admiration. Niccolini frequently asked Capponi's advice and leaned on him. Capponi thus writes of him: "Niccolini's was a strange temper; shy, reserved, and silent in moments of quiet; he was easily excited by things that appealed to him. Indignation was his muse; whoever wanted to bring forth the poet in him, had but to stir his wrath." Other contemporaries speak of Niccolini's timidity and of his sudden transformation into an eloquent speaker if the conversation stimulated his feelings. In his youth, Niccolini had a biting tongue and pen; in later years he grew more retiring, drifting into sullenness when the Neo-guelf tendency detached him from former friends.

About 1825, Niccolini inherited from his maternal uncle, Alamanno Filicaia, a small property situated between Prato and Pistoia on the banks of the river Agna. Here he offered a modest hospitality to his friends, and here he could rest in the solitude of shady *selve* and find refreshing diversion from strenuous work.[5] The intense intellectual combat preserved him from other desires. The lifelong attachment to Maddalena Pelzet, leading actress in his most successful plays, was sober friendship—gratitude to the artist on one hand, devotion to the master on the other. He visited at the house of Carlotta Cortellini, and finally settled with her and her aged sister in a sort of Joan and Darby affection, when age and melancholy had darkened his life. Niccolini never moved outside his habitual haunts. He was persuaded once to travel by rail to Pisa, but never repeated the experience.[6]

To the physical causes for Niccolini's premature aging, there was added his antagonism to the Neo-guelfism sponsored by Vincenzo Gioberti, which acquired tremendous momentum when Europe was startled by the miracle of a liberal Pope! Metternich, who was not easily surprised, said in 1846: "Nous avions tout prévu, mais pas un pape libéral."[7] Pius IX had granted a political amnesty; he had blessed the banner of Italy! "Viva Pio Nono!" rang all over Italy, and startled Princes and Potentates. Niccolini alone doubted the pope's sincerity. Broken in health and spirit, he shook his head and monotonously reiterated: "Non puo essere" (that cannot be). Events proved he was right.

The author of *Arnaldo da Brescia* did not trust the promises of a masquerading Pope. In 1846, he published a poem in the *Rivista di Firenze:*

> Dai sacerdoti libertà non voglio,
> E libertade non avrem giammai,
> Se salite a ginocchio il Campidoglio,
> Gridando: errai.

In the same poem he thus expressed the general feeling:

> Noi siamo un peregrin che si riposa,
> Ma non s'arresta.

and with poetical inspiration:

> . . . il secolo compiango
> Ma non disperso, perchè sta la vita
> Anche nel fango.

During the false appearance of liberalism in 1847–48, while the public shouted his name in every noisy meeting, while his *Gio-*

vanni da Procida was repeatedly performed and the audience called for him, Niccolini closed his doors to even friendly visitors and reiterated his dismal "non puo essere."

When the Grand Duke returned, biting epigrams, attributed without proof to Niccolini, were circulated. The Grand Duke is called "Broncio" (the sullen), and the rime is "concio" (manure). Niccolini lingered in solitude and sadness, seeing few friends, seldom leaving his rooms in via Larga for a drive in the Cascine.

Mario e i Cimbri is the last effort of his dramatic muse. An antipapal sonnet dated November 30, 1860, is probably the very last fruit of his pen. It contains the apostrophe: "Cedi insensato che to credi un dio . . . nè s'oda dal tuo labbro; il re son io."

Political and military events in 1859 were puzzling to most Italians. Niccolini must have been sorely perplexed by Cavour's subtle policy; Mazzini's and Garibaldi's trammeled activities; and even by the intervention of Napoleon III, who promised to be the liberator of Italy only to disappoint those who trusted him, and, as payment, exacted Nice, the birthplace of Garibaldi, and Savoy, the cradle of the Italian monarchy.[8] What must have been Niccolini's emotions when he saw the national flag flying over the ancient Medicean residence in via Larga? What his surprise if he saw from his window Florentines wearing a *coccarda tricolore!* His voice was not raised in the hour of triumph. Cantu relates that Niccolini, tottering and dazed, was taken into the presence of King Victor Emanuele and repeated some passage of his *Arnaldo.* Florence grieved at the death, in January, 1860, of that grand old man, the apostle of Italian unity, Giovanni Niccolini. He was buried in Santa Croce.

NOTES

CHAPTER X

1. Vincenzo Filicaia (1642–1707), Macaulay declared, was the greatest lyrical poet of his age. His inflated and austere odes, songs, and sonnets are now forgotten. His only surviving sonnet is thus translated in Richard Garnett's *History of Italian Literature* (Appleton & Co., New York, 1906, page 284):

> Italia, O Italia, doomed to wear
> The fatal wreath of loveliness, and so
> The record of illimitable woe
> Branded forever on thy brow to wear!
> Would that less beauty or more vigour were
> Thy heritage! that they who madly glow
> For that which their own fury layeth low,
> More terrible might find thee, or less fair!
> Not from thine Alpine rampart should the horde
> Of spoilers then 'descend, or crimson stain
> Of rolling Po quench thirst of Gallic steed;
> Nor shouldst thou girded with another's sword,
> Smite with a foreign arm, enslavement's chain,
> Victor or vanquished, equally thy need.

This gives faint reflection of the faultless perfection of the original Italian. *See* in D'Ancona e Bacci, *op. cit.,* Vol. III, page 534.

2. Giovanni Fantoni—better known as "Labindo"—was born in Fivizzano in 1755, a favored poet with princes and rulers, though often in trouble for his extravagance and his liberalism. He was a prisoner in Grenoble, for opposing Bonaparte's views for Piedmont. In 1800 he was professor of letters in Pisa, and a favorite with students. He died November, 1807. The University of Pisa was active in all Italian political movements. Its students fought with rusty fowling-pieces and ornamental swords, and died like heroes at Curtatone and Montanara. Out of these halls, there spread over Tus-

cany poets, lawyers, doctors, and political leaders who afterwards filled important places. Niccolini, once a student there, was always enthusiastically welcomed.

3. In 1799 General Gauthier came in the name of the French Republic. "Trees of Liberty" were planted in several *piazze;* Pius VI was arrested while in the convent *la Certosa.* Galleries and museums were ransacked and robbed. After a short interval of Austrian rule, on October 15th, 1800, General Miollis entered Florence for the French. He pretended to be a protector of fine letters. In March, 1801, Murat made one of his spectacular "progresses" which earned for him—from his Imperial brother-in-law—the nickname of "roi Franconi." On the 12th of August, in the same year, the Bourbons inaugurated the Kingdom of Etruria. In 1803, Louis of Bourbon died, and his widow was proclaimed regent for her infant son. December 10th, 1807, Marie Louise and the infant Charles Louis were taken from Florence to reign over the so-called Kingdom of Lusitania; while the French general Reille presided at Palazzo Pitti.

March 24th, 1809, General Menou proclaimed the annexation of Tuscany to the French Empire. It was divided into three "departments": Arno, Ombrone, and Mediterranée. Elisa Bacciocchi, totally eclipsing her unimportant husband, drove into Florence with great pomp. Pretty, bright, and gay, she was heartily welcomed by the Florentines. Beautifully gowned, in her elegant carriage "a la Baumont," with a youthful Moor as a groom, she was a great contrast to the late queen's deformed figure, toothless mouth, and shapeless sombre gowns. (For many amusing details of these successive court manners, *see* Pier Filippo Covoni: *Cronachette Fiorentine,* Firenze, Cellini, 1814; also *Histoires des salons de Paris,* by Madame la Duchesse d'Abrantès.) July 14th of the same year, she fled to Lucca during the night. Other French Generals passed in and out of Florence until the last troops were recalled to fight other battles; and, finally, in May, 1814, Don Giuseppe Rospigliosi assumed the power for Ferdinand III. In 15 years Florence had endured ten different rulers. Ferdinand III was heartily welcomed by a delegation at Porta San Gallo. The Gonfaloniere, who should have read an address, was so affected that he wept for joy and could not speak. Much has been written in condemnation of the Congress of Vienna. Witty Prince de la Ligne said: "Il ne marche pas, mais il danse"; and Niccolini: "Onta e catene; ecco dei re la pace." (Shame and fetters, such is the peace of Kings.) Yet La Sainte Alliance gave Europe peace for forty years, and contained the germ of the League of Nations.

Ferdinand loved his Tuscan subjects and they loved him. From 1814, to his death in 1824, this brother of the Austrian Emperor kept out Austrian garrisons and Jesuits. To the Austrian Ambassador he answered firmly, "Your *Sovereign* and my *brother*," and insisted on absolute independence. Democratic Ferdinand III enjoyed informal visits to "i signori" in their *villegiature*. He also followed the Italian custom of visiting ladies in their theatre-boxes. He generally sent in a bouquet of flowers, then came attended by S. E. Rospigliosi. If a visitor were already in the box and rose to go, the Grand Duke bade him stay. When in 1819 the King of Piedmont went into exile, Ferdinand III offered him hospitality in the villa of Poggio Imperiale. In the nearby Certosa, Pope Pius VI found a refuge. To a people governed so mildly, to a State already delivered from Jesuits, the inquisition, feudal privileges, and excessive taxation; the French republicans brought heavy taxes, enforced military service, and wholesale plunder.

His son and successor Leopold II is one man up to 1846; after 1849, he is quite another man. In the first years of his reign he possesses the qualities of a tolerable *paterfamilias,* but no kingly gifts. He was thrifty, ruling his family with great economy. Wrathful Metternich called this good-natured sovereign: "Traitor, heretic, unworthy to belong to the Hapsburg Lorena House." After 1849, he became the passive instrument of Austrian tyranny, unworthy of either love or hatred.

Florence was smaller than the Florence of today. The Lung Arno extended only from Ponte alla Carraia to Ponte Santa Trinita. The spot where the railroad station now stands was then covered with *orti* (orchards), as also the space between Borgo Pinti and Borgo la Croce. The Post-Office was in Vaccareccia (tettoia de Pisani). The stage-coaches started from there twice a week. The first *carrozze di piazza* were seen in 1824. The shops were similar to those now on the Ponte Vecchio: a low stall in masonry, protected by a lid of greenish glass. Popular amusements were many: *Corse di Barberi* (riderless horses); military parades; illuminations for San Giovanni, San Lorenzo, and other saints, enlivened by the *rificolone* (elaborate lanterns carried on top of poles, still in use); fireworks on Saturday before Easter; *scoppio del carro;* many fairs for every feast—Annunziata, Assunzione, San Giovanni; and also for the seasons of nuts, grapes, etc.

When Ferdinand III died in 1824, Leopold II continued his father's efforts to repress malaria and to promote agriculture. He provided Leghorn with canals and a reservoir; and granted protection to the Jewish traders who now almost monopolized the commerce of Leghorn with the East. Fossombroni, who had directed the Grand Ducal government with mildness, died in 1844. He was succeeded by men like Rospigliosi, who were devoted to Austria or feared revolutionary ideas. With the election of Pius IX in 1846, flamed the first war for independence. Gino Capponi was Premier of a liberal Tuscan Cabinet; but both his and the Montanelli ministry were soon overturned. A short revolutionary *dittature Guerrazzi,* in March and April, 1849, ended in civil conflicts and treason. The Grand Duke returned and abolished the Constitution and the national colours.

The history of Italy during the ensuing ten years is crowded with important events; but Tuscany did not share in them. Life went on quietly if not happily in Florence, until the revolution, in 1859, when not a gun was fired, not a cry uttered, and the grand-ducal government crumbled. Niccolini, broken in body and spirit, was unable to realize the final triumph of his lifelong desire. In 1849, when Austrian sentinels were guarding Palazzo Pitti, Niccolini's friend, Vincenzo Salvagnoli, wrote this prophecy in the album of Eleonora de Pazzi: "To-day, May 10th, the Austrian militia have entered Florence, to-day, ten years hence, the son of Charles Albert will be King of Italy."

In September, 1837, Giuseppe la Farina wrote to his father: "Here I am in my new dwelling. It is in via Ognissanti, one of the most central and beautiful streets of the city. I have a bedroom and a parlour furnished with carpet, mirrors, a bronze stove, etc. I pay for it fifty lire a month, besides six lire for a servant, who does all the cleaning and serves at meals, remaining in the house from the morning until after three, when I have dined. I pay to the *padrona,* three paoli and a half per day for my dinner; a soup of good broth, boiled meat, and roast or fried fish, a dish of greens, cheese and fruit."

Allowing for the difference in purchase value of the Tuscan lira at that time and the Italian lira of to-day, la Farina could then live in comfort for a month for less than he would now pay for the same lodging and menu for one day. At the Cocomero theatre (now Niccolini), one could listen to the best artists: Adelaide Ristori, Tommaso Salvini, Ernesto Rossi, and Clementina Cassola for a small fraction of the price to-day. La Quarconia was the most popular theatre in Florence. In the same night a tragedy, a farce, a ballet, acrobatics, pantomime and a violin concert were given. In the pit families would eat heartily, reserving the orange-peels and similar projectiles for use against the actors.

Nor were the amusements of fashionable society much more expensive. After the traditional drive round the Cascine, society stopped in front of the Bottegone—corner of Piazza del Duomo—to have ice cream, "gelato in pezzi" or "gelato al bicchiere," served at the carriage-door by *camerieri* or attendant *cavalieri,* even long after Niccolini's days. Countess d'Albany and Madame de Staël always stopped for their "gelato" after driving in the Cascine.

4. All men of good-will were attracted to Capponi, and he gave every liberal initiative encouragement. Gian Pietro Vieusseux, a Swiss tradesman, founded a liberal literary review, "l'Antologia"; but it was Capponi's mind that guided the undertaking. A popular Bank was founded. It was Capponi's idea; and his participation supported the effort. Enrico Mayer and a small band of patriots founded schools, and promoted popular instruction; but it was Capponi's patronage which made the endeavor successful. Capponi appreciated the Grand Duke's refusal to obey Austrian orders against persons suspected of carbonarism. Of the Florentines he said: "We have plenty of brains and knowledge; but we lack both character and force of will."

5. Niccolini never accepted payment for his tragedies. His salary as a teacher, and the small inheritance from his uncle sufficed for his modest needs. His sole extravagance was entertaining his friends at his country place, Popolesco, on the banks of river Agna. Here the frugal meals were prolonged by literary discussions, with little more than a book of history for reference, and glasses of cold water for thirsty speakers. About those nervous fits and other physical troubles, Niccolini writes his friend, Angelica Palli: "It would take me very long to speak of my illness, which I could not wish to my worst foe. You partly know what brought it about; add to these causes a passion which my duty bids me renounce. My soul is filled with sadness, but I must come out of this mire. Only my body was weak; in those days I was very near madness, not death."

Like many a gentle, poetic soul, Niccolini appreciated the friendship of high-minded women. In another letter to Angelica Palli, Niccolini writes: "I feel sure it is possible to have a very tender sentiment untainted with desire; you are wrong when you believe that a great love, such as I conceive it, is dominated by self-love. If there is a passion that makes man forget his own self and live entirely for the beloved one, that is love. It is absolute sacrifice; it is utter devotion. But this love, which is somewhat like a worship, is not to be found in our time." The same letter contains an allusion to a love-affair when the poet was sixteen, and a clearer reference to the friendship "of a person who nursed me during my late illness, the person whom I frequently see. It binds me with such strong ties that I would rather die than break them." The *person* is, evidently, Carlotta Cortellini, whom, in later letters to his brother or to intimate friends, he mentions as "La Signora Carlotta," or "la mia amica," as a husband would send regards from his acknowledged wife. Many portraits of Niccolini show him wearing a skull-cap. Some of these caps were plain black silk, others were delicately embroidered, the gift of a *ricamatrice* who divided her affections between Niccolini and Foscolo, and kept a sweet remembrance of both.

6. Enrico Mayer writes to Daniel Manin, in Paris, June, 1852, "G. B. Niccolini was always of a sensitive disposition, his nervous system is unable to control the force of Genius dwelling in his body. Hence the singular contrasts between his mental energy and the weakness of his character; between the courage displayed as an Author and the shyness of his habitual demeanor. These contrasts sometimes amounted to terrible fits, causing physical and moral crises of such violence that we feared either suicide or madness must be the result. Such things were not always kept so secret that his foes should not hear of them, and Niccolini has many foes, among persons who will have no scruples, if they have the chance to injure those who expose their wickedness and dishonourable intrigues. . . . One of his colleagues of la Crusca went so far as to charge him publicly with immorality.

"Niccolini could not obtain an apology, and ever since, he has reproached his friends with being lukewarm; he has shunned them even more, when he saw that they were all inclined to adopt towards Rome, the opinion of Gioberti, in direct opposition with his own. . . . He was not so much deserted by his friends as he stood aside from them, obstinately repulsing them. . . . 'If I am wrong,' he would say, 'then I have lived in vain; the guide of history has waylaid me; the light of philosophy has betrayed me; the ideas that have inspired my words were all illusions; I can do nothing better than recant publicly.' A few days later I saw him in Pisa, and he embraced me on my leave-taking, and exclaimed: 'Tell your professors that they must cover Galileo's statue with a shroud, because if Gioberti is right, then Rome was right in sentencing Galileo.' "

7. Vincenzo Gioberti and Cesare Balbo were the promoters and leaders of the Neo-guelph movement, but with slight differences; Gioberti (1801–1852) aimed at an ideal reconstruction of Italy (*Primato morale e civilie degli Italiani,* 1843), which is opposed to French philosophy, to Mazzinian internationalism, and to Jesuit intrigue. It rests on the superiority of Piedmont and the supremacy of the Church. It is recorded that when Cardinal Mastai went to the conclave, whence he came out Pope Pius IX, he carried with him Gioberti's *Primato.* The first acts of his pontificate justify the story. Cesare Balbo, his disciple, aimed at political and national independence first, and then at reforms. ("Le Speranze d'Italia"; issued in Paris, 1855.)

8. Napoleon III at the New Year's day drawing-room, Paris, 1859, said to the Austrian Ambassador: "I regret that our relations are not so good as I wish they were. . . . " At the end of the day, Paris was in consternation; and the telegraph had spread the report throughout Europe. On January 10th King Victor Emanuele, opening his Parliament in Palazzo Madama (Turin), declared: "While we respect the treaties, we are not insensible to the cry of suffering which is raised towards us from so many parts of Italy." (*See* Life and Times of Cavour, by William Roscoe Thayer, Vol. I, p. 552, Houghton Mifflin Co., The Riverside Press, Cambridge, 1911.)

About the fall of the Grand Ducal government in Florence, Ferdinando Martini writes: "Confessioni e Ricordi—Firenze, Grand

Ducale" (Firenze, Bemporad & Figlio, 1922). "The evening of 26th April, 1859, the Tuscan Ministers held their council [in his uncle's house], in the room contiguous to the one wherein, behind closed doors, the fate of the Grand Duchy probably, certainly the fate of the Cabinet, were discussed; friends chatted and waited for news. I told what I had seen in the streets; in the next room some of my words were heard, and my uncle's voice called out: 'Ferdinando.' I went in, as you may think, rather embarrassed. President Baldasseroni interrogated me: 'What were you saying there, what hast thou seen?' I repeated my tale about the gathering of a silent crowd in the Piazza. 'When did that happen?' 'Half an hour ago, Eccellenza. . . .' Shortly after the Ministers came out, first Baldasseroni: I remember that turning to his colleagues, with an air of superior, smiling irony, he exclaimed: 'We'll see, we'll see.' " During the night this boy was sent from one to the other sleeping minister, to tell them that without one cry, without one shot, the revolution had been made. The Grand Duke accepted his fate when Don Meri Corsini said: "Your Highness, the coach is ready!" How the berline rumbled away, as if for a simple drive; not a hiss, not a jeer from the assembled crowd. But when the Grand Duke saluted with the usual "Arivederci" (till we meet again), a voice from the crowd answered cheeringly, "in Paradise."

CHAPTER XI

THE PLAYS OF NICCOLINI

In all his plays Niccolini sought for an historical basis for his ideal of Italy's independence: Niccolini was morbidly sensitive to criticism of his plays: Niccolini's real début was his play *Nabucco*: It is intended to be an historical picture of Napoleon: As a political pamphlet, *Nabucco* has sincerity and courage: In the dispute between classicism and romanticism, Niccolini never seems to have made up his mind: Both schools claimed him: Some of his plays are called classic and others are called romantic: His play *Antonio Foscarini* was hailed as a masterpiece: There are many incongruities and inconsistencies in this play; but passion and patriotism give it reality and beauty: The play *Giovanni da Procida* was violently discussed, praised, and blamed: Niccolini's next tragedy, *Lodovico Sforza*, is one of his best works: Niccolini poured out his soul and some of the speeches are truly eloquent: Its theatrical performance was prohibited: His tragedy *Arnaldo da Brescia* had an enormous success; it was hailed as a gospel of liberty, justice, and nationalism: Its characters are symbols: The complex conditions of Italy are discussed by Pope Adrian, by Arnaldo, the Emperor Frederic, and many others: The author of *Arnaldo,* though unmolested in Tuscany, would have been imprisoned or murdered elsewhere in Italy: Niccolini's last tragedy, *Mario e i Cimbri*, printed after his death, does not answer to the sublimity of its aims.

NICCOLINI was a born teacher. His lessons at the *Accademia,* his speeches before "La Crusca," were praised for their earnestness and learning. His aim was lofty: he sought for an historical basis for his ideal of Italy's independence; but also he knew that within the rich treasury of the classics were to be found models and inspiration. His whole life was an apostolate of these principles.

Many sought his friendship; they haunted the houses that were honored by his presence. In the modest lodgings in via Larga that he shared with his mother and brother, his own little room was almost filled by a writing-table. Within this narrow space, the flower of Italian and foreign intelligence passed. Yet neither the praise of friends nor the rush of dilettanti could make him vain. Criticism wounded him deeply. In later years he became morbidly sensitive.

Praise poured in, even from the beginning. On receiving the poem, *La Pieta,* inspired by the pestilence that had lately devastated Leghorn, Foscolo wrote (September, 1807) expressing approval mixed with a few friendly hints as to the metre and inveighing against that inharmonious *ottava.* When Foscolo's *Aiace* was censured and prohibited, Niccolini was preparing his *Polissena.* He regretted his friend's imprudence; that he had "not sufficiently considered that if we say too much we may be prevented from saying anything at all." *Polissena* was performed in January, 1813, and immediately attracted the attention of scholars and poets. A translation of Sophocles, *I Sette a Tebe,* was praised by scholars.

Niccolini's real début was *Nabucco.* As a political pamphlet, *Nabucco* has sincerity and courage. The prisoner in St. Helena was an easy prey for bilious and malevolent detractors; but Niccolini strove to draw an accurate historical picture. When it is said that Nabucco was Napoleon; Vasti, Madame Mère (Loetitia Bonaparte); Amiti, Marie Louise; Mitrane, Pius VII; Afene, Caulaincourt; and Arsace, Carnot, the whole plot is told. Niccolini tried to reconstruct the character of the fallen Emperor, avoiding adulation and dispraise. The second scene, in which Pope and Emperor stand face to face, may be compared with the almost equivalent situation in *Arnaldo da Brescia.*

Nabucco to Mitrane: "Prophet, hearken—Thou boastest of humility; but amidst thy Magi the first honours thou usurpest; and wouldst reign from the altar as I do from the throne. Perils and bloodshed earned my sceptre; to thee white haired age, false or vain virtues and subtle arts, laid the great mantle on thy shoulders. Midst mysteries and crimes, is your empire. Wherever a host of priests is met terror is master, and decides the vote. Thou numberest thy slaves and I my rebels." In the third act, the speeches of Arsace (Carnot) impersonating the republican spirit, and the answers of Nabucco (Napoleon) impersonating power and glory were applauded. Arsace: "True glory thou hast lost when thou ascendest the throne. When Nabucco would equal the Kings he became meaner than himself." To which Nabucco proudly retorts: "I was born for the throne; I am the necessary tyrant, the only one whom the world can obey without shame."

Grand Duke Ferdinand praised this play. His Minister Rospigliosi—a clerical conservative—having criticized it, the Grand Duke smilingly suggested: "You had better read it again, I am sure you will like it." Yet the Grand Duke knew that Niccolini gave this definition of the Congress in Vienna—"Onta e catene, ecco dei re la pace," and perhaps this other epigram: "Ecco d'Italia i Fati, Tifo, Tedeschi e Frati." The Grand Duke was mild; and also he knew that Niccolini was esteemed by the whole literary world, and that every pen would be raised in his defense.

While the disputes were going on about classicism and romanticism, though Niccolini hesitated to break with the classics, he was hailed as a champion by the romantics. For the classics, he was the professor who *ex cathedra* exalted the power of poetry and the great Greek poets as "the inspirers of immortal masterpieces." He was the translator and imitator of Sophocles and Euripides. At the same time, he accepted the fundamental principles of the neo-romantic school. He exalted Orcagna and the awakening of art under his impulse. He considered Michelangelo an example of power and virtue and inexhaustible genius. All these qualities of Niccolini's mind and heart blended to make *Nabucco* a compound of classicism and romanticism.

In December, 1818, when he writes Gino Capponi of the impossibility of having his *Nabucco* printed, he terms this play "un aborto," and adds, "As for romanticism, that also is a folly which prompts the Lombards to ape the Germans. We must neither be classics nor romantics. Whoever is gifted with genius will make his food of the ancients. . . ." He seems never to have really made up his mind on this disputed question. In a letter to Niccolo Puccini dated 1830, Niccolini writes: "I know how difficult it is to give tragedies to Italy. If you outstep the traditions which are called rules, you have all the Classicists on your back; if you follow them, all the Romantics will call you a merchant of old clothes, an imitator of Alfieri. I think that our century demands a tragedy different from either the French or the English, but who will be fortunate enough to hit on it and to conquer the public opinion which sees nothing beyond Alfieri?"

Most of Niccolini's biographers and critics have marked a division in his works; some of his first plays they call classic, and others, like *Nabucco, Matilde, Antonio Foscarini,* they call romantic. This division is more formal than fundamental. According to the inspiration of the moment or the choice of subject, Niccolini adopted some of the precepts of each school. He frequently confesses the impossibility for him to make a definitive choice. "Io non sono da tanto" (I am not equal to) is the phrase that usually closes his discussion of the topic. Two other plays of classical character, *Medea* and *Edipo,* were performed with great success.

Antonio Foscarini burst on the Italian audience as a wonderful masterpiece—which it is not. The subject was in the air; Ippolito Pindemonte had lately published a *novella in versi* chronicling the misadventures of Teresa Navagero Contarini and Antonio Foscarini; the French court-poet, Arnault, had given a play, *Blanche et Moncassin,* which told the same story and discredited the Venetian government. In his letters, Niccolini disparages the French play and compliments the author of the *novella.*

Niccolini, holding *per fas et nefas* to the rules of the unities, revealed his own uncertainty. But *Antonio Foscarini* answers most of the demands of the romantic school: a pseudo-historical foundation, contrasted passions, and those "sinuous lines intertwining and mingling," as De Sanctis says. The first fault is a double motive.

Antonio Foscarini, son of the Doge, has just come home from Switzerland. He learns of the marriage between Teresa Navagero, the girl he loved, and Senator Contarini, in a talk with his father about the Venetian oligarchy. An example of this tyranny is a decree of the Council making it treason for a Venetian to be discovered in the dwelling of a foreign Ambassador.

Act II shows Teresa enduring her aged and unloved husband's reproaches, and betraying her pain when she hears that Antonio Foscarini has returned to Venice. The scene between Teresa and her confidante Matilde is romantically interrupted by the song—behind the scenes—of Antonio Foscarini, pathetic in his reminiscences of past love, darkly threatening in his purpose of suicide. Act III is in Teresa's garden: the usual love-scene. Teresa tells how she has been persuaded to marry Contarini in order to save her father. She refuses to elope with Foscarini, but hopes to meet him in heaven. These ethereal endearments are shattered by Matilde's cry that Contarini has surrounded the palace with his guards. The only other exit is through the adjoining residence of the Spanish Ambassador. While Contarini and his men rush on the stage, a pistol shot is heard; and Teresa faints, thinking Antonio has killed himself.

Act IV: Antonio Foscarini is not dead; he is only slightly wounded, a prisoner in a room adjoining the secret tribunal in which Loredano, Contarini, and Senator Badoero are meeting. The culprit is introduced and questioned. Antonio declines to explain his behaviour; Badoero urges the young man to explain. The Doge, aged and powerless, kneels, imploring his son to reveal the secret which he suspects. The fifth act is crowded with breathless events. The Doge is informed of his son's doom. The terrible "Three" sentence Antonio to death within one hour's time. The sand drops from the hour-glass; a tumult is quieted. Attended by the Doge, a veiled woman, Teresa Contarini, enters and insists on giving evidence. Senator Badoero is for hearing her. Teresa is still speaking when Contarini, who has already ordered the execution, throws down the hour-glass. A black curtain is pulled aside, and the headless corpse of Antonio Foscarini is revealed; Teresa stabs herself.

Inconsistencies there are, and incongruities in this play. Antonio's double motives: love and liberalism, are both too powerful and too different to be thus mingled. There are weak lines and bombast; but passion and patriotism give the play reality and beauty. The contrast between the grandeur of the Doge and his helplessness, the conflict between his official duty and his paternity, is dramatic. The three Judges present three embodiments of almost absolute power and its reaction on three different spirits. Teresa is consistent. Through filial duty she sacrificed her love to her father's safety; nor does she waver when duty towards her lover arouses her husband's jealousy.

Niccolini wrote: "the time is past for the classical tragedy, the time is past for Racine; yet the romantic Shakespearean tragedy does not suit our time. . . . The public must be educated; the author and the actors must be educated by the public; but where is this public in Italy?" (To Salvatore Viale, July, 1828.) A year later, Niccolini wrote to Maddalena Pelzet: "Please do not believe that I am satisfied with my works; I know but too well that I am a second-rate writer [*uno scrittorello*]. . . . I have reaped nothing but bitterness from my miserable profession; the persecutions for my Foscarini are not finished. . . ."

In October, 1829, he wrote Viale that he was preparing a play about the Sicilian Vespers. "The subject is most difficult, and I will reap out of the literary and political disputes, nothing but persecutions." The subject was difficult and dangerous, since the author meant to show Italians revolting against a foreign tyrant. Unfortunately Niccolini lacked adequate historical data. *Giovanni da*

Procida, however, created a great sensation. It was violently discussed, praised, and blamed.[1]

When the actor uttered the apostrophe "Il Franco Ripassi l'Alpe e tornerem fratelli," Bombelles, the French Ambassador, said to Monsieur, the Austrian representative: "L'addresse est pour moi, mais la lettre est pour vous." The fault of showing a double motive is here more obnoxious than in *Foscarini.* The heroic figure of Giovanni da Procida impersonates his people and their rights. The Sicilians rising suddenly, daggers in hand, to destroy oppressive French garrisons, would always make a dramatic picture. But Niccolini must mix with the grand historical passion of an enslaved nation an intrigue of adultery and secret marriage, converging into the shocking horror that Procida's daughter has unknowingly married her own brother. And there is a child on the stage to bear witness! Because Niccolini, one of the purest of men, lacked creative imagination, he searched through his classics; and out of the Greek plays he took the idea of innocent incest and inserted it into a pseudo-historical, pseudo-romantic tragedy, wherein it was utterly unsupported by the sense of fatality that pervades Greek tragedies.

The subject of Niccolini's next tragedy, *Lodovico Sforza,* was well chosen. This period, end of fifteenth century, was not unfamiliar to cultured Italians. Lodovico Sforza, "Il Moro," has opened the doors of Italy to French King Charles VIII; and, at the same time, has obtained from Emperor Maximilian the investiture as Duke of Milan, and thus recognized the supremacy of the Empire. In the sombre castle of Pavia, Lodovico Sforza imprisons Gian Galeazzo—the legitimate heir—and his wife, Isabella d'Aragona. Gian Galeazzo is slowly dying; and Isabella lavishes on him the sweetest expressions of her devotion, and watches over him lest Lodovico should give him more poison.[2]

In another part of the castle, Lodovico and his wife, the celebrated "Beatrice d'Este," hold their court attended by the courtiers Belgioso and Calco. Charles VIII is convalescent in Asti, but presently comes down on the castle. Charles VIII wavers between his affection for his cousin Gian Galeazzo and the promises of Lodovico Sforza. "Il Moro" proclaims himself Duke of Milan, and Gian Galeazzo dies. Over the dead body of Gian Galeazzo, Isabella prophesies Lodovico's captivity and miserable death: "If within the treasuries of eternal wrath there are worse evils which I forget to implore, may they all be thine." Lodovico replies: "Impreca, io regno." The tragedy is one of Niccolini's best works. Some speeches are truly eloquent.

The theatrical performance of *Lodovico Sforza* was prohibited. The characters are abstractions, uttering the aspirations and desires that were intensely real in 1837, and Italians applauded. Niccolini poured out his soul. Critics questioned his facts, and disputed about his romanticism and his borrowings from Victor Hugo and Casimir Delavigne.

Niccolini owed little to French romanticism. An intense nationalist, hating Papacy, he abhorred the religious element which appears in Chateaubriand's prose and in Delavigne's poetry. That hybrid composition the dramatical poem, borrowed probably from Byron, suited his manner of constructing and developing a plot. It concealed the excess of episodes, and encouraged that lyricism that easily expressed ideas of independence. Moreover, since his best plays could be printed but were not permitted on the stage, Niccolini naturally composed them in the form most fitted for reading.

The Tuscan Grand-ducal officials were tolerant; the people understood; and his audience applauded those other plays of his whose performance was permitted.

Criticism of *Arnaldo da Brescia* must reckon with the environment which caused its enormous success. Niccolini was the passionate champion, the apostle of his people, proudly declaring both their hopes, and their hatred of papal and imperial despotism. *Arnaldo da Brescia* was accepted as a gospel of liberty, justice, and nationalism. Its characters are symbols; the events are shadowy outlines projected on the reader's imagination. Two Roman patricians, Giordano Pierleoni, Leone Frangipane, dispute the claims of Empire versus Papacy; then Arnaldo appears to plead for the Italian people.[3]

The second act shows Adrian in the Vatican "near the temple, far from God," as Arnaldo will say. The pontiff explains his politics to Cardinal Guido: "The fates of Europe I must overrule; the Kings are part of the fold once entrusted to Peter, not the best part; I stand in Italy undecided between Frederic and the Lombard cities. If I stand by Caesar, I become a slave and I reduce the Church to its antique servitude." In many other speeches, the complex conditions of Italy are discussed by the pope and his partisans, by the followers of Empire, and by the Romans who strive to recover their ancient civic rights. For these, Arnaldo fights both with spiritual weapons and patriotic appeal to Roman traditions.

Adrian has sent his *salvacondotto* to Arnaldo, because he hopes either to persuade or to bribe him. The Pope prays for Divine assistance: "He who carried the cross, heavy with all the world's sins, may help him to bear the load of that cloak which crushes the strongest shoulders, and that tiara which burns the brow I raise in tears to Thee!" When Arnaldo is introduced, the Pope expects the sinner to kiss his feet and speak to him "from the dust. . . ." Arnaldo answers with equal pride. It is the prelude to the duel. Arnaldo argues as a theologian; Adrian thunders from the fortress of his supreme power.

"Always," Arnaldo says, "between peoples and tyrants, is ever the Church—cruel with the weak, and coward with the strong. Thou art in thy desire so discordant with thy words, that out of truth thou makest a lie, and then a lie is truth." "The servant of servants, thou claimest to be, and art the tyrant of tyrants." The Roman Church is "used to giving little and exacting much. . . . Trading in terrors and lies, enriched by the blind rabble that runs from crime to the altar, from the altar to crime." Adrian's answers are weak. He supports the rights of the Church by Neo-guelf or Giobertian arguments: "I am above all parties like God in Heaven, the Judge of all—none to judge me—to peoples and Kings. The Principle and the font am I, of that life, all powerful and unique, which is the Church of God." "Abelard is come back to life and speaks through thy lips. Thou wouldst oppose to Faith proud Reason; wouldst make a queen of this slave of God."

Adrian allows Arnaldo to return whence he came; Cardinal Guido announces to the multitude that unless Arnaldo is given into his hands, the Pope will not come to receive consecration in the Lateran. The rabble throw stones and darts: Cardinal Guido falls dying on the church steps. Suddenly the Pope appears, pronouncing interdiction on the city. The third act suggests the Greek Prometheus, while it announces Shelley's impersonation of man facing supernatural powers. Arnaldo is assaulted by friends and foes. Giordano would persuade Arnaldo to side with the Emperor, against the Pope. Then the Swiss soldiers who had followed Arnaldo from exile, and are now leaving Rome, offer to escort Arnaldo to Switzerland. Arnaldo merely accepts their escort to the castle of Astura where Ostasio, Adelasia's husband, will give him asylum.

Impressive is the encounter between Arnaldo and a friar who offers him refuge in a cloister. The narrative of Abelard's death, poisoned by consecrated wine, is a blast of trumpets denouncing papal methods. The fourth act opens with scenes of misery and terror announcing the approach of German troops, echoing the lamentations of refugees from the destroyed cities of Tortona. In the fifth scene, Frederic enters attended by his uncle Ottone di Frisinga, by the Norman Duke Sergio of Naples, the Ghibelline admirals of Pisa, a group of bishops. Frederic Barbarossa holds a council, boasts his past prowess, and announces further triumphs. Ottone urges Frederic to rest satisfied with having secured the Lombard iron crown. But Frederic wants the Roman consecration, and the death of Arnaldo is the price to be paid.[4]

But the ghost of Hildebrand still haunts the political horizon. The Emperor is in doubt. Will the Pope present the Imperial crown as a gift, or as his right? Here, if the play were ever performed, a grandly spectacular pageant should be seen. The Pope advances proudly on his white steed, crowds of kneeling faithful prostrate and kissing his foot. Frederic has alighted; and Adrian expects him to pay homage, to hold his stirrup and attend him to the *faldistorio* or throne. But Frederic stands aside, then comes forth to receive the Papal embrace of peace, which Adrian refuses.

"Thy refusal shows thee to be my foe"—says Frederic: to whom Adrian replies, "To God I secretly prayed; I only threaten the son I ought to punish." No greater situation, no grander tragedy than this face to face encounter of the two "Suns" was ever attempted by a poet. Ottone persuades Frederic that by changing some words in the formula of homage, the honour of the Empire will be saved. Thus Frederic, taking the crown from the hands of the Pope, utters the words: "To Peter and not to Adrian I bend." The Roman Patrician Giordano threatens Frederic with the Normans. Such threats bring about the reconciliation of Frederic and Adrian.

Adelasia comes to the Pope in agony for her husband's sin in giving hospitality to Arnaldo, and promises his delivery to the Pope. The scene of Arnaldo in prison awaiting death is worthy of fame. It is the confession and prayer of a mind that has accepted martyrdom yet faces death with the unanswered question trembling on his lips. "Almighty God, that which Thou art I do not know. I am going soon from this last doubt to the first Truth."

The vision of the Lombard League triumphing over the Imperial army was the flourish of trumpets that stirred Italian hearts. Arnaldo's last word expressive of his sure trust in the sanctity of his opposition to the Church, was Niccolini's challenge to those who dreamed of a federation of free Italian States under papal supremacy. In the finale, Adrian and Frederic rejoice over their united triumph; and Adrian absolves those soldiers who had killed and plundered in the cause of Empire and Holy Church. Then turning to Frederic: "Joined at last. Let the Church and Empire be like one substance the two who are on earth . . . in that unity that is like God's."

The author of *Arnaldo* remained unmolested in Tuscany although lighter offence would have meant imprisonment, perhaps death, anywhere else in Italy. Florence became the center of nationalistic activity. Niccolini stood apart, dissenting from the Giobertians; and grew old and broken in health. Yet his example was not lost: other leaders kept alight the sacred fire of nationalism. When the Grand Duke returned under the protection of Austrian troops, Niccolini submitted sullenly. A few parasites attended official functions and fawned for favour. Niccolini continued to write. The final effort of his wearied muse, the tragedy *Mario e i Cimbri*, was printed after his death. It does not answer to the sublimity of its aim.[5]

NOTES

CHAPTER XI

1. The spectacular fifth act of Niccolini's *Giovanni da Procida* is in complete accordance with the romantic school. Yet it is typical of Niccolini that he also wrote a classical ending to his play "In order" says he, "to facilitate the actors' task." Niccolini's chief authorities for *Giovanni da Procida,* are Giovanni Villani, and Boccaccio; from the latter, he borrowed the story of Procida's wife. Yet, though he thus accepted an unhistoric episode, Niccolini read widely about Sicily and the "Sicilian Vespers."

    Niccolini might better have adopted the simple lines of de Blasi's narrative (*Storia di Sicilia,* Lib. viii): "On the day 30th of March, 1282, it being Good Tuesday, the Palermitans were in the fields gathering flowers, hailing with gay songs the return of Spring, when, provoked by the impudence of a Frenchman named Drovetto, they rose in tumult, and made that memorable vendetta."

2. The Milanese Dukedom, ruled by Lodovico, "il Moro," as guardian of his nephew Gian Galeazzo, comprised the land between the rivers Adda and Sesia, besides Valtellina, the Ticinese, and the cities of Tortona, Parma, Piacenza, and Cremona. In 1495 Lodovico dreamed of uniting different Italian States in a league. Piero de Medici opposed this idea. Then Lodovico formed a secret league with Venice and the Pope. He asked Emperor Maximilian to give him the investiture of Milan. At the same time, he persuaded Charles VIII to invade the Kingdom of Naples.

    Lodovico, "il Moro's" fate is prophesied by Isabella in Niccolini's play. Deprived of his duchy and deserted by his people, he fled to Emperor Maximilian. In 1500 Lodovico tried to recover his Dukedom. Betrayed by his Swiss mercenaries, he was seized and imprisoned in the castle of Loches; and there died after ten miserable years.

Niccolini saw in Lodovico Sforza only the murderer of his nephew and the ally of France. It was an incomplete interpretation of a powerful personality.

3. The play *Arnaldo da Brescia* was printed abroad (1843) and shipped to Tuscany in sheets concealed within balls of sugar. The sale of it was prohibited by *Censura*. In September, 1843, Niccolini wrote to S. Centofanti, "Arnaldo is in prison, that is to say, not on the market. Were I the government, I would have done the same."

Arnaldo da Brescia, born in Brescia about 1105, died in Rome, 1155. He studied theology and philosophy in Paris. Like St. Bernard de Clairvaux he was a disciple of Abelard. He was the nationalist leader against Pope Adrian and the German Emperor Frederic. For nearly seventeen years, Arnaldo fought for democracy and the reform of the Church. Arnaldo, already excommunicated, was banished by Pope Adrian IV; but was still supported by the common people and some of the aristocracy. In a Roman popular tumult, a cardinal was killed; and Pope Adrian pronounced the "interdiction" or wholesale excommunication of the city. No one could be christened, married, admitted to communion, or any religious office; no dead body could be buried. This awful malediction Adrian pronounced during the Easter week, when Rome was full of pilgrims from every part of the world. The Romans dared not revolt; Arnaldo da Brescia was betrayed; brought in chains to the gates of Rome (porta del Popolo); and there burned alive; and his ashes thrown into the Tiber.

4. Frederic of Hohenstaufen represented both Ghibelline and Guelph houses. He was elected Emperor in 1152, being then thirty years old, strong in body, proud in spirit, and athirst for glory. He first came to Italy in 1154 with a strong army, and wasted the territory of Milan. Next year he crossed the Ticino and destroyed Novara, Vercelli, Torino, Chieri, Asti; and completely razed Tortona. In-

vested in Pavia with the iron crown of the Lombard Kings of Italy, he proceeded to Rome. Frederic received the imperial crown in Rome, June 18th, 1155. But when the Roman citizens revolted, and there was bloody fighting, Frederic left in haste; destroyed Spoleto on his way, then, through Ancona and Verona, he returned to Germany.

5. Niccolini's plays were widely discussed, translated, and praised by French, English, and German writers. Theodosia Garrow translated *Arnaldo* into English in 1846. *La Revue des deux Mondes* published a study by the editor, Charles de Mazade (1845), which contains the following passage: "Ce qu'il faut louer ce qu'il faut aimer en Niccolini, c'est cette constance qui ne se dement pas, cette aerenite, pour ainsi dire, qu'il montre dans la colere, cet ensemble de qualités qui ont survécu a des deceptions nombreuses, et, en un mot, le rajeunissement progressif de son talent." Apropos of Arnaldo, Marc Monnier in his book, *L'Italie est-elle la terra des morts?* (Paris, 1860), has the well-known boutade: "Il y avait une fois un prince allemand et un prêtre italian qui se mirent d'accord par un arrangement singulier. Le prince prit des terres qui ne lui appartenaient pas, et il en fit un present au pretre, L'Italien, reconnaisant, prit une couronne qui ne lui appartenait pas d'avantage, et la mit sur le front de l'Allemand. De la sont venus tous les malheurs de l'Italie."

Many Italians have written about Niccolini's works and his life; among the first and best is "Ricordi—della vita e delle opere di G. B. Niccolini—raccolti—da Otto Vannucci." (Le Monnier, Firenze, 1866.)

CHAPTER XII

AN OUTLINE OF POLITICAL EVENTS IN ITALY

The contribution of Bonaparte to the Italian State: Italy after Napoleon's fall: The Congress of Vienna: Reaction in Italy: Oppression of political prisoners: Election of Pope Pius IX: Beginnings of an organization for a united and independent Italy: Garibaldi's "Thousand": Recovery of Rome: The Italian *Risorgimento*: Patriotism among the dramatists: Growth of Romanticism: Alfieri, Foscolo, Mazzini, Niccolini: The realism of D'Annunzio, Verga, and De Roberto: The work of Gazzaletto, Battaglia, and the end of the historical drama: Giacometti's *La Morte Civile*: The patterning of comedy after Goldoni: The work of Giraud and the French influence.

THE first fifteen years of the nineteenth century are overshadowed by Bonaparte. Though he brought misery, though he drafted the Italian youth into his armies, though he pillaged Italian art-galleries, though he cruelly taxed every city, yet Bonaparte was Italy's benefactor, the promoter of her *Risorgimento*. He destroyed the Holy Roman Empire. He limited the temporal power of the Papacy.[1] The many changes of government and the uniting together of various petty states gave to Italians a sense of national unity. In November (18 Brumaire), 1799, Bonaparte secured almost absolute power in France; in May, 1800, he crossed the Alps and won great victories.

In 1801 the treaty of Luneville settled the position of Italy under Bonaparte's control: Venice was abandoned to Austria; the republics of Genoa and Cisalpina were re-established; Tuscany was granted to Louis of Bourbon, with the title of King of Etruria; Ferdinando IV was King of Naples and Sicily, and Pope Pius VII was master in Rome. A little later Piedmont was annexed to France, King Carlo Emanuele IV being allowed to reign over Sardinia. Bonaparte having signed the "Concordat" with the Church, obtained the Imperial Crown in May, 1804. He took the iron crown of the Lombard kings, in Monza, in 1805, uttering the historical words: "God gave it me, woe to whoever touches it."

This *Regno d'Italia* with Eugène Beauharnais as viceroy; the kingdom of Naples with Joseph Bonaparte as king; the duchies of Lucca and Piombino given to one sister, and Guastalla to another sister, did not satisfy Bonaparte's greed of power. He annexed Tuscany and laid hands on the provinces of Parma and Piacenza. He bade his brother Joseph take the crown of Spain and leave Naples to Joachim Murat.[2] After Napoleon's fall, if Murat and Eugène had joined forces they might have saved Italy, for both possessed high military qualities. Eugène Beauharnais, menaced by Austrians and Neapolitans, departed. Murat tried to keep his crown and was shot.

Thus at the end of 1815 the whole fabric of French reconstruction was swept away. But some of its material and moral effects remained. Napoleon had gripped and tortured Italy but he had also reawakened the nation. Under French rule, that which was the Kingdom of Italy, and also the Venetian provinces, and Piedmont, though battered and tossed by political changes, were benefited. Besides the enormous numbers of new bridges, roads, and buildings constructed, schools were opened, and were freed from clerical dominion; the legal codes were reformed, convents suppressed, and every form of activity encouraged. There was intellectual and scientific progress. The literature produced was not always imitation, and the theatre was not entirely moulded after the French.

The decision of the Congress of Vienna represents the lowest ebb in the history of Italy. It seemed like a return to irredeemable servitude and division. Austria seized Lombardy and Venice; Parma was given to Marie Louise, ex-empress of France, Modena to Francis IV of the house of Lorraine; Tuscany, Rome, Naples, and Piedmont received their former rulers. Schools and universities were closed; Jesuits were recalled; convents were returned to the monks and nuns; feudal privileges were restored. In Tuscany Leopold and his minister Fossombroni ruled on the plan summarized in the motto "il mondo va da sè" (the world goes of itself). Pius VII vied with secular princes in obscurantism and tyranny.

The fanaticism which inspired the Holy Alliance in Europe, the reinstatement of foreign dominion in Italy, had for its counterpart a fanaticism of revolt that assumed many names and aspects, but was always a reaction against intolerable conditions. Carbonarism was a school of endurance and courage which everywhere maintained the idea of Italian unity. On July 2, 1820, the revolution against Ferdinand I, King of the Two Sicilies, obtained the promise of a constitution. After taking his oath, the King entrusted the regency to his son and went to the meeting of Kings in Laybach, in order to call in the Austrians. In the same year, Piedmont demanded a constitution. Rather than grant this demand, Victor Emanuele I abdicated in favor of his brother Carlo Felice, in whose absence Carlo Alberto, prince of Carignano, was made regent. On Carlo Felice's return, the constitution was annulled.

In Lombardy, liberalism found expression in the literary periodical *il Conciliatore;* but the movement was stopped by the trials and condemnations of Silvio Pellico, Maroncelli, Andryane, and others. Encouraged by the French revolution of July, 1830, several Italian cities attempted rebellion. The cruelty of repression in Modena under Francis IV, in Rome under Pope Gregory XVI, excited the pity of the civilized world. A memorandum signed by reigning princes was directed to the Pope, who took no heed. The Austrians occupied part of the Papal States and France garrisoned Ancona. Misery and oppression and torture of political prisoners had reached the limit of endurance. Giuseppe Mazzini[3] began the secret association *La Giovine Italia,* on the fundamental principle "God, the People, Liberty, Unity." The Mazzinian association floundered in useless bloodshed and used doubtful weapons, but it was a most noble experiment.[4]

Then an unexpected event startled the world. Metternich exclaimed: "We had foreseen everything, but not a liberal Pope!" G. B. Niccolini shook his white-haired, tired head and muttered, "Non può essere" (it cannot be). Yet the news spread that the newly elected Pope Pius IX had issued a political amnesty (June, 1846), the first of several liberal measures. His example urged other potentates to grant reforms. Ferdinand II in Naples was faced with a revolt of his Sicilian subjects. Venice and Milan rose in arms; Tuscany and Lombardy followed. The five heroic days which saw the Milanese holding out against the trained troops of Radetzki, the first victories won by Carlo Alberto with the support of the Tuscans at Curtatone and at Montanara, then at Goito, echoed the movements in Vienna, Berlin, and Paris. For Italy it was only a bright interlude, and then came the realization that military forces cannot be improvised, and that armies must have experienced leaders in order to win battles.

With the three Giuseppes—Garibaldi, Mazzini, La Farina—Cavour began to organize for an independent and united Italy. Most Italians agreed as to the common end, but disagreed over the means to accomplish it. Some desired autonomy; Mazzini's ideal antagonized Gioberti; Garibaldi did not encourage obedience; there were Republicans of every shade, clericals of every hue, disputing about constitution, monarchy, republic. In Milan the Austrians flogged men and women publicly. King Ferdinand (Bomba) and the once liberal Pope, vied in repression and vengeance. Piedmont faced many obstacles, the most formidable being the sullen opposition of Rome. Carlo Alberto departed from the scene. Vittorio Emanuele, a bluff soldier, was loyal and knew men.

D'Azeglio was the Premier appointed to initiate the reign and arrange peace with Austria.[5] Cavour soon came to the front, and held the helm of government with a strong and able hand. He relied on France and her enigmatic ruler, Napoleon III. One of

Cavour's first acts was the sending of a corps of Piedmontese soldiers, commanded by their own general, to the Crimea to fight beside French and English troops, and to conquer a place in council with other free nations. From almost every part of the country support came to Cavour's plans. A French army crossed the Alps to help Italy in her struggle against Austria. From May to June, 1859, battles were won. Vittorio Emanuele and Napoleon III made a triumphal progress through the streets of Milan. Garibaldi's volunteers had fought with the regular troops, and this alliance reconciled many republicans.

The expedition of the Thousand (*I Mille*) reads like a legendary episode—Garibaldi's ragged volunteers first fighting trained soldiers on the terraces of Calatafimi and stirring all Sicily to revolt, and then that great patriot giving to the King the island of Sicily and the Neapolitan realm that his warriors had redeemed. Again an emotional progress through the streets of Naples: Garibaldi riding at the stirrup of his king, amid crowds of southern peoples in the first joy of release. But Rome and Venice were still under the yoke of foreign rulers; order and unity were not yet attained in this new kingdom of Italy. Vittorio Emanuele had on one hand the Pope wielding the weapon of excommunication, and the republican democrats on the other, threatening to plunge Italy into renewed war. In Florence on the 27th of April, 1859, the grand-ducal government fell and the Grand Duke left Palazzo Pitti never to return.

A first Italian Parliament met in February, 1861, in Turin. There were members from all parts of Italy, representing almost every policy. Things did not run smoothly; but though Garibaldi uttered his recriminations, and Brofferio, Guerrazzi, and other Democrats hated noble born Cavour, in every mind there was a deep desire not to destroy united Italy. The army was reorganized and the position of the clergy regulated. Hovering clouds were still on the

Italian horizon. The Republicans were dissatisfied; the patriots claimed Rome and Venice. Garibaldi tried to conquer the Tyrol and Rome. Italian troops were sent against him at Aspromonte; he was slightly wounded and confusion spread among Italian Liberals. Nor was this confusion dispelled by the Convention signed with Napoleon III in 1864.[6] Vittorio Emanuele agreed to move his capital from Turin to Florence (November, 1865).

In 1866 Prussia was at war with Austria. Vittorio Emanuele was allied with Prussia, and once more the Italians expected to win their unredeemed provinces. Garibaldians fought once more beside the regular army. The defeat at Custoza by land, at Lissa by sea, crushed all hopes. Yet by the treaty of Vienna, Austria gave Venice to Napoleon III, and the French Emperor immediately gave it to Italy. In September, 1870, France called back the garrison in Rome: thus giving to Italy the opportunity of acquiring its capital. After a two days' quiet siege, the Italian army entered the city through a breach in the Roman wall near "Porta Pia." While every heart in Italy rejoiced over the fulfilment of the national union, the Roman Church appealed to the whole Christian world. The sullen Pope remained a voluntary prisoner within the Vatican.

The Italian *Risorgimento* was not merely proclaimed through voice and pen by the intellectuals, but these same intellectuals willed, directed, suffered, and died for it.[7] In Italy every action was first an idea. All progress toward Italian freedom and political unity was first a dream, then a literary expression, and finally an accomplished reality. Mazzini's mysticism and Garibaldi's imprudence, Cavour's diplomacy and Gioberti's Guelfism, the conspiracies of youthful enthusiasts and the plottings of oppressed intellectuals—all were needed to prepare and to achieve the liberation and unification of Italy, and all are represented in the Italian Theatre. Patriotic passion filled the hearts and minds of these dramatists. Each had his viewpoint and anticipations—republics, federation, kingdom, democratic or aristocratic rule; every form of government, every plan of policy was discussed, professed, and praised. This preoccupation determined the choice of episodes, of characters, and left no place for real psychic interpretation or for true historical reconstruction.

This current of nationalism found its earliest expression in the writings of the so-called "purists." First came Pietro Giordani (1774–1848). More discussions arose over the newly introduced word "Romanticism." The thing was not new; the plays of Carlo Gozzi, Giovanni Pindemonte, and others had introduced the principal elements of romanticism; its rejection of fixed rules and limitations had become a popular form of expressing Italian political independence. Madame de Staël's books and her visit to Italy in 1817 gave the signal and suggested the method. In Lombardy the Austrian government pretended to protect and encourage Italian letters. The periodical *La Biblioteca Italiana* was encouraged by Austrian authorities to support literary classicism. It was opposed by the patriotic periodical *Conciliatore,* which Austria suppressed thirteen months after its foundation. Great was the confusion between the classical and romantic schools and their ideals.

Following the blast of Alfieri's trumpet, Foscolo, Pellico, Niccolini, and many other playwrights, and even timid Manzoni risked prison or exile in proclaiming Italian liberty. Romanticism voiced the turmoil, the contradictions and uncertainties of a national and social revolution. Romanticism partook of the mysticism which Mazzini and other prophets of revolution preached, while, on the other hand, it inspired extravagant ideals of duty, as represented in secret plotting and romantic episodes. Another foundation of romanticism, which brought about its final transformation, was the reverence for national history. History is a stern Muse; even if courted at first for its picturesque colours, history soon proved to be *magistra vitae,* a sober teacher of reality.

Realism produced the stories and novels of G. Verga and De Roberto, and D'Annunzio's first manner. The first stimulus came from abroad, but the realistic or verist movement soon assumed a national character. Italian playwrights presented life as comprehensively as they could, giving garish pictures of violence and rudeness. Even before the end of the century a reaction had started which inclined towards sentimentalism. D'Annunzio struck a line of his own, profuse in images and poetic flights, and other writers of plays strayed into different channels. During this entire intellectual movement, starting with French liberalism, and growing through the pangs and struggles of nationalism into the sober consciousness of freedom and power, the Italian Theatre has echoed and mirrored the evolution of the nation. It has blown the trumpet of warlike patriotism, it has soared on the wings of romanticism, then sobered into the observation of customs, in the analysis of characters, in the didactic satire of social evils. Each author has brought some contribution to Italian progress. The inclusive impression which their compositions leaves is that without reaching sublime heights of excellence, they have created a modern Italian Theatre that is worthy of comparison with the theatre of any other European country.

Paolo Gazzoletto in 1857 published a rather good play *Paolo*. The central figure is St. Paul. The scene is in Rome; Nero, Seneca, and a pair of lovers; Giunia and Eudoro, moving about in a reconstruction of Roman gardens, of catacombs, orgiastic feastings; such as ensured the success of *Fabiola* and *Quo Vadis*, such as Chateaubriand poetized in his *Martyrs* and Flaubert pictured in *Salâmmbo*. Honest-minded, industrious Giacinto Battaglia, accepted the heavy burden of continuing with the *Compagnia Sarda*, the management so gloriously held by Gustavo Modena. Modena possessed *le sens du théâtre;* Battaglia was a man of letters. He admired Victor Hugo and imitated his plays.

With Battaglia the historical drama came to an end. After him came the tendency to adopt subjects out of everyday life. One of these dramatized social theses is Paolo Giacometti's *La Morte Civile*.

The central personage, like Victor Hugo's Jean Valjean, is an escaped convict. Corrado has killed the man who loved his wife, Rosalia. He escapes from prison and finds that this Rosalia is the governess to a supposed daughter of a Doctor Palmieri, although she is in fact Corrado's own child. Her husband believes that the doctor is Rosalia's lover. Corrado is "civilly dead" and cannot assert his rights over his child, who shrinks from this ragged, hungry looking wretch. Corrado loves his wife and his daughter, and commits suicide.

Giacometti was born in 1816 and died in 1882. He wrote many popular plays of the type called *Teatro da Arena* meaning—good for Sunday matinées in popular theatres, and appealing to simple minds and honest hearts. *Il buon Giacometti* is known all over Italy. Tragedy asserted its classical origin by assuming dignity of versification and solemnity of style.

The comedy remained a genuine representation of Italian life and manners and held to the Goldonian principles, even when it imitated French models. It was very easy to say: "follow Goldoni and reproduce the life of your contemporaries; make them speak as they speak on their doorsteps, in their drawing rooms, and in the cafés." But from what city, what province, what class of citizens were the models to be selected? The truest picture of Florentine characters and speech would not have been understood even in neighboring Pisa; and in Milan and Turin would have been less intelligible than French plays. Those autochthonic audiences who refused to understand and sympathize with Italians of other provinces gladly adopted everything that came from beyond the Alps. The optics of a theatrical audience are peculiar. They do not see things as they are, but as they are perceived by the author and expressed by the actor. There was no common viewpoint, moral standard, or æsthetic preparation in divided Italy. Italian dramatists were forced to imitate French models. Giraud's *Don Desiderio disperato per eccesso di buon cuore* is a real Italian character. This busy-body who does endless mischief by blundering into other people's affairs, is charmingly natural, and amusingly exaggerated. Giraud's attempts at tragedy or drama are forgotten while his comedies are still performed.

NOTES

CHAPTER XII

1. By the treaty of Tolentino, 1797, the temporal power of the Holy See was virtually abolished. Romagna and other territories were formed into the "Cispadana" Republic; the Pope paying with cash, pictures, statues, jewels and other treasure for the Consul's permission to exist. In February, 1798, the Roman mobs in the Campo Vaccino proclaimed their independence, hailed with exultant cries the planting of a tree of Liberty, and voted a charter that reproduced the French Constitution. Pius VI died in exile. His successor was Pius VII (Chiaramonti). Once more a Pope was dragged from Rome. Then Bonaparte summoned him to the ceremony of coronation and the official blessings of the Church were negotiated in a concordat. When Bonaparte set upon his head the iron crown of the Longobard Kings, he followed his Italian instinct.

   When the Congress of Vienna gave peace to Europe (1815), Italians welcomed back the princes and the forms of government which they had so gladly overthrown at the bidding of French invaders. Piedmont welcomed home the Prince of Savoy, a vassal of Austria. Tuscany gladly welcomed the return of Ferdinand the mild Grand Duke. If only Eugène Beauharnais had been more of a man, Milan might have remained the capital of a greater Kingdom of Italy; yet she gladly accepted her fate.

2. Literature and living, what men do and what men think, are the warp and woof of all social organization. Confused and complicated was the Italian pattern at the close of the eighteenth century. At the very time when foreign armies invaded Italy and new ideas of iridescent brightness came from abroad, they were contradicted by the acts of these reformers. Brescia, Bergamo, Verona, were already garrisoned by French troops. In April, 1797, the Venetian form of government was changed, the treasures accumulated

through centuries of power and art were plundered. Every ship, everything removable was stolen from the *arsenale*. The museums and galleries were robbed, the granaries emptied, heavy taxes levied; the dominion of Venice over the isles, and over the opposite Adriatic shore was abolished by the treaty of Campo Formio. Eleven centuries of glory and affluence were destroyed. Even before he left for Egypt, Bonaparte had demolished the ancient frontiers of Italian States, and established several so-called independent republics. The most important, longest lived and most fortunate was the Cisalpina—afterwards the Kingdom of Italy— which comprised all Lombardy and part of the Venetian state with Milan for its capital.

3. The grand figure of Mazzini has been summarized in one immortal line of Carducci's:

    To solo, Ei disse, O Ideal sei Vero.

Mazzini aimed at a goal that is not within the reach of mankind. All his political mistakes cannot obliterate his spiritual leadership. In his program for *Giovane Italia,* he says, "A revolution ripens through education, is prepared by prudence, is accomplished by energy, and sanctified by being directed towards the welfare of all."

4. The silence of exhaustion fell over the whole peninsula. Much facile and fantastic romance has been added to simple reality about the Italian Patriotic Societies. The odds against them were tremendous, the dangers great, the penalty for failure appalling. The true story of these first movements has not been written. The real hero who risked death or life-long imprisonment in an Austrian dungeon, neither blazoned his own feats nor revealed the treachery or the cowardice of his associates; spies and traitors were encouraged to invent conspiracies. Obnoxious persons were sentenced to "carcere duro," like Silvio Pellico, or shot like the brothers Bandiera; priests were hanged like common villains, yet gleams of hope flash through the gloom; Giuseppe Mazzini's winged words breathed

valour into fainting hearts. Pius IX issued an amnesty for all political offenders, and extended his hand to bless the people of Italy,
and then retracted. Winged aspirations, unbounded hopes, romantic dreams, were quenched in blood and stifled in prisons; Italy
sank back into the slumber of misery and exhaustion.

5. Massimo Taparelli d'Azeglio (1798–1866) of an ancient noble family is one of the most attractive personalities of his time. He left
the comforts and pleasures of home for the "vie de bohême" of a
painter, tramping in the Roman campagna. He did not always
agree with Cavour, but never refused to cooperate, when it was for
the nation's good.

6. Napoleon III issued a proclamation to the Italians, from Milan,
dated the 8th of June, promising that he would liberate Italy "from
the Alps to the Adriatic Sea." On the 24th of June the victories of
his troops and of the Italians over the Austrians at San Martino and
Solferino were announced by Napoleon to Empress Eugenia in
these terms: "Grande bataille et grande victoire." Yet on the 11th
of July the two Emperors signed the armistice of Villafranca. Cavour, on hearing of the armistice, was so incensed that he stormed
against the King in language that no official historian has dared to
record.

7. Presently a new dawn pierced the night; a dawn that lacked some
of the illusive romance of 1848, but promised more lasting splendour. Great leaders came forth at the appointed time, Garibaldi,
Cavour, Victor Emanuele, presided over the *Risorgimento*. But a
time comes when events overrule men. When United Italy became an accomplished fact, when accepted authorities ruled, when
public opinion was limited to the rôle of spectator and critic, when
the best blood of its citizens was no longer being shed in the struggle for liberty, the Italian Theatre ceased to be directly affected
by the course of political events. The era of heroism and romance,
of rebellion and enthusiasm, closed in 1848.

Monti

CHAPTER XIII

MINOR DRAMATISTS

Vincenzo Monti: his verses in connection with the new Italian State: His life in
Rome: His poem *Bassvilliana*: His enthusiasm for Napoleon: His family: His
tragedies: *Aristodemo, Caio Gracco*: Monti as a writer of tragedy: Giovanni Pindemonte: his ancestors, early life, marriage: Influence of the French upon his writing:
His *I Baccanali*: His *Ginevra di Scozia*: *Cincinnatus*, his most classical play: Ippolito Pindemonte: his life: Influence of Rousseau and Pascal: His *Armino*: Ugo
Foscolo: His *I Sepolcri*, a glorification of his country: His birth and youth: His
career in politics: Exiled to foreign lands: His death in poverty: The popularity of
his *Ajace* among the literati: His *Ricciarda*: Silvio Pellico: early life, journalistic
adventures, political activities and imprisonment: The great success of his play,
Francesca da Rimini: His lighter tragedy, *Eufemio da Messina*: Allessandro Manzoni: his early and uneventful life: His marriage: Influence of Romanticism and
religion on his plays: His *Conte di Carmagnola*: Influence of Schiller: His second
tragedy *Adelchi*: Carlo Marenco: his *Pia dei Tolomei*: The patriotism of his
Arnaldo da Brescia: Paolo Ferrari: his realistic comedies of social life: *Roberto
Vighlius, Cause ed effeti, Il Ridicolo*: His reliance on Goldoni: His best plays:
La Satira e Parini, Goldoni e le sue sedici commedie nuove.

IT was amid the tumult, agony, and uncertainty of the French invasion under Bonaparte in 1796 that the first signs of a national
consciousness began. Lazzaro Papi, the future historian and severe
judge of the French Revolution, ends one of his sonnets thus:

> Tu che dell' avenir nel grembo oscuro
> Spinger sai l'occhio dell' acuta mente
> E cio che e dubbio altrui, vedi sicuro,
>   Dimmi: quel che dall' Alpi ora descende
> D'armi e d'armati inondator torrente
> Ceppi a noi reca, o libertà ci rende?

> Thou who the dark secrets of the future
> Canst pierce with thy mind's eye so keen,
> And see'st clearly what to others is dim,

Tell me: that which now descends the Alps,
This inundating torrent of arms and armed,
Brings it chains to us or liberty?

Within four months after the invasion was founded the Cispadane Federation in Reggia Emilia. Thus after many centuries there issued an Italian State. The blind enthusiasm for military glory, excessive faith in Bonaparte, and lastly despair, terror, cowardice, following upon the tragic downfall of so much greatness, all these are expressed by Vincenzo Monti in the finest verses heard for centuries.[1] Carducci made a complete edition of Monti's poems. "His verses," says Carducci, "overran the beautiful kingdom of Italy, as bewildering in impetus and splendour as King Murat's squadrons of cavalry. When the literary history of the great century extending for Italy from 1750 to 1850 shall come to be written with objective serenity, and without party bias, Vincenzo Monti will be given the place he deserves as a prince in the art. . . ." But Monti the man, his life, and the relation of his poetry to his time, are also important. Monti was violent like all weak natures, and weak like all violent ones, with perpetual alternations of self-abnegation and egoism, audacity and fear, anger and tender-heartedness, generosity and meanness. Cantu has written of him with ultra-catholic prejudice and political virulence; Achilli Monti, his nephew, has written with passionate idolatry of his glorious kinsman. Apologist and detractor are both equally wrong.

When in May, 1778, Vincenzo Monti came to Rome, he was a handsome youth of twenty-two, bearing the title of abbot which implied few duties and secured many advantages. As a seminarist in Faenza he had won the favor of his masters. He was invited to Rome by Cardinal Legate Scipione Borghese, formerly a resident of Ferrara. No moral atmosphere was ever more destructive of conscience and soul than this Roman mixture of tyranny and lewdness, that was covered by the robes of cardinals and priests, nuns and monks. Pope Braschi (Pius VI) was reigning. He was no bigot. He was vain of his beauty and elegance, ostentatious in adding the eagle of the House of Austria and the lilies of France to his coat-of-arms, in undertaking great public works, and in enriching his nephew Luigi Braschi Onesti, an animal of a man, to whom he gave in marriage a very pretty Roman girl with a pair of black fulminating eyes and the figure of a Canova Venus.

By patronizing letters and art, Pius VI imagined himself another Pericles, Augustus, or Leo X. But the times were changing; ominous novelties of scientific discovery and philosophical doctrines stirred the air. French ideas came to Rome with the swarm of emissaries, of emigrants and other visitors, each having some new report about events in Paris and Northern Italy.

Monti, besides fooling with conspiracy, glided from one love-affair to another, ending with a liaison with the Princess Costanza Braschi-Onesti, and then, to ward off the scandal of his amours, he suddenly married Teresa Pickler, a beautiful Roman girl who was certainly ignorant of serving as a lightning-conductor for the safety of his political and erotic deceptions. But what a beauteous lightning-conductor was Teresa Pickler! And Monti fell in love with her in earnest, which was more than the Duchessa Braschi desired.

It was during the time of these intimate and secret conflicts between personal terror, guilty passion, legitimate love, and patriotic illusions and disillusions that *Bassvilliana* saw the light. The poem has splendid style, harmony, purity of language and composition. It is a true historical poem of the Italian counter-revolution. But the invectives of the *Bassvilliana* against the excesses of the French Revolution were not sufficient to allay the suspicions of the Pontifical government. Monti fled from Rome in the night of March 3, 1797, in the carriage of General Marmont, one of Bonaparte's aides-de-camp, who had come as the bearer of the Treaty of Tolentino.

From the dissolute oligarchy of priests, from classical Arcadian Rome to the bracing intellectual climate of Milan and the industrious plentifulness of Lombardy, the change was enormous. Life in Milan during this *Regno Italico* was both splendid and pleasant. Eugène Beauharnais was a man of pleasure; he liked a brilliant court, and his example encouraged the Milanese wealthy or noble Houses to imitate him.

Already tottering through violence, corruption, robbery and every kind of excess, the Cisalpine Republic was buried under the victorious Austro-Russian reaction, and Monti fled to France, till the victory of Marengo offered him the occasion to intone the splendid hymn of his return to Italy:

> Bell' Italia, amate sponde,
>   Pur vi torno a riveder!
>   Trema in petto e si confonde
>   L'alma oppressa dal piacer.

> Beauteous Italy, beloved shore,
>   Yet to see thee I return!
>   My spirit trembles in my breast
>   Perplexed, oppressed by joy.

And now Monti is carried away by another enthusiasm. Who has enkindled it? Napoleon! And so he wrote his Napoleonic poems: *Prometeo, Bardo, Spada di Federico,* and the *Palingenesi politica*. But after Napoleon becomes intoxicated with power and glory, Monti refuses to follow him. "What he does," he writes to Lampredi, "is enough to cool a volcano. He prepares his own fall and ours who are faithful to him. Only one good thing has he done, the organization of this kingdom, but then, what treatment does he give us Italians? He is making enemies of all the kings of Europe, who will triumph in the end. And we shall fall with him."

Count Cavour himself could not have foreseen more clearly and reasoned more accurately than this poet! And was Monti the only one in the terrible European catastrophe of the Napoleonic Empire who believed in the benefits of peace and in the moderation of the allied liberators? No! It was an entire generation that, amid accumulated ruins, acclaimed peace and him who promised it with deceptive words.

When the Congress of Vienna met in 1815 and divided up the peoples like flocks of sheep, Monti sang the *Ritorno d'Astrea* for the Emperor of Austria, and this, without a doubt, together with the letter to Salfi, is one of his most repugnant acts. After the restoration, Monti's literary career was ended, though he wrote poems for small occasions or in defence of his old art. Monti was now but a shadow of himself. For him all hopes, tenderness, and glory were centered upon his wife and daughter Costanza, who married Perticari in 1812, and for whose wedding the poets of Italy called upon all the gods of Olympus.

His wife, Teresa Pickler of Junonian beauty, whom Cantu ironically calls "the flower of virtue," was not spared in the bitter polemics sustained by Monti. Foscolo, that impenitent Don Juan, solicited her favours but was denied, though she is the alleged heroine of the first edition of his *Jacopo Ortis*. Monti loved her dearly and immortalized her in the following tender lines:

> . . . La stella
> Del viver mio s'appressa
> Al suo tramonto: ma sperar ti giovi
> Che tutto io non morrò: pensa che un nome
> Non oscuro io ti lascio, e tal che un giorno
> Fra le italiche donne
> Ti fia bel vanto il dire: "io fu l'amore
> Del cantor di Bassville,
> Del cantor che di care itale note
> Vesti l'ira d'Achille.

> . . . The star
> Of my existence is about
> To set: but thou must hope
> That not the whole of me will die: think that I leave thee
> No obscure name, and one that some day
> Among Italian women
> Thy glory it will be to say: "I was the love
> Of the singer of Bassville,
> Of the singer who, with dear Italian notes,
> Clothed Achillean wrath."

Monti's idolized daughter Costanza was a notable figure. She was witty and wonderfully beautiful. Like her father she was the object of much love, but also of furious hatred. She became a widow in 1822, and was even accused of having poisoned her husband. It was infamous calumny. Monti died in 1828, Costanza in 1840, and the epilogue to all the poet's vicissitudes was unconsciously written by Niccolini in a letter to Maffei: "Within a short span of time Monti, his wife, and his daughter have passed away: few speak of them at all and most of these badly. Oh the vainglory of human greatness!"

Monti was an authoritative representative of classicism. His tragedy *Aristodemo* (1786) was a great success. Aside from that which passes in the soul of the protagonist, there is almost no action. *Aristodemo* is of the classic school, but it is also the sepulchral tragedy *par excellence*. For four acts the open tomb of Dirce is in view, and Aristodemo's thought is a perpetual anguished colloquy with the shade of his slain daughter. The pallid king of Messena, who craves the oblivion of death, who questions the great mystery of the "to be or not to be," and finally commits suicide, is kinsman to the pallid prince of Denmark; yet he also retains something of the Alfierian Saul. The play remained popular upon the Italian stage even when classic tragedy was already passing from favour.

Many of its lines have become proverbial, as "Se Sparta Piange, Messene Non ride."

The *Caio Gracco* (Caius Gracchus) is better versified. Begun in 1788 and completed before 1800, it had a clamorous triumph largely due to its many patriotic expressions. There is little action in the *Caius Gracchus,* but much oratory. Opimio, the aristocratic consul, descends from Alfieri's stereotyped tyrants. Lavinia, Gracchus' wife, is a pallid shade who pours forth tender griefs, and strives to restrain her husband from certain death. Cornelia is the legendary Roman mother, the *donna forte*. Her strength is the studied attitude of an ambitious soul. In the third act are several splendid orations. The end of Opimio's speech, an invocation of the gods, an apostrophe against Caio, so appeals to the listeners that Caio with difficulty obtains permission to speak. Caio pleads passionately for those popular laws which the Senate had formerly accepted. He brands the wealth, luxury, and lewdness of the *arpie togate* (harpies in toga) weltering in a flood of Falernian wine, amidst lascivious dancing, reeling in drunkenness and feeding on the flesh and blood of the people.

The people are stirred by Caio's speech; there is a rush upon Opimio; weapons are drawn; lictors are called upon to quell the rebels; and Fulvio strikes down the chief of these armed guards. But Caio bids his friends to refrain and "leave the tyrant to the torture of his remorse." Opimio meditates a dire revenge. In Act IV, Cornelia points out the error of allowing Opimio to escape. She urges him to fight against all odds. The last act shows Caio pursued by Opimio's lictors, rushing to his mother, and asking her for a dagger. He stabs himself rather than be captured by his foes.

Here ended Monti's activity as a writer of tragedies. If his plays have survived their first success, it is because they offer splendid speeches for actors.

Giovanni Pindemonte

During the Roman Empire, Verona was an important city, a stronghold against invasions, a center of intellectual life. It was the royal residence of King Theodoric. Legend relates that Pepin le Bref is buried under the carved images of Roland and Oliver in front of San Zeno. From gentle Catullus down to Scipione Maffei, from Liberale da Verona to Paolo Cagliari (Veronese), it has given birth to famous poets and artists. Longobard blood has mingled with the Latin to strengthen without impairing the gentleness of this people.

The Pindemonte came of an ancient stock: they possessed land, wealth, and influence sufficient to support their hereditary title of marquis and the dignity of Venetian patrician. Giovanni was born on December 4th, 1751; Ippolito two years later. On the death of their father, both boys were sent to finish their education at the celebrated college of San Carlo in Modena. In these colleges, directed by priests, the sons of great families were taught Latin and Greek and the social graces. In 1772 Giovanni returned to Verona. Lavish with his money and light of love, Giovanni became entangled in an affair which ended in the ecclesiastical divorce court. The verdict and the peaceful ending of the story showed that Giovanni gathered willing fruit, and also provided for the lady.

Giovanni had social and political ambitions, and entered the Venetian *Maggior Consiglio* by marrying a patrician lady. Vittoria Widman Pindemonte, like every Venetian lady, did not expect to occupy entirely her husband's affections. In a letter dated Venice, 1793, "Nane" tells a friend of his that "These last twenty days my beloved wife has been ailing. . . . Look here what a mishap! At the same time, my actual lady-love has fallen ill with the same cough. . . . I have been dividing my time exactly between conjugal and amorous attentions; now sitting by one bedside and then by the other one. Thus I spend my whole time." Giovanni by his attitude in the *Maggior Consiglio,* by his tragedies *Mastino della Scala,* and *I Coloni di Candia,* had already given offence to the *Inquisitori di Stato* who domineered all Venetian life. There was also a quarrel with an injured husband. This coffee-house broil was just the pretence required, and the marquis, Venetian patrician, Podestá di Vicenza, Giovanni Pindemonte was condemned to eight months seclusion in the fortress of Palma. In January, 1803, Giovanni Pindemonte was back in Milan, and resumed his seat in the *Consiglio dei Juniores.* He was still there in 1805 when Bonaparte came to be crowned King of Italy. Pindemonte returned to Verona, where he lived quietly and died in January, 1812. Giovanni Pindemonte is of his time and social rank; like a gay butterfly he flirts and endites in Arcadian bowers. He still impersonates the Venetian of the late eighteenth century, when he is pricked by the ambition of partaking in public affairs.

Giovanni looked to France as the source of philosophical ideas and political reforms. Almost every other Italian shared this illusion. His imagination was kindled by the halo of glory surrounding the brow of Bonaparte. He welcomed the conqueror, but warned him to come like Caesar or Alexander, not like Attila. Like many other Italians, he hoped that the Republics founded in imitation of the French, would prosper. "Cittadino Pindemonte" participated in the government of the Cisalpina, and soon realized the fundamental weakness of such an impromptu constitution. It was reformed; it changed its name; it was gilded with high sounding titles and grandly liberal speeches; but it was built on moving sand.

Giovanni Pindemonte never outgrew his aptitude for improvisation, nor did he tame his impulsive temperament. He plunged into a tangle of political allusions, historical reminiscences, philosophical polemics, in his very first plays: *Mastino della Scala, I Col-*

oni di Candia, I Baccanali. Giovanni Pindemonte never wavered in his fight against clericalism. The great struggle against the Jesuits, their expulsion from France, 1764, then Bonaparte's dealings with the Popes, had given an actuality to the question of theocratic authority. Pindemonte opened his campaign against priestcraft with his second play *I Baccanali*.

I Baccanali is a classical tragedy where every rule and tradition is carefully observed; where the Roman toga, the lictors and their fasces, represent immanent justice and power; while intriguing priestcraft, secret torture, and treachery are represented by the bacchantes. Sempronio, an important member of the sect, tells Minio the chief priest of Bacchus how, during the orgies of their worship, Eburzio was murdered, so that Sempronio might marry his widow and become trustee for his son. The boy is coming of age; he may ask his guardian to return his estate; Sempronio would kill the son as he murdered the father. Minio consents to this plot. Eburzio Junior will, this very day, be initiated into the mysteries of the Bacchanalian worship and be murdered. The only obstacle to this plan is Fecenia, a young woman formerly a slave. Fecenia loves Eburzio Junior, and she witnessed his father's murder. She has even been entrusted by the dying man with a written message for his son. All through the tragedy horrors are committed within the secret bowers. Minio has undermined Eburzio's piety by false arguments that were interpreted by the audience just as Pindemonte wanted them to be.

Adelina e Roberto is an even more virulent attack against clericalism. Torments are inflicted on husband, wife, and father-in-law by the Spanish Inquisitors in Flanders. Pindemonte no longer attacks his theocratic adversary in the name of Bacchus, or in the temple erected to Apollo, but in the Tribunal of the Inquisition, and in the characters of a Father Vicario and a Grand Promoter of the Inquisition.

For his *Ginevra di Scozia* Pindemonte adopted the story as told by Ariosto in his *Orlando Furioso*. Polisseno is introduced from the first, and his hateful figure is always conspicuous. He is Dalinda's lover; he uses her as his advocate with her mistress Ginevra, royal princess of Scotland. But Ginevra loves Ariodante the brave commander in her father's army. Polisseno plots to ruin Ginevra's honor. Dalinda promises that she will that night lower the silk ladder from her room in Ginevra's apartment, and that she will represent the Princess. Thus Polisseno plays Iago to Ariodante, who witnesses the opening of a window—as he thinks—by Ginevra, a silk ladder lowered, and Polisseno clasped in a tender embrace. Ariodante maddened with jealousy rushes out and is understood to have jumped in the river. Lucarnio, Ariodante's devoted brother, has also witnessed the scene. He summons the King to enforce the law that punishes with death a girl's transgression unless she is saved by a champion who fights in the lists and wins for her the "Judgment of God." But Ariodante is not dead. Clad in sombre armour, bearing no device on his shield, he has entered the lists to champion the cause of the woman he loves, even though he believes her guilty. Polisseno is killed.

Evidently this spectacular performance is not classical tragedy. But his *Rappresentazione Spettacolosa* was applauded and was repeated.

In *Cincinnatus,* Pindemonte discerned the career he would willingly have pursued himself. Even in this most classical play, amidst these most classical personages and events, some breath of romanticism found its way, as in the fourth and fifth acts when the action is swollen with fightings and burnings. The first act shows Cincinnatus in his home, tilling his own land, lovingly building his household, courteous to his more worldly successor in the command of Roman armies. Then suddenly the prudent farmer is raised to the highest plane of political importance. This change is brought about by the simplest means. Postumio, sent by the Senate, directs Cincinnatus to put on his toga before hearing the message. The toga here is a symbol; when Cincinnatus has donned it he is the Dictator, the King. But one moment before, when he desired Rascilda to bring him the Senatorial robe, he was a simple landowner; from the moment he has listened to the word of Rome he is transformed.

Ippolito Pindemonte

"I am proud to say that I never wasted a moment of my time when at school," says Ippolito. And he might have said the same of his whole life. He was a scholar by disposition, training, and imitation. Ippolito Pindemonte pursued his quiet round of studies, composing occasional pieces of poetry, and also a tragedy *Ulisses* which won for him the applause of Arcadians. The day that Vincenzo Monti delivered his *Stanzas to Virgin Mary* before the shepherds of Arcadia, Ippolito was admitted within their fold under the name of Polidete Melpomenio. Ippolito Pindemonte was a man of many faithful friends. Alfieri called him his "lavandaia" (laundress), meaning that he entrusted his manuscript to scholarly Ippolito for correction. Foscolo by addressing him in the first lines of his *Sepolcri* has immortalized his name. Pindemonte is an aristocrat, conscious of his intellectual superiority and of his gentle birth.

When Pindemonte came to Paris, he was welcomed by Countess d'Albany and Alfieri. In Ippolito's eventless life the visit to Paris was a milestone, and the visit to London in the ensuing year was another capital event. When Pindemonte landed in England, he admired the English gardens and—a young English lady. Each inspired some of his poems, but neither troubled his tranquillity. From London he travelled to Berlin, Vienna, and back to Italy.

In 1793 Ippolito Pindemonte was back in Venice, a constant attendant on Isabella Teotochi Albrizzi, whom he often addressed

Foscolo

in poetry as "Temira." "Temira" may have granted something more than friendship to Ippolito. In Venice such amours or their poetical equivalent were garlanded by gallantry, incensed with approval. Her description of Pindemonte shows him "a most discreet and valuable friend." But also she tells of his scrupulous partition of his time so "that every hour of the day one could tell what he was doing." Unwilling to remain in a Venice ruled by Austrians, he went to Verona and then to his villa. "It is well to go on dreaming, since reality is so sad. It is well to live by imagination, so as to forget the ill-fortune which surrounds us."

Ippolito Pindemonte does not soar to spiritual heights. He has read much and remembers his readings. In his writings there is constant echo of Rousseau's *Promenades* and of Pascal's *Pensées*. Ippolito Pindemonte chanced to step upon the stage of life at a moment of the most pregnant innovations in almost every branch of intellectual activity. French invasions, plundering soldiers, and undigested philosophical principles poured into Italy and destroyed much of the past; but when these receded they left behind ideas, experience, and hopes. The Italians were recovering their national pride. Worship of the classics, eager investigation of historical events, mark this turning point of Italian evolution. Scholarly Muratori, sturdy Pietro Giannone, G. B. Vico, and Cesare Beccaria are the harbingers of the movement which spreads and expands under the magic pens of Alfieri and Foscolo.

What does Pindemonte achieve or attempt? Almost nothing. Rigorously observing the sacrosanct unities of time and place, Pindemonte constructed the tragedy *Arminio* which has as its central feature the struggles between public duties and private affections. The scene is laid in a German forest. Arminio suggests Julius Caesar. Like the Roman dictator, the leader of the Cherusci is opposed by friends and relations who admire and love him, but who love liberty more. His son Baldero kills himself rather than fight against his father, leaving Telgaste, the friend and almost son-in-law of Arminio, to vanquish the tyrant, who dies repentant. When Pindemonte selected Arminio as the protagonist of his tragedy, he failed to realize his own limitations. He was bound to show a warrior, a leader of men, an ambitious despot, aspiring to dominate, and with slight moral consideration or family affection. What could peace-loving scholarly Pindemonte do with such a subject?

The tragedy, however, has a few redeeming qualities. Besides the sustained dignity of style, and the accurate versification, and the clever division of acts and scenes, there are traces of a new dramatic school, new sources of inspiration.

Pindemonte's last utterance in verse *Il Colpo di Martello* is dedicated to Isabella Teotochi Albrizzi (Temira). As the stroke of a hammer tells of the hours, so the poem is a review of his whole life, a preparation for death. The religious feeling is shallow. The philosophical theories, which had shaken the whole Christian world during this time of rebellion against all traditions, have not troubled him.

Ugo Foscolo

"Due secoli l'un contro l'altro armati" is Manzoni's description of that period of vague endeavour, dazzling hopes and bitter disappointments which are exemplified in the life and work of Foscolo. Monti, Cesarotti, the Pindemonte brothers, the Verri's were moulded and sometimes deformed by their environment; but Foscolo shines in his own light, interpreting the national soul, voicing national aspirations, proclaiming: "Our Past is the rock on which our future must be built."

Foscolo's *I Sepolcri* is a masterpiece; some of his sonnets, his odes to Luigia Pallavicini and to "L'Amica risanata," and the fragments of his *Carme* are among the most perfect specimens of Italian poetry.[2] But it is because he was a spiritual leader that his name is immortal. "Mankind is incurably religious. All the world seeks after God. When there is no vision, the people perish. Man-kind demands the prop of faith." When the French Encyclopedists had battered the philosophic basis of the Catholic Church, when Bonaparte had given to the world the spectacle of two Popes dragged in exile and accepting terms from him, when upon every renewal of Austrian tyranny the church had lifted its head to incite bloody reprisals, it was but natural that the flame of faith should flicker low in the Italian soul. In 1800 men had been intoxicated by the bright vision of immediate liberty only to have their expecta-tions shattered, had been freed from tyranny only to be fettered in heavier chains.

Vico had the vision, he saw mankind developing through pangs of pain, through throbs of joy. Foscolo grasped the philosophical principle and moulded a shining phantasmagoria. In the chain of great men rising out of the common herd to point the way, he se-lected first the Greeks, then the Italians as their natural successors, tracing in *I Sepolcri* the lofty centuries expanding like an arch built upon the virtues of great men across which humanity marches towards perfect ideals. Man was the new idol; the antique soul of the race was heir to classical ideals. The inspiration of *I Sepolcri* and the emotional alarum of *Jacopo Ortis* shaped imaginations, directed aspirations, and for two generations expressed the emo-tions of Foscolo's countrymen.

I Sepolcri will take up the Imperial theme and swell the an-them of his country's glorification by a most classical interpretation of that which the tombstones of great men may mean. Like an an-tique Greek, he gives a longing, loving look at life when he must leave it and the things that make it dear to him. Like an antique Greek he knows that even "Hope the last goddess avoids the grave," that the "sleep of death is hard." Can the funeral rites, the flowers and wreaths soften this "hardness?" He has no ready answer; he wonders and passes on to that which is the predominant theme of his poem—the memory of the great as inspiration to great deeds, splendid evocations of Italian poets who are recalled to even more glorious life in Foscolo's lines. Glory to those who have earned glory: part of this glory is the grief they leave behind them. Images as terse and forcible as they are harmonious are blended together in an almost faultless poem.

Nicolò Ugo Foscolo was born in a humble home in a small Ionian islet, January 26th, 1778. He was the eldest child of Andrea Foscolo, a physician of Venetian origin, and of Diamante Spaty who was of pure Ionian descent. Foscolo attended the Catholic seminary in Spalato and remained there after his father's death in 1788. He joined his mother in Venice about 1793 to live with her, his two brothers, and sister in decent poverty. Foscolo attended the University of Padua. He was a timid youth, neither tall nor well built. His hair was reddish, his shoulders slightly stooped, yet he attracted women and had many amours. Fair Isabella Teotochi Albrizzi, like him half a Greek, who was the leader of Venetian intellectual society, smiled on the timid student, spinning the first threads of an ardent friendship that lasted long after distance of time and place had sobered their feelings.

Ugo was soon caught in the political whirlpool. An ardent patriot, he first enlisted in the legions of the Cispadane in 1797, then, after the treaty of Campo Formio, he fled to Milan and entered that circle of intellectual activity which centered round Parini, Vincenzo Monti, Pindemonte, and others. Ugo served the Cisalpine in various capacities. He was sent to Florence where he knew and admired Alfieri and became the friend of Niccolini. He also fell desperately in love with a Pisan young lady, Isabella Roncioni, whom he would not marry because she was rich and he was poor, but whom he has celebrated in many of his poems. In 1798 the Austro-Russian sent him to prison with many other Italian patriots.

On Bonaparte's return, Ugo was once more in the Cisalpine

legions, fighting bravely, enduring the hardships of the siege of Genoa with Massena. One of his many love-affairs was with an English girl, Sophia Emery. A daughter was born and was brought up by her mother's relatives. His career in Milan and Pavia as professor and author was varied with more amours. Impulsive but fickle, Ugo Foscolo was easily allured by sentimental women who wished to be praised by the popular poet.[3] Foscolo was then poor, having lost his salary as professor. Besides these passing liaisons, there was the lady he ever graced with the title "Donna Gentile," the sweet Quirina Mocenni, who remained his friend through all the misadventures of his later years.[4]

On the fall of the Regno Italico in 1815, Foscolo fled to Switzerland and then to England. These are the darkest years of Foscolo's life. As long as he mixed in Italian circles, as long as he dwelt with people of his own creed and breed, there are few flaws in his honour from the Italian viewpoint, though there was youthful folly and extravagance. But no sooner does he cross the Alps than, in the atmosphere of a Swiss provincial townlet, he begins the series of blunders that will finally discredit him. It was still worse in England. Foscolo was by turns lionized and ignored in the "Mare Magnum" of London. He was tossed from luxury in fashionable rooms, attendance of a liveried groom and riding his own horse, to the shifts of wretched lodging-houses. When his daughter Floriana brought him money inherited from her grandmother, Foscolo indulged in dreams that brought only ruin and disgrace. To provide a bright home for himself and his daughter, he plunged into extravagance, and it ended in a narrow escape from the debtor's prison.

Thus after the first years of chequered splendour, when he was the honoured guest of famous personages, Foscolo dropped into poverty and obscurity, brightened alone by his daughter's affection and the fitful remembrances of a few friends. Hudson Gurney, faithful and generóus, provided him at last with a decent dwelling in Turnham Green, where he died of heart-disease on the 10th of September, 1827. From the churchyard of Chiswick, his last remains were transferred to the Italian Pantheon of Santa Croce.

Those whom the gods love die young, in ancient Greece it was said. An appropriate belief for people who admired the gifts which nature so lavishly grants to youth, so scantily to maturity. To Foscolo, early death should have come as a token of love from the Muses. If, like Byron, Alfred de Musset, or Shelley, Foscolo had been cut off before reaching middle age, how much brighter would his fame appear! Some men are born old; others cannot age. Foscolo remained young and romantic, irrational and poetic, when world-wisdom decreed that he should be respectable and thrifty. There were pathological explanations for some of Foscolo's actions. The family, a very old stock of Venetians contaminated by the East, was infected with suicidal mania; and Foscolo was further impaired by the intermarriage with morbid Diamante Spaty, already a widow. Foscolo could not free himself from hereditary germs, or fail to be influenced by the excitement and unbalanced changes of his environment during that stormy period.

Ugo Foscolo in 1797 dedicated to Alfieri the *Tieste,* written in the Alfierian style, and stated that "for the simplicity of the design and the severe parsimony of the dialogue, the tragedies of the ancients, and hence the Alfierian, are the only ones to imitate." The *Tieste* has a broad political purpose. Altreo is the symbol of perfidious tyranny; Tieste is the vindicator of justice and liberty.

Foscolo's next tragedy *Ajace* may have seemed dull to the merchants, soldiers, and provincial landowners that compose a Milanese audience; but literary circles appreciated its quality, and posterity has endorsed their judgment. It is an heroic poem with many faultless lines. How lofty and musical is the metrical theme, how splendid the descriptions, how stirring the narrative of com-

Pellico

bats, how magnificent the speeches of Greek kings, priests, and heroes! The very spirit of antiquity has been reproduced.

The plot was already maturing in Foscolo's mind when he composed his *Sepolcri*. It is here developed on lines that would have been appropriate if the epic plan had been adopted. For a tragedy, the woof is too slender and the warp of episodes does not fill it. Ajax claims the arms of Achilles; Agamemnon denies them. Ulysses entices Agamemnon to resistance, while he plots the destruction of Ajax by sending Teucro, Ajax's brother, on a secret expedition which can be turned into the appearance of treason. The whole camp is in arms; the Trojans are coming. Ajax is charged with having sent them his brother and his "salamini" to reinforce their ranks. Tecmessa, a Trojan princess, wife of Ajax, is a prisoner in Agamemnon's tent. The battle rages fiercely; Ajax will not survive the defeat of his people by the Trojans and by his own brother; he stabs himself. Before dying, he hears Teucro explaining that, far from betraying the cause of the Greeks, he has largely contributed to their victory by a diversion. The capital fault of this plan is that nothing happens on the scene; everything is narrated. But what superb beauty is there to counterbalance these faults!

In the second act another beautiful passage is spoken by Calcante to Agamemnon. The spirit of epos breathes in every line. The struggles and glories of the past are conjured up in magnificent images: the awful night, when the infuriated Greeks entreated Calcante to placate the Erinyes, and Iphigenia, crowned and veiled at the altar, clung "with cold, trembling hands clasping mine, raising her eyes to heaven." To which Agamemnon answers that the torment inflicted on him by the Erinyes, he will force upon all others. "I alone will be my judge and my executioner. . . . I scorn both your tears and your praise; I want only your terror." In the third act, Ulysses' narrative of the assembly is a magnificent description so perfect in every detail, so complete as a whole, that no partial rendering can be attempted. The fifth act is most beautiful. Besides the description of the fight as seen by Calcante and deplored by Tecmessa, it contains Ajax's dying words: his farewell to the sun.

This was the last and perhaps the best of a long series of Italian tragedies, a splendid gem comparable to the best of Alfieri's. Comparison between Ajax and Saul is inevitable.

The *Ricciarda* was composed in 1813 at Florence and was printed by Foscolo in London in 1820. In the story, Guelfo and Averardo are brothers who for many years have struggled for the paternal inheritance since Guelfo would not divide it with Averardo, as their father had decreed. The *Ricciarda* deserves a notable place in the history of the Italian tragic theatre. The appeal to national sentiment exceeds that contained in the Alfierian theatre.

SILVIO PELLICO

Nature and education intended Silvio Pellico to lead a humble and quiet life. Yet he was tossed into the stormy sea of conspiracy and experienced the horrors of an Austrian prison. His youth was a bright poem, his trial and prison a wicked tragedy, his last years a dirge.

Silvio Pellico was born on the 28th of June, 1789, a puny babe whom his mother barely kept alive. Poverty sent Silvio to Lyons where he remained four years with an uncle. When his father obtained a clerkship in the Ministry of War, he returned to Milan, and was warmly welcomed by Foscolo. In 1816 Silvio became private tutor in the house of Count Luigi Porro Lambertenghi, and was plunged into the seething waters of conspiracy. Against the semi-official classicism of *La Biblioteca Italiana,* the literary clan of *casa Porro* joined in publishing the *Conciliatore*. Among the contributors to its 118 issues were Romagnosi Berchet, Sismondi, and Niccolini. Pellico devoted most of his time to the periodical.

By the intervention of literary protectors, Pellico's tragedy *Francesca da Rimini* was performed by the famous actress Carlotta Marchionni; and Pellico was invited to the hospitable house of the artist; and fell in love with the great Carlotta's cousin Teresa, "Gegia" Marchionni. While Pellico courted "Gegia" Marchionni, Piero Maroncelli was making love to Carlotta Marchionni. Maroncelli, a genuine *bohéme*, found responsive enthusiasm in Pellico, Porro, and others. These foolish plotters provided themselves with absurd diplomas framed in symbolical figures, worded in high-sounding terms. Maroncelli wrote to Bologna for these papers; the letter was seized, and Porro and Pellico were involved. Pellico was arrested October 13th, 1820. In his reminiscences Pellico never blames Maroncelli; his most affecting passages are in honour of his friend and companion. This serene position *au dessus de la mêlée* is the attitude of a Christian soul; but if Italy had been peopled by saintly martyrs like Silvio Pellico, Austrian officers might still be swaggering about the streets of Milan, their governors still be ordering Milanese ladies to be whipped publicly and their husbands to pay for the lashes.

On the 22nd of February 1822, from the balcony of the Ducal Palace, the sentences of death were commuted to fifteen years *carcere duro* in the horrible dungeons of the Spielberg.[5] Here Pellico dragged out his sickly existence; here good Count Oroboni died with words of pardon on his lips; here Maroncelli after long months of suffering had his leg amputated, and tendered to the barber who performed the operation that rose which Pellico has immortalized in his simple tale. Well could Gioberti dedicate a book to him as to "The first Italian patriot."

Although his patriotism was opposed to his attachment to the Roman Church, Silvio Pellico did not realize this antagonism. His brother Luigi was a Jesuit, and his sister Maria a nun, and he composed his book under the supervision of his confessor. It is remarkable that Silvio Pellico, afflicted with consumption, shattered nerves, and weak heart, managed to live in the horrible prison and on scanty diet, or that he did not become insane under the torture of long solitude, broken only by the sight of suffering, sickness, and death. After his release, he lived with Marchesa Baroli in Turin, declining all honours but the "Croce del merito di Savoja" which was pressed upon him by Massimo d'Azeglio. He died in January, 1854, aged sixty-five.

His play *Francesca da Rimini* had a tremendous success, yet the plot is weak, the versification poor, and there is some ranting and much padding. Francesca loves Paolo who, after killing her brother, has fled and left Francesca to nurse her sorrow. Finally she is persuaded to marry Paolo's brother, Lanciotto. Francesca weeps and talks about her grief for her dead brother, and her hatred for Paolo his murderer, who has suddenly returned from the East. Here comes the first tirade which was to become a war-cry for years: "For whom was my sword tainted with blood? For a stranger. Have I no country for whom her sons' blood should be sacred? For Thee, for Thee, My Italy, will I henceforth fight, if outrage is done to Thee by envy." Such a passage spoken wildly, compensated for any amount of nonsense. Francesca is ashamed to tell the real nature of her grief, yet consents to see Paolo. Act III contains the other tirade. Paolo breaks upon Francesca's solitude, and the classical *scena d'amore* is performed, and finally that cry of passion which every Italian has repeated at least once in his life, "T'amo Francesca t'amo e disperato e l'amor mio. . . . Even if it must be punished by everlasting chastisement, this love will endure in everlasting passion." Such a paraphrase of Dante's reticent episode caused enormous applause. In Act IV Lanciotto becomes suspicious and orders his brother to be held in custody. In Act V Paolo again expresses his passion. Lanciotto enters and kills both Francesca and Paolo.

Manzoni

Pellico's light tragedies are forgotten.⁶ *Eufemio da Messina,* however, was a milestone in tragedy's progress. The scene is crowded with combatants. The whole arsenal of romantic contrasts, surprises, mistakes, sinuosities, lines and colours and historic references gives an appearance of life to this medley.

But historical documents alone will never make a literary production. When Sophocles, Shakespeare, Corneille, and Alfieri have spoken through one of their characters, they reveal the spirit which informs the reconstruction of the historical episode. Pellico, in narrating the struggle round Messina, has left it doubtful whether he sides with passionate, love-sick, treacherous Eufemio, or with sturdy, implacable Teodoro; whether he means to plead for patriotism or for love.⁷

ALESSANDRO MANZONI

Manzoni's uneventful life reaches from the Austrian dominion, through the French invasion, the Austrian restoration in 1814, the convulsions of Italian Nationalism, the agonizing oppression that followed the dreams of 1848, up until the campaign of 1859 brought Italian independence and unity. Through all those years of light and shadow, of hope and despair, Manzoni gave timid approval to the general struggle for liberty. In 1782 Manzoni's father, Pietro Manzoni, blundered into a marriage with the fair and witty daughter of Cesare Beccaria. Their only son, Alessandro, born in 1785, was early entrusted to two maiden aunts, then sent to Jesuit colleges.

Giulia Beccaria—she dropped the name of Manzoni—was a planet of first magnitude in the intellectual constellation in Paris. Manzoni merely hints at the evils of his education by priests. Giulia Beccaria fostered the ingenuity of her son. Manzoni preserved an uncommon mental chastity. In his letters to Arese, he assures him that Paris is the abode of virtue. In 1807 Manzoni and his mother returned to Italy. Their letters to Claude Fauriel are filled with expressions of attachment to France, and contempt for Italians. On March 9th Manzoni wrote from Genoa: "Je vous dirai a vive voix tout le mal que je sens de cette belle Italie et les raisons qui me font lui préférer la France." One of these reasons for disliking Italy was Pietro Manzoni. His son avoided Milan until he heard that his father was dying. When he purposed to see him, it was too late; the deserted husband and father had died; and Manzoni does not seem to have attended his funeral.

Neither the solitude of Manzoni's estate of Brusuglio, nor his unsocial disposition, nor the doubtful virtue of his mother, prevented Henriette Blondel from marrying Manzoni. A frail, delicate blonde, aged sixteen, belonging to a Calvinist family of French Switzerland, submissive enough to satisfy "ma Mère qui a parlé avec elle plus que moi," Manzoni gladly mentions that she is neither of noble birth nor a Roman Catholic. The marriage was celebrated by a Calvinist. Yet in 1809 the Manzoni trio, once more settled in Paris, were intimate with Abbot Dègola. His austere life, his gentleness, attracted Henriette towards his cult, but more was needed to subdue the imperious will of Giulia and the enlightened mind of Alessandro Manzoni. Henceforth the abbot dominates the Manzoni household. In 1814 Manzoni settled in the house in Via Morone, Milan, where he continued to live until his death. In 1831 Manzoni's eldest daughter married Massimo d'Azeglio. In 1833 his wife died, deeply regretted by her husband. Three years later, he married Teresa Stampa, a widow of energetic temper. Manzoni was tried by many early deaths and by the slender success of his sons. Even his second wife and his son Pietro preceded him in death; his daughter Vittorina alone outlived her father.

From his first settling in Milan and the publication of his first poem until his death, Manzoni was beloved by every Italian writer. His modesty, his abhorrence of crowded places, and of every excitement, would not admit of his taking an active part in political events. There is a good portrait of Allesandro Manzoni by F. Hayez. The delicately chiselled features, smiling lips, and taper-fingered hands show his sensitiveness, while his intellectual expression, the beautiful shape of his head, reveal his mind.

In March, 1816, Manzoni planned his first play, *Il Conte di Carmagnola*. Manzoni's program for a Romantic tragedy is fully expounded in his later *Discours sur les trois unités*.

The revival of religion and the cult of Romanticism were closely allied. In Italy and in France this religion was not quite the same religion that poets and artists had professed in the past. Mysticism gave place to philosophy and humanitarianism. This blending of realism and piety, of liberalism and religion, produced varied results. Almost everyone professed it according to his own predisposition. Manzoni's religion is the keystone of his intellectual activity, the basis of his life and of Romanticism. Romanticism everywhere supported the religious revival. Chateaubriand and Manzoni are its apostles, but they differ widely in their interpretation of it. Romanticism turns towards the past. Poetical evocation rejected critical investigation. The centuries which classicism had branded as the darkest were now idealized. Thus the Middle Ages were now represented as the cradle of nationalism, as the spring of all that was best in human progress. The so-called Manzonian reform repudiates the cumbersome unities of time and place and the other rules, which constituted the main body of classical tragic poetry. It abandons mythological and classical subjects, and substitutes national, medieval, or modern historical subjects, faithfully reproduced in substance and character.

Il Conte di Carmagnola, dedicated to Fauriel, was published in 1820. The subject of the play is Carmagnola's career during the seven years of his rise and fall in the service of the Venetian Commonwealth. Francesco Bussone, better known as Carmagnola from his birthplace, was one of those *capitani di ventura* who carried the service of their mercenary troops from one prince to another. In times when no State kept a national army, the importance of these *venturieri* was very great: hence their insolence and rapacity was almost unlimited. Modern historians know that though Carmagnola was brave in battle and shrewd in council, he was as ready to shift his political views and sell his sword and his men as his compeers were. He first fought for Filippo Maria Visconti, who rewarded him largely and gave him in marriage one of his nieces. Visconti however dismissed Carmagnola and attempted his murder. Carmagnola then offered his service to the Venetian Commonwealth and served the Republic. Then the Senate arrested him and condemned him to death.

In the *Conte di Carmagnola* there is much history, and the action which extends from 1426 to 1432 includes salient facts in the life of Francesco Bussone, from the moment of his entering the service of Venice up to his execution. There is also Venice with her devious aims and policy. In trying to reveal the soul of Carmagnola, the poetical, high-minded Manzoni has obscured history, and has represented a spiritualized Christian character very differently from the fifteenth century soldier of fortune.

Manzoni's play opens with a sitting of the Senate: the Doge proposes an alliance with Florence in order to make war against Filippo Maria Visconti, and suggests that Carmagnola should be called to command the Venetian army. Carmagnola gives his advice and receives the Senate's commands. In the second act, Carmagnola's captains are discussing whether the moment is favourable for attacking the enemy entrenched in the village of Maclodio: A lyrical chorus describes the battle and closes the act. In the third act Carmagnola rebels against orders from Venice. He releases his prisoners without exacting ransom, saying that such was the custom among mercenaries. In the Council of Ten, Senator Marco, Carmagnola's friend and protector, is charged with excessive leniency towards the *condottiere,* whom the council now considers a traitor. Marco must immediately leave for a distant colony and must first sign a solemn agreement that he will give no warning to Carmagnola.

Carmagnola in his tent rejoices over the honour of being summoned to the presence of the Ten. He expects thanks and rewards, but he walks into a trap. The Venetian Senate charge him with having lost opportunities, with having shown clemency towards war-prisoners, with having caused the loss of the fleet by his tardy movements, and finally they charge him with treason. Carmagnola pleads for a fair trial, but is answered by the entrance of guards who lead him to secret prison and more secret tribunal. At the end of the fourth act Carmagnola's wife and daughter appear anxiously awaiting his return. Gonzago comes to tell them the awful news of Carmagnola's impending fate. The fifth act is entirely pathetic, the adieux of Carmagnola to his dear ones. *Il Conte di Carmagnola* disregards the unity of time and the unity of place. The scene shifts constantly.

What sort of man is Carmagnola? A Christian hero who walks to the scaffold with words of pardon on his lips? Or is he a Wallenstein grandly ambitious and grandly dreaming? In obedience to the dogmas of Romanticism, the character is traced by means of intertwining lines, of contrasting colours. Though the name of Wallenstein is mentioned only once in Manzoni's letters, the influence of Schiller's masterpiece is evident in *Il Conte di Carmagnola* and especially in the delineation of the hero's character. Yet, when in his *Discours sur les trois unités* he reviewed the principal masterpieces of the theatre, he selected Shakespeare, Corneille, Racine, and makes no mention of Schiller. While Wallenstein is following a great dream and is a powerful factor in Imperial events, Carmagnola is now but the instrument of the Senate, and lately of Visconti.

In Manzoni's tragedy neither the captains nor the Venetian *Commissari* nor any other of the less-important personages add much to the painting. In *Adelchi,* his second tragedy (1820–1822), Manzoni searched for solid "historical foundations." His conscientious preparation is evidenced in the *Discorso sopra alcuni punti della storia longobardica in Italia* (Discourse upon some points of the Longobard history in Italy). The drama begins when Vermondo announces the imminent arrival of Ermengarda. Her father King Desiderio awaits her with outraged heart. Adelchi also feels the insult done by Carlo to Ermengarda, but he is not a good hater. This criticism applies to the whole play. Where is the fierceness of conflict between two nations? Where is the patriotism that should have lent dignity to the Longobard's fight against the invaders? Where the religious enthusiasm that might have justified Charlemagne's advent? Furthermore, Charlemagne's invasion is not connected with the repudiation of Ermengarda. Charlemagne comes because Pope Adrian has sent for him in order to oppose him to Desiderio. He comes also because he does not trust the Pope, and fears that he may crown one of Carloman's sons, Gerberta. All these historical complications may be perfectly true; yet a poet should have made a selection and not have left the figure of Charlemagne so indistinct.

Desiderio is traced with more vigour though he too shows a superfluity of tenderness. As for all those warriors, so ready to betray their king, they are as unreal as they are unhistorical.

The episode of Ermengarda is most attractive. Her situation suggests comparison with Catherine of Aragon in the Shakespearean play. Catherine has the firm outline of a Shakespearean creation. She is a queen in every attitude towards king, cardinal, and grim death. "When I am dead, good wench, let me be used with honour; strew me over with maiden flowers, that all the world may know I was a chaste wife to my grave. . . ." Ermengarda also protests her chastity but she envies the nuns who "have offered their hearts to the King of kings, and thrown the shadow of a veil over their eyes before setting them on the face of any man." Catherine of Aragon is a living, throbbing, suffering woman who strives to assert her rights, her royal prerogatives; she appeals to our sympathy because her feelings are intensely human. Ermengarda is an ideal heroine: her meekness is poetic but hardly human. The chorus is the fittest expression of that vaporous sweet vision of feminine delicacy. Manzonians have disputed about the significance of this chorus. Whatever the interpretation, this lyrical interlude is beautiful.

To Adelchi death comes as the sweet hour of liberation (Act V, sc. 8). This melancholy hero is the champion of "a people that breaks up" (Act II, sc. 5). His sorrow is for the dissolution of a people corrupted by base desires and base envies, corroded by discords, allured by gold, and intimidated by arms. But his sick soul would, in any case, have been almost equally unhappy, because between him and the world "possessed by brutal force which gets itself called right" there would always have been an incurable dissension. In Manzoni's tragedies there are beautiful episodes, but theatrical art demands unity of design and vitality, and this is lacking in the *Adelchi*.

In Carlo Marenco's *Pia dei Tolomei* Ugo declares his love to Rinaldo's wife Pia, and is disdainfully repulsed. Upon the return of Rinaldo, revengeful Ugo suggests that Pia has betrayed him. She is dragged to that castle of Maremma which is to be her tomb. Ugo appears before Rinaldo "worn and ghastly pale, in pilgrim garb all torn in front," and confesses his treachery. Ugo forestalls Rinaldo's vengeance by tearing the bandages from his wounds, and expires. Pia, broken by the Maremma fever, seeks relief outside the castle in the deadly cool of the evening. Rinaldo finds her too late. She dies, sweetly blessing, pardoning.

Heroic and patriotic sentiments abound in his *Arnaldo da Brescia*. Comparison between this piece and Niccolini's has often been made. Marenco's is an Arnaldo less elated with hopes and enthusiasms, less iconoclastic in regard to the papacy and the empire, but more concrete psychologically and perhaps also historically.

The doleful tragedies of Marenco present the love of country in a kind of romantic languor. It is elegiac, shines like a tear, sounds like a lament, but it aroused echoes in many hearts similarly disposed. Marenco died in 1846.

After 1870, Italian tragedy was bankrupt. The Italian *Risorgimento* was accomplished. Tragedy lost its last reason for being.

Paolo Ferrari

Ferrari, writer of Italian comedies, was born in Modena in 1822 and died in 1889. Ferrari's first plays correspond to the last wave of romanticism; he then composed pictures corresponding to the new realistic movement.

His *Roberto Vighlius* gives a chapter of the history of the Flanders of 1566, so as to interpret the patriotic feelings of modern Italians; his *Vecchie Storie, ossia Carbonari e Sanfedisti* is a wild nightmare of improbabilities.

A peasant nurse substitutes her own baby girl in the lordly castle, and the noble born child is brought up in poverty. A bastard is the head of the *carbonari,* and his father is the judge who sentences him to death. Two girls love Sergio, the *carbonaro;* one becomes temporarily mad, the other appeals to the sovereign and obtains his reprieve at the last minute.

Ferrari soon drifted into the mood which answered to his natural tendency. He discussed moral or social theses in plays that did not always give a solution to the problem. Duels, suicide, illicit amours, jealousy, all those plagues of social life he studied and represented. Ferrari adopted some of the realism then so popular in Italian literature. Ferrari's many plays, based on social problems, are too superficial or too conventional for modern readers.

In *Cause ed effeti* Ferrari grappled with the protean problem of marriage. An innocent high-born girl, Duchessina Castellieri Estensi, is married to Marquis Olivaria Gonzaga. By the usual arrangements between family lawyers, every item of the settlements, every consideration, has been taken into account with the exception of the feelings of the young people. The natural result is that a good wife is unjustly suspected, a profligate husband spends most of his time with Countess Eulalia. In the fourth act the little child of the lawful wife dies on the stage. The audience applauded and wept floods of tears. Guilty Eulalia also dies, while a reconciliation between the repenting husband and his forgiving wife makes up the happy and illogical ending.

Il Ridicolo, a complicated chain of mistakes, shows that a husband is foolish when he unjustly suspects his wife; and that this terror of becoming ridiculous may bring about greater mischief than her actual guilt could have caused. *Il Suicidio* is even less persuading, since it is not a real but a supposed suicide.

Ferrari is at his best when he copies Goldoni. *Amore cenza Stima* is closely imitated from Goldoni's *Moglie Saggia.* He has exaggerated the faults of his model, but failed to grasp the beauty of its plan. In Goldoni's play, when Pantalone's daughter becomes the "grande dame" and shames her noble rival, there is a meaning that extends beyond the limit of the footlights. Ferrari describes a wife's resentment of a vulgar intrigue.

Ferrari's best play is *Goldoni e le sue sedici commedie nuove.* All the elements of a good comedy were to be found in the picture which Goldoni traced of his players as living persons. Just a little change of spelling and the anagram of Carlo Gozzi will provide Ferrari with a grumbling, envious, treacherous rival to Goldoni. The Sant' Angelo theatre provides a background for amusing scenes: rehearsal of plays, squabbling of actresses, jealousies of husbands, all the *brio* and vivacity of Venetian life, supporting and adorning this reconstruction of episodes that were familiar to the audience; all of them sanctioned by the judgment of posterity as part and parcel of the Goldonian tradition. This play had a lasting success.

The success of *La Satira e Parini* was almost as lasting. An historical reconstruction of the Milanese set with Parini for its central figure, had many chances of success. Parini's immortal poem of *Il giorno* and the episodes of the poet's struggle against the immorality and superficiality of his time make good comedy material. Moreover Ferrari introduced a humorous character which had obtained great popularity. Marchese Colombi is an Italian Mrs. Malaprop who blunders with the best intentions.

La Satira e Parini, Goldoni e le sue sedici commedie nuove, and a few bright plays written first in Modenese dialect and afterwards translated into Italian, are still performed.

The Italian dialect theatre has no exact counterpart in other countries. The divergence between Italian provinces—so lately independent Italian States—is greater and deeper than that between parts of any other country. A difference of language and of manners means a different conception of life.

When Ferrari composed a play in his native dialect his heart and mind found their opportunity and his deficiencies were hidden.

Even when translated into Tuscan Italian, *La Medicina d'una ragazza ammalata* and *Il Codicillo dello Zio Venanzio* continued to please. The medicine which cures the sick girl is a nice young man. The obstacles to this union form a series of amusing episodes. Ferrari, kept within the limits of his power, seldom strays beyond that *aurea mediocritas* of goodness or wickedness. Ferrari was a man of courage; through all his long and honorable life he showed steady purpose and endurance of persecution. His *Gol-*

doni is a jewel, and the whole play a valuable historical compo-sition.

Parini was more difficult. The more one realizes the grandeur of Parini's character and of his work, the less one should place him within the center of petty intrigues. Alfieri appears as a fop, a slave to a love intrigue that has no basis of genuine passion.

NOTES

CHAPTER XIII

1. Monti attacks the "pleasing life" of the Cisalpine Republic with the tremendous force of invective that makes his poetry both historical and human, a reflection, that is to say, of the present, and a prophecy and solemn warning for other times, should they perchance ever resemble the present:

> Altri stolti, altri vili, altri perversi,
>> Tiranni molti, cittadini pochi
>> E i pochi o muti, o insidiati o spersi.
> Inique leggi e per crearle rochi
>> Sulla tribuna i gorgozzuli e in giro
>> La discordia co'mantici e co'fochi,
> E l'orgoglio con lei, l'odio, il deliro,
>> L'ignoranza, l'error, mentre alla sbarra
>> Sta del popolo il pianto ed il sospiro.
> Tal s'allaccia in senato la zimarra,
>> Che d'elleboro ha d'uopo e d'esorcismo;
>> Tal vi tuona, che il callo ha della marra;
> Tal vi trama, che tutto é parossismo
>> Di delfica mania, vate piú destro
>> La calunnia a filar che il sillogismo;
> Vile! tal altro del rubar maestro
>> A Caton si pareggia e monta i rostri
>> Scappato al remo e al tiberin capestro.
> Oh iniqui! E tutti in arroganti inchiostri
>> Palar virtude e sé dir Bruto e Gracco
>> Genuzi essendo, Saturnini e mostri.
> Colmo era insomma de'delitti il sacco;
>> In pianto il giusto, in gozzoviglia il ladro,
>> E i Bruti a desco con Ciprigna e Bacco.
>
> . . . .
>
> Dal calzato allo scalzo le fortune
>> Migrar fur viste e libertá divenne
>> Merce di ladri e furia di tribune.
> V'eran leggi; il gran patto era solenne,
>> Ma fu calpesto. . . .

Vota il popol per fame avea la vena;
        E il viver suo vedea fuso e distrutto
        De'suoi pieni tiranni in una cena.
Squallido, macro il buon soldato e brutto
        Di polve, di sudor, di cicatrici,
        Chiedea plorando di suo sangue il frutto;
Ma l'inghiottono l'arche voratrici
        Di onnipossenti. . . .

        .   .   .   .

Sai come s'arrabatta esta genia,
        Che ambiziosa, obbliqua e penetra
        E fora e s'apre ai primi onor la via.

Some are fools, some debased, some depraved,
        Tyrants in plenty, citizens but few
        And these few speechless, watched or scattered.
Iniquitous laws and to create them
        Hoarse throats on the tribune, around them
        Discord with bellows and embers,
Haughtiness, hatred, delirium,
        Ignorance and error, while at the barrier
        Wait the sighs and tears of the people.
One in the senate dons the cassock
        Who hellebore needs and exorcism;
        There thunders one with pickaxe warted hands
Another machinates, all is a paroxysm
        Of Delphic mania, calumny
        As soothsayer more dextrous is than syllogism;
Villain that other, who a master in robbery
        Compares himself to Cato, and mounts the rostra
        Escaped from the galley and gibbet.
Oh iniquitous! And all in arrogant ink
        Speak of virtue and call themselves Brutus and Gracchus
        Being Genuzi, Saturnini and monsters.
Overflowing, in fact, with crime was the measure
        In tears the just, in revelry the thief,
        Brutuses feasting with Ciprigna and Bacchus.

        .   .   .   .

From the shod to the unshod, fortunes
        Were seen to migrate and liberty became
        Thieves' ware and tribune frenzy.
Laws there were; solemn the great pact
        But it was spurned . . .

The people's courage had oozed with hunger
    All his goods he saw melted and destroyed
    By his fell tyrants in one supper.
Squalid the good soldier and thin and ugly
    With dust and sweat and wounds,
    He asked and implored the fruit of his blood;
But swallowed it is by the ravenous coffers
    Of the almighty. . . .

    .   .   .   .

See how these vile ones toil
    Ambitious and crooked, they enter and penetrate
    And burrow their way to the highest honours.

2. It would be impossible to condense into a few pages the literary activity of Foscolo. His romance *Le Ultime Lettere di Jacopo Ortis* is the most important novel of his time. Foscolo has left many excellent translations from the classics. He was an eloquent orator; his critical essays are remarkable for original views and extensive information. His translation of Sterne's *Sentimental Journey* is a jewel. His letters are almost incomparable in their outpouring of passion and enthusiasm; of delicate feelings and exquisitely shaded gradation of emotions, expressed fluently and in beauty of style. His loves are always dignified by a masterful imagination which spreads the veil of illusion over even the sensual episodes; while in many cases the "Amitie Amoureuse" reveals the delicacy of his soul.

3. Countess d'Albany is not an attractive personality. Foscolo felt bound to show his regard to Alfieri's pseudo-widow. In order to attract him, Countess d'Albany introduced Foscolo to many pretty coquettes and encouraged his amours. Cf. *Lettere inedite di Luigia Stolberg Contessa d'Albany a Ugo Foscolo,* published by Camillo Antona Traversi and Domenico Bianchini, Rome, Molino, 1887; also *The Countess of Albany,* by Vernon Lee, London, Allen and Co., 1884 (page 210 and *passim*); *Gli Amori di Ugo Foscolo,* Giuseppe Chiarini, Bologna, Zanichellu, 1892—a voluminous book with quotation from Foscolo's and his many friends' letters.

4. Quirina Mocenni was predestined to literary amours. She married idiotic Maggiotti and promised to watch over and protect him. Such a marriage was not considered very binding. Countess d'Albany introduced her to Foscolo. She immediately loved him with an intense devotion and utter self-denial. Yet, after a short episode of passion, Foscolo drifted into the attitude of a grateful and tender friend. She accepted the rôle and never swerved from the painful path. She served him in every possible manner. She provided him with money when he was in want in London, pretending that it was from the sale of his books. Foscolo was deeply touched by her constancy and delicacy; he gave her every possible endearing name, "sister, mother, wife, lover," and he proposed several times to take her as his companion first, then, when her husband died, as his wife. Quirina knew better than to submit his affection to such an ordeal.

5. Pellico was arrested on the 14th of October, 1820, sentenced on 22nd of April, 1822, reached the castle of Spielberg in September of the same year, and was released in September, 1830. He died in Turin on the first of February, 1854.

Brünn, residence of the Governor—capital of Moravia—is situated in a pleasant valley. The castle of Spielberg on a mountain close by, was the most terrific prison of the Austrian States. Within it were then imprisoned some three hundred wretches, for the most part robbers and murderers. Some condemned to "carcere duro" others to "carcere durissimo." "Carcere duro" meant compulsory hard labour, the wearing of chains on the legs, sleeping on hard boards, and loathsome and scanty food. The "Carcere durissimo" signified that one part of the iron was fixed on the wall and the other fastened round the prisoner's waist so that he could not move further than the boards of his bed. Pellico was sentenced to "carcere duro," and not obliged to work, which was an aggravation of pain, since labour in the fields would have meant diversion, and some sort of companionship.

In Chapter LVIII he describes his first night in the Spielberg. "When I found myself alone in that horrid cavern, heard the closing of the iron doors, the rattling of chains, and by the gloomy light of a high window saw the wooden bench destined for my couch, with an enormous chain fixed in the wall, I sat down, in sullen rage on my hard resting place." The heavy fetters chaining his legs prevented him from sleeping. He was refused a straw bed when he was very ill.

The most cruel torture was the deprivation of all news from home. The only letter Pellico got from his family was entirely obliterated by ink across the writing. Not one single word was left visible, but the "Dear Silvio" of the beginning and the last salutations of the end. In ten years at the Spielberg he was allowed to write once, because they thought he was dying.

6. In his later tragedies Pellico did not greatly depart from the classical school. The *Gismonda da Mendrisio* is politically the most significant of all Pellico's tragedies. Conte di Mendrisio is father of two very dissimilar sons. One, Ermanno, is most loyal. Ariberto, on the contrary, though valiant and generous, despises the hallowed rights of the empire; he is a firebrand, a heretic. Ariberto has gone to Milan to marry a Torriani and to fight for the rebel commune against the imperial eagle! The Count disinherits and curses him; but when he learns that the Milanese have been dispersed and that Milan is destroyed, he pities this misguided son, who is perhaps dead or at least a wretched fugitive. Ariberto arrives at the paternal castle, throws himself at the feet of his father, who pardons the prodigal son and gives him his blessing.

Pellico's theatre is dominated by hatred of the German or Guelf idea.

7. The letters of Silvio Pellico are collected in an *epistolario* edited by Guglielmo Stefani, Le Monnier, Firenze. Unfortunately they have been revised and corrected under the prejudice of religious

motives. There are several portraits of Pellico taken at different
moments of his life. In all of them his features have a moody,
sullen expression. Even in his youth he must have looked aged.
His head is small, above a thin short throat, a square jaw, firmly
set lips, large eyes, and a brow of ample proportions.

See Alfani, "Silvio Pellico" in *Vita Italiana,* a brilliant *Conferenza* delivered at Palazzo Riccardi in Florence. It contains a certain
amount of information but mostly a bright, comprehensive, interpretation of the man Pellico. See also in *Revue des deux Mondes,*
September, 1842, a paper by Charles Didier; and *My Ten Years'
Imprisonment,* by Silvio Pellico, translated from the Italian by
Thomas Roscoe, Cassell's National Library, 1886.

BIBLIOGRAPHY OF GIOVANNI PINDEMONTE

The first tragedy written by Giovanni Pindemonte was *Mastino della Scala*, but the first printed was *"I Baccanali,* tragedia di nobile autore, rappresentata la prima volta nel Nobilissimo Teatro di S. Giov. Grisostomo in Venezia," Firenze, 1788.

The editor, in a preface, declared that the MS. was not given him by the author. "Yet I mean by this publication to give him a token of my respect and admiration. . . . " Cf. *"Ginevra di Scozia,* rappresentazione teatrale, inedita del Signor Luigi Millo." Venezia, 1796. Luigi Millo was the name of Giovanni Pindemonte's valet.

Orso Ipato | tragedia del Cittadino Giovanni Pindemonte. In Venezia, 1797. Anno I della Libertà Italiana. Dalle stampe delli cittadini "Casali."

Elena e Gerardo | azione patetica | fatto nazionale tratto dalle novelle del Bandello | parte seconda, novella XLI. In Venezia, 1799.

Donna Caritea, tragedia inedita in Venezia, 1799.

Il Salto di Leucade, tragedia inedita in Venezia, 1800.

Agrippina, tragedia inedita in Venezia, 1800.

(Most of these plays were first published in the collection *Il Teatro Moderno applaudito* in the years 1799–1801.)

I Coloni di Candia, published under the false title of "Philadelphia in Verona."

Cianippo, tragedia di Giovanni Pindemonte, Venezia, 1806, presso Antonio Rosa.

Adelina e Roberto | dramma tragico di Giov. Pindemonte in Venezia, 1807, presso Antonio Rosa.

The author edited also complete collections of his works: Cf. Sonzogno ed., and Silvestri ed.

D'Annunzio

CHAPTER XIV

GABRIELE D'ANNUNZIO: THE MAN AND HIS PLAYS

Gabriele D'Annunzio is the most discussed of modern writers; the world watches him; the world applauds him as novelist, poet and playwright: In all his writings, his characters are puppets, each reflecting some phase of his own personality: With himself as the subject, he became the world's most successful publicity agent: D'Annunzio's last rôle is in Franciscan garb, and his motto "silentium" has become vocal over all the world: D'Annunzio's tragedies are simple in their structure: Their characters are dominated by lust, ambition, or cruelty: They are mere tools in the hands of Fate, and the lower nature always triumphs: D'Annunzio's plays present magnificent descriptions unsurpassed in any language: There is no real psychoanalysis: Primitive emotion requires no delicate investigation: D'Annunzio's play *Gioconda* deals with the familiar social triangle: It reflects Italian characters, manners, and social atmosphere: In his *Francesca da Rimini*, D'Annunzio has transformed Dante's sweet sinner into a fiery amazon who brandishes deadly weapons: She is filled with sensual desire: The play is full of brutal violence: D'Annunzio's fame will rest on *La Figlia di Jorio* when his other plays are forgotten: In D'Annunzio's masterpiece there is throbbing life: On his *Fedra* D'Annunzio has lavished æsthetic beauties: This classical mosaic, containing many fragments of antique plays, is drowned in the verbosity of episodes.

MUCH ink has flowed; thousands of pages have been printed in many languages about the greatest living representative of Italian literature. No other modern writer has been so much discussed. From his early boyhood D'Annunzio dramatized his personality. He sees himself as in a mirror. He treads a grandiose stage, before an enormous audience, while the world watches and applauds him.

Slight of stature, and low voiced, he is a remarkable conversationalist. He has much to say; and he says it well. His information is enormous; and his every word receives the full harmony of its sound. The most musical of languages is never so musical as when it drips in balanced accents from his lips. His gestures add significance to his speech. Those beautiful little hands move as if they held a pencil or a brush and painted the image he evokes in the mind of his hearer. With equal felicity, he plays the gamut of emotions. He is impressive or affecting, simple or strenuous, according to his mood and opportunity. In a word D'Annunzio has a superlative natural and cultivated histrionic aptitude.

If the work of a painter reveals the stigmata of his physical deficiencies—Andrea del Sarto's weakness, Luca Giordano's criminal tendencies, being discovered in their pictures—surely the poet will imprint his personality on the creatures of his fantasy. D'Annunzio's characters are stage puppets. Always he writes with a view of the effect on his audience. He never startles beyond the limit of an astonished but consenting surprise. Possessed of psychic sensibility to the currents of public emotion, D'Annunzio began by shocking the critic. He advertised his amours, his intrigues, his extravagant habits. He gloried in notoriety and became the world's most successful publicity agent. In Paris he adopted the Parisian system of réclame, but objected to the witticisms of Parisian *la blague,* and was glad of an excuse to leave Paris.

D'Annunzio returned to Italy to preach the gospel of the war that was to end all war. An apostle *nouveau style,* he was attended by fair ladies, was followed by dogs, horses, and a retinue. At every opportunity he exalted heroism and glorified force. D'Annunzio maintained this attitude during the war, and experienced some of the rude life of the combatants. He capitalized an injury to his eye. He published eloquent details of his illness and convalescence. A more important réclame was his Fiume affair: that improvised and unauthorized militarism under pretence of patriotism. His use of the Roman form of salute, and the rally cry of "eya eya alala," was D'Annunzio's contribution to Fascism.

D'Annunzio's last rôle is carried out in Franciscan garb in a splendid hermitage on the Gardone, under the protection of Saint Francis, and with the motto, "silentium." It was a "silence" that became vocal all over the world: a solitude that welcomes intrusions and secures publicity. Is this the last avatar of the protean artist? Is he finally sated with the fame he has received, and the enormous publicity he has secured?

D'Annunzio's tragedies are simple in their structure. An atmosphere is created which favors the most violent emotions. The scenes are laid in ancient times, or in some period of decadence when the crust of civilization is thin, or has been torn off by violence. In such a *fata morgana* he places people dominated by lust, ambition, or cruelty. These souls are not tortured by remorse, nor struggling against temptation. Such a conception ignores the classic notion that drama is a soul-battle between good and evil. D'Annunzio's characters have already experienced the first and most interesting phase of the everlasting combat. They are at the end of their "passio"; they have surrendered to the fiend that drives them. They are mere tools in the hands of some Erinyes or Fate that leads them to a tragic and inevitable end.

This conception is incompatible with a discriminating study of character or a consistent plot. The fatal course of a destiny is already fixed by its own ego. That dainty artist, informed antiquarian, creator of exquisite images (*l'immaginifero*), that is D'Annunzio, may accumulate incidents, multiply stage directions, empty the treasures of his descriptive style; he will never produce the catharsis which crowns the victory of the heroic soul over the animal instinct. Indeed the lower nature always triumphs in D'Annunzio's tragedies. Death for Francesca, Phèdra, Mila, is not purification or atonement. Such primitive characters cannot be set within the frame of modern life. When this anachronism was attempted in *La Città Morta,* the contrast between the sport costumes and the fatality overhanging the personages would have ruined the play, had it not been supported by splendid episodical parts.

D'Annunzio's plays present an enormous wealth of scenic ar-

rangement, magnificent descriptions colored by his magic vocabu-
lary, illumined by his unparalleled gift of evocation and by his
erudition. The treasures lavished in Flaubert's *Salâmmbo* or in the
Tentation de Saint Antoine, the dazzling descriptions in Huys-
man's *A rebours,* are perhaps surpassed by many descriptive passages in D'Annunzio's plays. Does this compensate for the absence
of human interest? Certain modern critics and also D'Annunzio
would smile at this question. What to them is the value of spiritual
emotion? "La divine bestialite," instinct, passion—that is all they
care to see or describe.

This simplification of psychoanalysis accounts for the sensualism
of D'Annunzio's plays. Primitive emotion is easily described and
requires no delicate investigation. It is picturesque; takes relief
from colorful surroundings; explains and is explained by anything
that is strange, weird. It revels in quivering noontide heat, in mysterious illusions; and extenuates an improbable plot. It suits D'Annunzio's aesthetical tendency, and hides his lack of real human
emotion.

D'Annunzio's voluminous work has not yet been critically clas-
sified. Without insisting upon different "manners," there is an obvious difference between those earlier plays, which were strongly
influenced by Nietzsche's realistic philosophy, and his later plays.
Gioconda is an attempt to blend these different conceptions. It is
the familiar social triangle: a man who is a profile of the author
and two women. Lucio Settala, a sculptor and aesthetic, worships
beauty and his own precious ego. His sweet devoted wife, Silvia
Settala, is a paragon of virtue, loved and respected by all, and in-
termittently by her husband. Gioconda Dianti is Settala's model.
Her plastic beauty inspires the artist and has sex appeal. Gioconda
impersonates Art and Sex; Silvia represents Duty.

Lucio Settala, torn between duty and desire, attempts suicide at
the foot of his finished statue, and near another one modeled in

clay. Silvia is telling Lorenzo Gaddi that she hopes for the total recovery of her dear convalescent, and for the return of his love. Then she discusses her misgivings with her sister, and with Cosimo Dalbo, her friend and fellow-artist. The curtain drops on a pretty love-scene between the repentant husband and the tender and forgiving wife.

In the second act, Lucio Setalla confesses to Dalbo his conflict between duty and desire. Lucio tells how he admires his wife, is thankful for her devotion; but . . . life with her is death to an artist; while Gioconda is inspiration! "She is always varied, like a cloud that, from instant to instant, changes without your seeing it changing. Every motion of her body destroys one harmony and creates another even more beautiful." Her whole form is endowed with that power of expression which, in common mortals, is limited to the eyes: "The life of the eye is the look, more expressive than any word, than any sound," . . . In Gioconda, that mystery "is all over her body." Gioconda returns every day to Settala's studio to wet the cloths that cover the moulded clay; thus preserving the unfinished work of the sculptor.

The third act is "le clou" of the play. In the studio, behind a heavy hanging is the statue. Here Silvia Settala, with her sister, awaits her rival. Exit Francesca, enter Gioconda. The duel begins: Silvia challenging Gioconda: "One of us usurps the right of the other. Which? I perhaps?" "Perhaps," echoes Gioconda. Silvia blames Gioconda for Lucio's attempted suicide. Gioconda retorts that in death he sought deliverance from an unbearable yoke. "He does not love you. Here, he told me how unbearable was his slavery . . . your hands of goodness and pardon prepared for him every night a bed of thorns." The lover stabs the wife in every most sensitive feeling. "You nursed him and watched over him; but I watched over his unfinished work. I was shut out. I could only secure, binding it with my own sorrow, the work of his hands

. . . nothing is more sacred than a work of art which has just started into life."

Silvia pleads her cause with dignified warmth; but, goaded by the taunts of her rival, wounded in her love, she shrieks out a lie: Lucio has sent her; Lucio wants the latch-key back; Lucio does not want to see Gioconda any more. Gioconda is furious. "Tell him I take with me all that was his—power, joy, life . . . and that statue which is me, which is mine, I will shatter it to pieces." She disappears behind the hanging, followed by Silvia crying out that she has lied. A crash, a shriek, Francesca Doni rushes in and drags Silvia from behind the hanging, fainting and bleeding. Her hands have been crushed by the fall of the statue. "It is safe," she cries; and faints.

Here the tragedy should end; Lucio and Gioconda have disappeared. Why should poor, crushed Silvia be kept before the eyes of the public, unless some symbolical meaning was intended? Is it the cruel Nietzschean philosophy that good is bad, and wrong is right, and that a feeble and well-meaning, simple heart has nothing to expect from overruling Fate? Or is it in the spirit of Maeterlinck, comfort coming to a bruised heart from the simplicity of nature, through half-awakened intellects? Silvia is attended by a babbling maid servant Sirenetta, who murmurs soothing lullabies, fragments of lyrical poetry, ineffective in this tense atmosphere, as is the conventional inrush of Silvia's little daughter, Beata.

Gioconda may never become a popular play. Yet its limpid style transmits every shade of meaning, and brightens every image. The harmonious prose reveals D'Annunzio's greatest gift: his Italianity. The play is a presentation of Italian characters, manners, and social atmosphere. The fault in *Gioconda,* as in most of D'Annunzio's plays, is the confusion of different elements. It is as if the cadence of some thrilling musical theme were suddenly interrupted by voices in familiar conversation.

On hearing that Silvio Pellico intended to write a tragedy about Francesca da Rimini, Ugo Foscolo wrote him, "I morti di Dante lasciati in pace." Pellico could have explained that his Francesca was not Dante's at all, but just a romantic maiden of the early 1800's, all innocence and timidity, listening in affrighted ecstasy to Paolo's ranting. In his *Francesca da Rimini,* D'Annunzio transformed Dante's sweet sinner. He so manipulated her story, accumulated episodes, as entirely to transform the personages of Dante's vision. D'Annunzio is an authority on ancient Italian customs. He may have documentary support for his interpretation of Francesca's and Paolo's characters. Yet one clings lovingly to the idealized lovers as immortalized by Dante.

How delicious are Dante's lines! What surpassing suavity in this tale of deathless love. "Like doves on the wings of desire" they come, chastised by the "Master of the Universe," by sinful love. Even in hell, Francesca is still the "grande dame," the gentle "signora" who welcomes the visitor and offers thanks for his pity. Courteously she answers; modesty makes her reticent. She does not extenuate. She exalts the power of love, "che non perdona," the love to which she clings. Even in this kingdom of punishment, even under the flail of the everlasting tempest, Paolo is hers; love is immortal. And, as the pair are driven by the chastising wind, the poet is overwhelmed with pity—pity and sympathy.

D'Annunzio's Francesca is different. She is beautiful; "there never was a sword that went so straight as her eyes go if they but look at you." She fights on the battlements; she plots and intrigues. Strong in mind and body, she is filled with sensual desire. Unlike Dante's Francesca, unlike Guinicelli's ideal, "Amor e cuor gentil sono una cosa," unlike the Francesca who "weeps and speaks" when urged to tell how she succumbed to "dubbiosi desirii"; she has none of the womanly delicacy and deathless love of the accepted legends.

D'Annunzio has introduced Francesca surrounded by the luxurious refinement, mixed with violence and cruelty, that will inform the whole play. The stage directions, splendid fragments of descriptive prose, will appeal equally to archaeologist and painter. To follow his directions, to interpret his archaic terms, to understand these strange objects and complicated architecture, is difficult. Within this terraced court of the Polentano stronghold, flit a swarm of gaily gossiping maids; while armed men march to and from the iron-barred posterns.

There is poetry in the songs; pretty speeches are spoken by Francesca and her sister. In contrast, there is brutal violence. Bannino the bastard is wounded by his half-brother Ostasio, the legitimate Polentano. There is vileness in the trick whereby Francesca is led to marry Gianciotto Malatesta while believing her husband is to be Paolo, the fair and gallant brother who negotiates the match. When she wakes on the first morning after her marriage, she discovers by her side the uncouth and brutal face of the lame Gianciotto where she expected to find Paolo. This strange dénouement admits of a symbolical closing of the first act, with Francesca holding out to Paolo a rose that has grown in an antique sarcophagus, and has been watered in bloody water, while the bleeding face of Bannino peeps through the iron bars of a dungeon. Altogether, a complete picture of times that are far enough removed to be painted with the colors of fantasy.

The elaborate and effective staging of the second act is an historically exact reproduction of an Italian battlemented tower of that period: a cross-shaped room, bristling with projecting beams; stone pillars supporting the tower where men at arms are watching; an enormous catapult stretching its framework of twisted ropes; a trap-door leading down to the dungeon. Here are square-topped bows, balistas, arcobalistas, and other primitive forms of artillery. D'Annunzio's picture is accurate.

Within this atmosphere of cruelty and violence, Francesca becomes a fiery amazon. She brandishes the deadly weapons. Joyously she plays with Greek fire, and exults in the suffering it will inflict.

> Swift through the night, swift through the starless night,
> Fall in the camp, and seize the armed men,
> Enswathe his sounding armour, glide between
> Strong scale and scale, burn down
> The life of veins, and break
> The bones asunder, suck his marrow out,
> Stifle him, rend him, but before
> The final darkness falls upon his eyes,
> Let all the soul within him without hope
> Shriek in the splendour that is slaying him.

It is a woman who speaks; and not under the madness of battle! She is not even justified by party feeling, since it is improbable that Francesca has espoused the cause of the Malatesta husband she loathes. The ensuing encounter between Francesca and Paolo may be inconsistent, even sacrilegious; but it holds the audience.

A strange meeting for strange lovers! Francesca reproaches Paolo for his treachery. Paolo's poor excuse is that he is miserable and sick. Has not his wife, Oldrada, some herb for his fever?

> Franc—I had an herb, a healing herb
> There in the garden when you came one day,
> Clothed in a garment that is called, I think,
> Fraud in the gentle world.

Paolo was so miserable that he killed several foes. To this unusual proof of devotion Francesca answers that "God will forgive him all the blood he has shed; but not the tears she has not wept." Paolo well understands the "rebuke so over-much cruel, so over-much sweet." He does not entreat a pardon, but offers his life in atonement. "How will you like me to die?" "Like the galley slave, rowing in that galley which is called despair."

The signal of battle is given; and Paolo, doffing his helmet, stands on the battlement under the shower of deadly missiles. Francesca calls him back; then, flinging herself on her knees, she prays, saying that this is the judgment; if Paolo be unscathed by those flying arrows, it will mean that he is forgiven. This scene, the turmoil of battle, the kneeling woman reciting the Lord's Prayer, is of great dramatic effect which does not slacken when, amidst wild cries of victory, blood-stained, smiling, Gianciotto comes in, and drinks with his wife and brother the cup of aromatic wine. He lifts it to his lips with the wish:

> May God make you fruitful to me
> That you may give me many
> And many a lion's cub.

After this unloosing of elementary forces in an intensely dramatic scene, it was a *tour de force* to reconduct the story into an atmosphere of poetical love. The unchained ferocity of lust and bloodshed hardly prepared the development of the idyll, such as Dante and Boccaccio had narrated. The difficulty did not dismay D'Annunzio. The love-scene in the third act could not be omitted, though it comes somewhat unexpected after the episode on the tower. With all its stylistic beauty and musical verse, the drama drifts into something like *le romantisme echevale* or of Italian *drama da Arena*.

The introduction of a third brother, also frantic with lust for Francesca, his wickedness and treachery, his cruelty in killing the prisoner he kept for ransom, his revelation of Francesca's intrigue, are all vulgar and discordant elements. Three brothers, all desiring the same woman, is horrid. True, Racine in *Mithridate* presents two brothers and their father sighing for the same heroine. But with what infinite art and delicacy were the divers hues of the same feeling painted! Here the three are like hounds chasing their prey. The husband is as brutal as the discarded younger brother; and Paolo, though married and a father, is but slightly less brutal in the explosion of his love, amidst the shooting of arrows and the crackling of Greek fire.

The absence of form and proportion, the passion and picturesqueness and strong contrasts, passing from dainty lyrics to darksome brutality, make this truly a romantic play. The inevitable dream of pseudo-classic tragedies has not been omitted by D'Annunzio. He has used the familiar setting of sombre forests or elfin haunted wilds, found in Northern ballads. Francesca tells it to her confidante, a Saracen slave, Smaragdi. It adds another note to the growing terror:

> I see it as it were in very truth,
> A naked woman through the depths of the wood,
> Dishevelled, torn by branches and by thorns,
> Weeping and crying for mercy,
> Runs, followed by two mastiffs at her heels
> That bite her cruelly when they overtake her;
> See, behind her through the depths of the wood,
> Mounted on a black charger,
> A dark knight, strong and angry in the face,
> Sword in hand, threatening her
> With a swift death, in terrifying words.
> Then the dogs, taking hold
> Of the woman's naked side,
> Stop her; and the fierce knight, coming abreast,
> Dismounts from off his horse,
> And with his sword in hand
> Runs at the woman so,
> And she upon her knees, pinned to the earth
> By the two mastiffs, cries to him for mercy;
> And he thereat drives at her with full strength,

Pierces her in the breast,
So that the sword goes through her; and she falls
Forward upon her face,
Still always weeping; and the knight draws forth
A dagger and opens her
By the hip bone and draws
Her heart out and the rest,
And throws it to the dogs that hungrily
Devour it of a sudden. But she has lain there
Not long, before, as if she were not dead,
She rises up and she begins again
Her lamentable run towards the sea;
And the two dogs after her, tearing her,
Always, and always after her, the knight
Upon his horse again,
And with his sword in hand,
Always threatening her.
Tell me can you interpret me my dream?

The last act, with its setting of trap-door and darkened lights, with Paolo's secret admittance to Francesca's room, with Gianciotto's inrush, with Paolo's escape hindered by his cloak catching in the lock of the trap-door, will add little or nothing to the fame of its author.

One at least of D'Annunzio's plays is entirely his, original in conception, in style, and in manner, and harmonious in all its parts. D'Annunzio's fame will rest on *La Figlia di Jorio,* when his other plays are forgotten. This dramatic poem cannot be approached with cold criticism nor dissected and anatomized by the rules of any strict school. Something of spiritual altitude is required, wherein the spirit of the poet is perceived. We are in dreamland, in the country of legends, of fantasia. Why dispute the morality or the consistency of *La Figlia di Jorio?* Why dissect a hieratic mosaic? Why correct the perspective of a glowing stained-glass window?

In D'Annunzio's masterpiece, life is transposed, distorted; but throbbing life is there. This transposed reality appears from the first scenes. In pastoral rites, mystic worship, and esoteric conjurations, the figures move in hieratic attitudes. The mother Candia della Leonessa is scattering wheat and benedictions on the heads of her son Aligi and of Vienda who is soon to be his wife. Like the chorus on an Etruscan vase, the women place their offerings before the pair who are sitting by the door of their nuptial chamber.

Suddenly unbridled appetites, lust, cruelty, roar outside. Mila di Codrio, the sorceress, rushes in, panting, begging protection from the harvesters, maddened by the glaring sun, by wine, and frenzied desire for her body. Her feet are bleeding, her hair dishevelled. She crouches on the sacred hearthstone while Ornella, virgin daughter of the house, bars the door. The raging mob claim their prey, blood has been shed for her possession: "Leonessa beware, it is your own husband, Lazaro di Croio, who was wounded!" Affrighted by these threats and by terror of Mila's witchcraft, the woman would open the door and surrender the victim; but Aligi, the bridegroom, the dreamy shepherd, lays the crucifix on the threshold, and, opening the door, orders the lust-maddened men to refrain. He has seen, seen with his mortal eye, the mute angel hovering above her and weeping. Awed by the miracle, the pursuers depart and the curtain drops.

The second act shows a cave in the mountain, where Aligi and Mila have sought refuge. They are living in the purity of their love, the hospitality they have granted to fugitives, the fervour of their prayers. The votive lamp is burning before the madonna, while Aligi carves the image of the mute angel: all is holiness and sacred peace.

Mila, however, feels that Aligi must now return to his home and his flock. "Where wilt thou go?" he queries. She neither knows nor cares. Her soul, purified by love, cares only for his safety. Aligi, dreamy poet, has a sense of duty towards the girl at home, but loves Mila, "who weeps unheard." He seeks advice from the wanderers refuged in his cave: Cosma, the Saint, as pure as snow, visited by prophetic dreams, who will not encourage, though he pities; Anna Onna, the wise woman, who knows every herb and its power for healing or destroying, who can deliver those whom the Evil Spirit possesses. Mila has listened and better interpreted the sayings of these two; and, though her heart is breaking, she repeats:

> "Venuta e l'ora della dipartita
> Per la Figlia di Jorio e cosi sia."

They kneel in prayer. It is a sacrament of love. Aligi departs, and Mila, absorbed in orisons, agonized by her self-sacrifice, forgets to fill the lamp, and the light burning before the Madonna goes out. How great the art which makes us feel the tragedy of such an incident! How delicate the art that traces the girlish figure of Ornella, coming to entreat Mila to depart. To depart, but without reproaches; even tendering provisions for the way. The musical beauty of description suggests a Beethoven *andante*.

Then suddenly the storm breaks. Even to this Alpine refuge, Aligi's father has pursued the coveted prey. Brutally he would lay hands on Mila and bind her with the rope. Aligi, pale and distracted, defends the woman he loves. Lazaro asserts his primeval right "to pass over thy body with my plow, to make a handle for my knife with thy thigh bone." Aligi kneels before him; but he will defend Mila. Lazaro's servants bind Aligi and carry him away. Alone with Lazaro, Mila struggles. Aligi rushes in and stabs Lazaro. As he falls, the voice of Ornella is heard shrieking, "I loosened his bonds."

The third act discovers the desolate home of Candia della Leonessa; surrounded by a chorus of weeping women, she awaits her son Aligi on his way to torture. She has prepared the potion that will dull his mind and body. The chorus of the Lamentatrici repeat the dirge on Lazaro's coffin; Candia della Leonessa in their midst is crushed by the violence of Fate. The procession advances, with the veiled form of Aligi as the central figure of the group which joins the feminine chorus and creates an ensemble, as classical in its arrangement as an antique bas-relief.

Aligi drinks the proffered cup that leaves him unconscious. Mila appears, protesting that she alone must suffer, since she alone has sinned. Her witchcraft has armed Aligi's hand, her magic art has dulled his conscience. Willingly believing this self-accusation, the chorus cry, "let the sorceress be led to the stake." Ornella, the pure virgin, only has pity: "I kiss those feet of thine as they go," she says; while Mila, in an ecstasy of self-sacrifice, cries out: "La fiamma e bella! la fiamma e bella!" This is indeed the "Teatro di Poesia." No synopsis in a foreign language can express the beauty of lines, the harmony of colours, the musicality of verse.

D'Annunzio refuses to imitate classical or pseudo-classical models. Aristotelian rules are as repugnant as are the limitations arranged by Corneille and Racine, and accepted by their English and Italian disciples. Yet a classical ideal illuminates his pathway. A classical ideal is more easily realized in Italy than in other countries. Within the ruins of antique amphitheatres, in Fiesole or Syracuse, or Verona, or Pola, thousands have seen splendid reconstructions of Aeschylus, Sophocles, or Euripides performed under the same sunlight and blue canopy, and with the same background of monumental walls and leafy trees, as adorned their original creation. No Italian poet could ever treat a classical subject as Racine did.

Racine wrote for a public that knew little and cared less for antiquity. The performance of one of these plays was a court function. Hippolitus transformed into a French courtier, in full bottomed wig, sighing his love to a captive princess, dressed in garments of court magnificence, aroused no protest. Racine desired the approval of his dear teachers of Port Royal; but he also desired the approval of Louis the Fourteenth, and of court ladies and "grands seigneurs." If in his preface, he mentioned his indebtedness to Euripides, that was for the scholars. When he protested that if this is not my best tragedy, it is that in which "la vertu est mise le plus en jour. Les moindres fautes y sont sévèrement punies. La seule pensée du crime y est regardée avec autant d'horreur que le crime même." That was intended for the ears of messieurs de Port Royal, and ensured his pardon for past offences.

D'Annunzio's *Fedra* has none of the reticence, none of the tormenting remorse, found in the French and Greek plays. Fedra is lustful and cruel. This is the capital fault of the play. This lack of emotional elements allows a freer concentration on the esthetical beauties so lavishly spread. D'Annunzio pours into the mould of his tragedy many fragments of other antique plays, many transpositions of poems, many allusions to mythological fables, and pseudo-historical narratives. To understand this classical mosaic would require a library of texts, comments, glossary, and a knowledge of modern archaeology and of the recovered originals of Sophocles', Euripides', and Aeschylus' plays.

Are these pieces of the *Supplici,* these fragments of Euripides' lost "Hippolitus the crown wearer," or "Veiled Hippolitus," these lamentations of Theban mothers, and similar reminiscences interesting; or are they obtruded episodes? In Racine's plays, the action revolves around the announcement of Theseus' death. Here it is drowned in verbosity.

The Greek Phedra is a victim of Fate. Racine's Phèdre is the Christian penitent who atones for her unavoidable sin caused by hereditary disease. Both these tragic endings appeal to our emotions, since they rest upon certain fundamentals. They are universally human. But Fedra feels none of the religious awe that crushes Pasiphae's daughter within the sacred bowers haunted by the goddess Diana. She ignores the remorse that rends the soul of the French victim, tortured by "Venus tout entière a sa proie attachée," an inherited leprosy, inflicted by supernatural powers; tortured by consciousness of her wrong-doing, which, if ignored by the Greek model, was perfectly understood and accepted by the French audience, moulded by centuries of Christian teachings.

D'Annunzio neither realized nor cared for these human motives, these human emotions. Satisfied with the masterful appeal to æstheticism he could always stir, satisfied with his power to thrill the sensualism of his fellow creatures, satisfied also with his unequalled gift of expression, D'Annunzio has produced several other dramatical poems—tragedies they are not—fragments of which are likely to live in anthologies; but *la Figlia di Jorio* alone is likely to reach the heart of any large audiences.

Racine's *Phèdre*, like M. Hewlett's *Hippolitus*, is a pious adaptation of Christian ideals to the legend of an illustrious victim of Fate. With the same *naïveté* and the same religious intentions, Racine shows Phèdre, "malgre soi" (Boileau), wickedly charging Hyppolitus with the sin he has never contemplated; and immediately afterwards, touched by "La grace," repenting and confessing. Racine did his best. His most musical verse splendidly supports the delicacy of his psychology. By the magic of his perfect style, and by his borrowings from Euripides, he has made his *Phèdre* almost as formidable a model for D'Annunzio to confront, as was Dante's Francesca. Racine has intensified the pathos of his Greek model, and transformed Phèdre into a Christian sinner of his time. But since he has preciously preserved that which was really feminine in the Greek character, he has appealed to the emotion of innumerable audiences. Every one must pity the woman who struggles between irresistible passion and an accusing conscience.

This human, feminine, tragedy was already in Euripides. From the first moment, Phèdre is so tormented by shame for the sin, which is as yet only in her thoughts, that she cannot pronounce the name of Hippolitus, though she does not forbid the nurse's endeavor to quiet her passion. Greek spectators were spared a stepmother's amorous entreaties to a reluctant youth. The same respect is shown by Racine, when in that splendid love-scene (Act II, sc. 5), Phèdre, believing Theseus dead, is persuaded that she can have an interview with her beloved stepson and implore from him protection for her sons.

If her passion expresses itself in burning accents, she arouses such sympathy that there is no place left for criticism. When, blinded by passion, she offers power and glory to Hippolitus, she does not intend to bribe him. Always she is ready to avoid temptation by suicide. She struggles against the sensuality that she inherits from her mother Pasiphae and from her father Minos. In this tragedy of Fate, the only crime is committed by the nurse. Phèdre lends it barely six lines (Act III, sc. 4) of incoherent equivocating support. In Euripides, she left a letter which is not read aloud by Theseus.

Abuse pours from Fedra's lips in splendid verse. Bitterly, she reproaches the Theban mothers, her faithful Gorgo, the mother of Theseus, and the goddess Aphrodite, cause of all infamy which has cursed her family. The murder of the fair slave sent by Adraste to Hippolitus is mere brutality. Jealousy of a slave, a captive, as yet unknown to Hippolitus, may explain but does not justify the crime. There is perfect versification, and there are many exquisite details; but the number of narratives is appalling. A conductor of chariots, who turns out to be an "aedo," tells many beautiful stories: how Capaneo challenged the immortals and fell like a hero of Homer, how Evadne his widow sought death within the flames of his funeral pyre. But epic poetry cannot make a tragedy.

The second act is more successful. The staging is splendid and faithful to antiquity. Fedra reclines on panther skins, while the "aedo" expresses his love for her who made a poet of him by giving him a cetra, and by bending towards him the flame of her looks. "She took within her hands my heart—like the cup of an everlasting feast."

Enter Hippolitus, almost naked, panting and exalted, after chasing and breaking the horse Arione. He too has a long story about the great feats he meditates. Fedra, listening enthralled, offers one thousand ships, and promises of further aid from her father Minos; but furiously recoils when Hippolitus proposes an expedition in "Amicle sull Eurota," in order to capture a splendid maid, as compensation for the Theban slave murdered by Fedra. The dramatic scene with Fedra's wrathful denunciation of Theseus and Hippolitus is interrupted by the admittance of a Phoenician merchant.

Here follows one of those gorgeous enumerations characteristic of most of D'Annunzio's plays. They differ in detail, in colour; but each forms an impressive picture. In *Francesca da Rimini,* the seller offers the finest produce of arts of the time, the "Serparo"; in *La Figlia di Jorio,* all the magical herbs and natural treasures of the hills and valleys; in *Fedra,* the Phoenician proffers strange goods in such superabundance that Hippolitus falls asleep. Fedra crawls to where Hippolitus is slumbering, tenderly caresses his hair and face, presses an ardent kiss on his lips. When he struggles for release she clings to him, uttering entreaties mixed with offers. He threatens her with the axe given him by his mother, the Amazon. And Fedra bids him strike, that she may die by his hand. Hippolitus drops the axe and flees. Then another shocking scene. Fedra tells Theseus when and how Hippolitus has violated her. "Non cessit animus: vim tamen corpus tulit," said the Latin, which, as Boileau decreed, is allowed to say such things: "Le latin dans les mots brave l'honnêteté." The axe dropped by Hippolitus is used as evidence of her story. Theseus utters the classical apostrophe to

Neptune entreating punishment on his son, recalling the God's promise of granting three demands.

Despite its gorgeous staging, the last act is cold and ineffectual. With the dead body of Hippolitus in full view, the narrative of his death is mere rhetoric. Fedra, swathed in white veils which she drops over the corpse, is not impressive. She has bitter words for Theseus, fierce invectives for his mother Etra, and lastly, she turns her bitterness against herself, proclaiming her treachery and Hippolitus' innocence. Then, with an invocation to the chaste goddess Diana, she drops dead.

CHAPTER XV

MODERN DRAMATIC REPRESENTATIONS OF THE TUSCAN CONTADO: THE GIOSTRE, BRUSCELLI AND MAGGI

Names of rural dramatic representations vary according to the part of Italy where they are given: The chief names are *Giuochi, Giostre, Bruscelli,* and *Maggi*: *Maggio,* the most frequently used, celebrates the return of the Springtime, and is very ancient: In Siena the Bruscello is a form of theatrical art given in rustic style and language: The music of the *Maggio* is always a slow song in four verses of eight beats: At first the *Maggio* was recited in the open country, without stage or curtain: Now it is sometimes given in theatres: The *Maggi* are either heroic, historic, or spiritual: The subjects of these dramas are paladins, saints, and martyrs: The *Maggio* is a fragment of history arranged in dialogue: The *Maggio* avails itself of the marvelous and the spectacular, all performed in the most realistic manner: Celestial and diabolic personages, strange animals, and even Divinity, are among the actors; especially the devil, who frequently takes a comic part: In the *Maggio* innocence and justice always triumph: For the rustic the *Maggio* is the mirror of life and of history.

Living survivals of the sacred drama are found everywhere in southern Italy: Sometimes they are mute, frequently they are spoken: Usually it is a procession which issues from the church, passes through the streets, and returns to the church: Christmas, the Last Supper, the Crucifixion and Resurrection are most often represented. At Arzans near Naples there is an elaborate performance of the Annunciation: Elsewhere they celebrate the festivals of the patron saints. In some parts of northern Italy they still arrange processions in which the Madonna and the saints appear in masquerade: At Sordevolo a *Passione* is magnificently performed every five years by about four hundred persons: Also in Sardinia like customs survive: The festival of the *Rua* of Vicenza is a singular blending of the sacred and profane: The celebrated procession of *Gesu morto* is given at Prato every third year: A similar *Processione* is still held at Grassina and at Galluzzo near Florence.

THE names of the dramatic *Rappresentazioni* of the *Contado* (countryside), vary according to the part of Italy where they are given. In the Brescian rural districts they are called *Giuochi,* which recalls the *ludi* of the middle ages; in Tuscany they are called *Giostre* in the Pistoja mountains; *Bruscelli* in the Sienese and

Amiatese districts; and *Maggi* around Pisa, Lucca, and other parts of Tuscany and in the Tuscan-Modenese Apennines.

Maggio is the most common word to indicate such spectacles. Celebrating the return of the spring and singing its praises is very ancient. In Florence in the *duecento* there were May festivities over which the *Signor dell'Amore* (Lord of Love), presided; in Bologna they crowned the *Contesse di Maggio* (May Countesses), which at Modena and Ferrara were also called *Regine* (May Queens). "It was a very ancient custom," says a Ferrarese diarist of the sixteenth century, "that on the day of the Ascension of our Lord Jesus Christ there used to be erected in various parts of the city certain *palchi* (stages), after the fashion of theatres. In the middle of the said stages, sat a young girl charmingly adorned, crowned like a Queen, served by many ladies-in-waiting. There were other maidens who, when they saw anyone appear, advanced dancing a certain song which began

Ben venga Maggio,

in which they asked for a gratuity, and he was held as discourteous who did not offer something." The Florentine festival of the *Calendimaggio* is represented in an ancient print which serves as frontispiece to the *Canzoni a ballo* of 1568. Therein is shown a dance of twelve women before the Medicean palace, in front of which stands Lorenzo. These maidens were probably singing the canzonetta

Ben venga Maggio.

The custom of singing and "setting up the May" has never died out. "In the city of Bari," wrote Gimma, "we see the *Maggiolate* sung also in our own times. Usually certain rustic poets 'sing the May,' as they call it, on the first and following days of the month, along the streets and in front of the palaces." Placucci, in describing the customs of the *contadini* of the Romagna, writes "In the night of the entrance of May all the youths hasten to sing the May beneath the windows of their favored ladies. At the same time young girls sing *canzoni,* sitting at the windows and doors with the saying *di aver piantato Maggio* . . . that they have 'planted the May.'" One of such songs is the following:

> "Ben vegna Maz
> > Che I'ha purtea i bei fiur;
> > Vegna la stezza a tott i murador;
> > Cl'a purtea La bella spiga,
> > Vo, Crest, de zil mandela ben garnida.
> Ben vega e vegna Maz,
> > Che Maz i l'e arrivea:
> > E se pu anc ardi che sia arrivea,
> > Fasiv qua fura, cui e la Majea,"

> "Welcome May,
> > Which has brought the fair flowers;
> > May it come alike to all;
> > It has brought the lovely ear of corn,
> > Grant, Christ, that it may be well filled.
> Welcome and welcome May,
> > For May has now come to us;
> > And if thou art joyous that she has come to us
> > Come then out here, thou for whom is the Maying."

From this ancient and widely diffused custom of singing the May, there emerged, the dramatic form of the same name. It would have its first germ in the May song which would be gradually amplified in the same way as the *Bruscello* of the Sienese country.[1] The *Maggio* is in poetry or, as the *contadini* call them, *stanze,* which are always of four verses of eight beats. The music of the *Maggio* is a *cantilena* (a slow song) which however does not wholly exclude some *bravura* and trills on the part of a good actor.

This *cantilena,* which passes from *Maggio* to *Maggio* and is the same in every strophe, the oldest *contadini* remember hearing always exactly the same. Possibly in ancient times the *Maggio,* based on spiritual subjects, was joined with the annual celebration of certain ecclesiastical festivals. With certain profane *Maggio* there were intermingled special dances, such as the *Moresca;* but to-day the scenic spectacle is without dancing and the art of *Maggianti* consists only in a dramatic action.

At first the *Maggio* had no fixed home, but was recited on a *piazza* or at the cross-roads, or under the shade of olive or chestnut trees, without stage or curtain. Where there has been a change, it is chiefly due to the building of theatres, often paid for by the villagers. It was necessary that someone should announce how the action had changed its place. Sometimes a placard was fastened upon a pole, with the name of the city from which the drama was supposed to have been transplanted. Some places have solidly built theatres. The stage is of stone, with tiers of seats as in an amphitheatre, and in the middle is the *platea* with its benches for the humbler public. A canvas attached to poles protects from the sun.

In the same manner as the classic drama and the *sacre rappresentazioni,* the *Maggio* has a prologue, delivered by a special personage. In the Versilia he is called *Principiante.* The most common title in the Lucchese and Pisan districts is *Paggio.* The speaker is usually a little boy prettily dressed, with a short skirt to his knees, and he carries in his hand a flowered sceptre or a little bouquet. He makes a bow, and sings the *Prologue* in praise of Spring, whose return is the occasion of the spectacle. The Prologue also sets forth the subject of the spectacle. Thus for example, in the *Maddalena:*

> "Era indegna peccatrice
> A ogni vizio accostumata,
> E da molti era lodata,
> Come il libro parla e dice."

"A worthless sinner she of old,
    Experienced in all vice's ways,
    And many people gave her praise,
    As in the book is said and told."

The *Paggio* concludes with a plea for silence, and he then retires behind the scenes.

The *Maggi* are either heroic, historic or spiritual. The subjects of these dramas are paladins, saints and martyrs. The Tuscan *contadino* lives in a world of martyrs and paladins and knights-errant. Speak to him of Christ and of those who shed their blood for the faith: speak to him of

Tristano,
Lancillotto e il forte Orlando
Con il Sir di Montalbano

Tristram,
Lancelot and the strong Orlando,
With the Lord of Montalbano

as the *Maggio of Ginevra* says, speak to him of Charlemagne, and of Saracens and Turks to be conquered, and he will understand. There are however some other *Maggi* such as: *Gli Eroi etruschi in Africa,* or, *Bona presa dai Cavalieri* ("The Etruscan heroes in Africa," or "Bona taken by the Pisan Knights") which, though they may seem to be neither melodrama nor tragedy, are conceived and represented in heroic style. Thus the *Maggio della Gerusalemme liberata,* which derives directly from Tasso's poem, does not depart from the usual order of cherished forms and ideas, since the heroic and religious are together united in it.

The only wholly modern *Maggio* is that of *Louis XVI;* and even in this, the events are reported as if they belonged to ancient history, and the actual facts are strangely travestied therein. The *Burning of Troy* is a Maggio which would seem to belong to the classic more than to the romance tradition. But this likewise, owing to the manner in which it is conceived and represented, does not depart from the circle of chivalric memories. In its dramatic form the *Maggio* belongs to the free or romantic theatre, to which also belong the Spanish and the English dramas. Hence the *Maggio,* like the *sacra rappresentazione,* extends over a long space of time, often has for its scene places distant from each other, and comprises a great variety of events. The *Maggio* is a fragment of history arranged in dialogue. Hence in the *Maggio* each personage, each event necessary to make the fact understood in its entirety, is introduced and set upon the stage.

In the bath of *Susannah,* she "strips herself nearly naked"; the martyred saints are quartered, burnt, decapitated upon the stage. The heroes of such dramas, like Christ in the Passion, the sons of Bovo, and the children of Flora in the *Maddalena,* are born upon the stage. Death is represented upon the stage, whether it takes place by crucifixion like that of Christ, or by hanging like that of Judas. Chronology is ignored. Bovo, a little child in the first act, in the second is already a knight. To render these incongruities less glaring, the authors of the *Maggi* confide in the imagination of the spectator. The frequent raising and lowering of the curtain indicated the division of the acts. In the more ancient *Maggi* the scene is a little world, divided into as many parts as are the various places where the action takes place and the various characters move. The imagination of the spectator increases the distance, converts a tree into a wood, a hut into a city, a group of persons into an army, a duel into a battle, and attributes to minutes the duration of hours and days. If there are two thrones, one on the one side and one on the other, that indicates that the scene represents two provinces, two royal palaces; of which the thrones are the visible symbol.

Two curtains hung one to the right, the other to the left, are the symbol of hostile armies which face each other. In the *Maggio di Bradamante,* one sees on the one side the camp of Charles, on the other that of Agramante, and each of these is surrounded by his warriors. The intermediate space will generally be the field where the armies will fight. At times a simple duel of captains is the symbol of a general battle. At other times, as in the *Burning of Troy,* and in the *Liberation of Vienna,* the scene represents in part an encampment and in part the walls of a city, where the besieged are talking among themselves and also with the besiegers. And in the *Antichrist* it is divided, almost as in the ancient *Mysteries,* into Paradise on the right and the Inferno on the left; in the intermediate space are the Devil, and St. Michael with the trumpet of the last day; and above, heaven with Christ, Mary, and the Angels.

Two dramatic elements of which the *Maggio* very often avails itself are the spectacular and the marvellous: extraordinary deeds of valour, great catastrophes and upheavals of Nature; the sight of Paradise and the Inferno; and the scenic action of celestial and diabolic personages. Here are battles, duelling, and the striking great blows with the sword, generally between Christian and Turk, to the great satisfaction of actors and spectators. The faster fall the sword-strokes, so much the more are their tongues loosened in magniloquent words and brave boastings. Thus, in the *Cleonte e Isabella:*

> —Or convien che tu ti arrenda:
> Trema, io sono il forte Arcano.—
> —Questo acciar che tengo in mano
> Non e spada, e falce orrenda.—
>
> Now it is fitting thou should'st surrender:
> Tremble, I am the mighty Arcano.—
> —This steel which I hold in my hand
> Is not a sword, but a horrible scythe.

Formulas are generally drawn from ancient history or mythology.

The following, in the *Mainetto,* is one of the customary formulas with classical reminiscences:

> Fossi tu Sterope o Bronte,
>   Io di te non temerei;
>   E ti giuro in faccia ai Dei
> Che spezzar ti vo' la fronte.

> If thou wert Sterope or Bronte
>   I of thee should have no fear,
>   And before the Gods I swear
> That I wish to cleave thy head.

and in *Louis XVI:*

> Vostri corpi in queste strade
> Serviran di pasto ai cani;

> Your bodies in this road
> Will serve as food for dogs;

and in *Giant Goliath:*

> Ma vedra da queste mani
>   Vostre viscere sbranate,
>   E la carne insanguinate
> Darle in cibo ai cervi, ai cani;

> But thou shalt see by these my hands
>   Thine entrails torn asunder,
>   Shalt see them give the bleeding flesh
> To stags and dogs to plunder.

And so also in other *Maggi,* with slight variations. Another favorite form of combat in the *Maggi* is the *giostra.*

Besides these frequent scenes of warlike display there are in the *Maggi* others more peaceful; as in the last scene of the *Santa Oliva,* where one sees "the great piazza of Rome illuminated. A magnificent throne in the centre, under which there will be set magnificently dressed the Emperor, Roberto, Oliva, Fulvio, Diego: and at the sides of the throne guards and the populace." Other forms of spectacle are the tempest at sea, as in the *Presa di Bona* (Taking of Bona), in the *Bovo,* in the *Maddalena;* and the fire of the *Oliva,* of *Bonifacio,* and of the *Maggi* relating to Troy. The more spectacular scenes, executed with industrious mechanism, for which the theatre of the *contado* is not inferior to that of the city, are generally the final scenes: as, in the *Maddalena,* the ascension to heaven of the saint "in the midst of the angels with garlands of flowers in her hand and one upon her head." Strange animals appear upon the stage such as the lion who guides *Giosafat* (Jehoshaphat) and the wild beasts which in the circus lick the hands of four martyrs. The sacred personage who most frequently intervenes in the *Maggi* is *Angiolo* (Angel), the messenger of God. Nor are scenes of enchantments, sorceries, or magic lacking. In the *Presa di Bona* there is a scene in the *Inferno.* The Devil is also perpetually on the scene in the *Flavia,* and enflames the lust of her brother-in-law against her, and guides the hand of Alberto to the assassination of his nephew.

Intermingled with the serious and the heroic we often find in the *Maggi* the jesting and the comic. The comic part in the *Maggio* is very often entrusted to a special personage who has the generic name of *Buffone,* corresponding to the *Stultus* of the Mysteries and to the *Clown* of the English theatre. In the *san Pellegrino* this part falls to the Devil, who has come with the intention of beating the pious Hermit, and is derided by the Angel. Thus also in the *san Bartolommeo,* the Devil is embarrassed how to carry away so many new subjects. Sometimes the comic part is acted by Physicians who talk with great gravity and long words, citing Aristotle, Plato, Hypocrates, Galen, and Aretæus, although they do not understand where the disease lies.

The *Maggio,* especially if its subject is religious, stresses its moral. Usually it is the glorification of the Christian faith, for which knights contend, martyrs suffer, and innocents escape from the snares of the devil and from the persecutions of the wicked. In the *Maggio,* innocence always triumphs over wickedness, justice over oppression. There is never applause, but the progress of the *Maggio* is followed by the audience with eagerness. For the rustic spectator it is a mirror of life and of history, and a serious thing. The moral at the end of the *Maggio* introduces the *Licenza,* or farewell taken of the spectators, by the same person who spoke the prologue. Mingled with the good wishes, there is sometimes the announcement of returning another year, promising to do still better. Considering them as a whole, there is no *Maggio* of which the subject and dramatic web are the original invention of the rustic poet. Generally they are a reduction into verses of eight feet and into dramatic form, of previous verse or prose writings.

The *Maggio* is for the *contadino* what Tragedy was for the Greeks and the *liturgical Mystery* was for the early Christians. The *contadino* witnesses the *Maggio* with attention, almost with devotion. What the *contadino* wishes to see upon the stage is a man of superior holiness and courage. The personages and actions of ordinary everyday life find their appropriate place in the *Buffonate* and the *Contrasti;* both of which are sung in the open air in the piazzas. The *Contrasti* are recited in carnival instead of in the spring season. The *Buffonate* have the usual invocation to the Spring, and are perhaps recited before chanting the *Maggio.* Although the *Maggi* that are now performed date no farther back than the early nineteenth century, the *Maggio* is not of recent invention. It is probable that the *Maggio* may be a twin form, rather than a second form, of the *sacra rappresentazione*. Neither the characters nor the dramatic situations nor the scenic arrangement, and often not even the phrases have been changed. The *Maggio* probably originated in the fifteenth century, as do the *Rappresentazione* in *ottava rima*. Among the *cantici* of Jacopone are compositions in dialogue form which were perhaps actually represented by living persons.

In all the southern provinces of Italy are to be found living survivals of the sacred drama. They are traditional fêtes, which are dramatically executed on special occasions, with the participation of the people. At times they are mute, at times spoken. Occasionally the fête is in the church, as at Calvanico, at Castellamare di Stabia, and at Procida; and the preacher's word illustrates the events which are set before the people's eyes. Usually it is a procession which, issuing from the church and finally returning to it, passes through the streets and piazzas, bearing with it the *barette de' misteri*.[2] The occasions of this popular rejoicing are Christmas, the Last Supper, the Crucifixion, and the Resurrection. At Pietrapertosa in Basilicata, the ecclesiastical office of Christmas night is a true liturgical drama: pastorals are sung, bag-pipes are played, the star moves through the air from one end of the church to the other, and the *Bambino* is presented to the people in a little basket full of straw. In Atessa a youth, an old man and a child, selected from among the poorest, are led into a great hall where they present gifts to the *Bambino,* and three boys give him gold, silver, incense and myrrh, the whole finishing up with a dinner to the holy family and with distributions of money and bread to the poor.

More frequently the various episodes of the Passion are represented. At Gagliano in the province of Catanzaro on Good Friday they perform a *Pigghiata* which lasts six hours; the characters mount on to the stages when they have some part to play, otherwise they stand among the crowd. The public is most attentive;

the women weep and beat their breasts; and sometimes, all kneeling, they pray and moan. Then when the spectacle changes its place, the public follows the actors processionally. The women's parts are acted by men clean-shaven and with ample black mantles. Upon the stage are executed those scenes which require an enclosed place, such as councils of demons or of priests, or the Last Supper. For the arrest, they go out of the village about half a mile, where the garden of Gethsemane is supposed to be; and a little girl dressed as an angel, descending by a rope stretched between two trees, presents the chalice to Jesus. Returning to the *piazza* the people then witness the trial and scourging; then away, another half mile up a hill, is Golgotha, where the two thieves are already crucified. Christ is stripped of his tunic and a flesh-colored one is put on him: then the cross is raised, Longinus gives the spear-thrust, and from a prepared bladder the blood flows forth. They represent also the hanging of Judas, which is not without danger. In the episode of the Last Supper, Christ and the Apostles eat bread, fried fish, and *torte,* and drink good wine; and Judas, having eaten his share, goes around filching that of the others.

The *Mortorio* is celebrated in many places, by carrying in procession either the instruments of martyrdom or the dead body of Christ. But the gloomy rite is scarcely suited to the gay people of the south, and the festival of the Resurrection, the seeking by Mary, and her meeting with the risen Christ, is more popular. At Capistrello in the Abruzzo the crucifixion is represented; soldiers being sent on Good Friday around the *paese,* who, when they find Jesus, seize him, bind him, insult him, and set him on the cross, where he remains until the *gloria* of Saturday. Others are dressed as Herod, as Pilate, as Priests, Apostles and Marys: but this representation is silent. In Lanciano, the Resurrection is celebrated with the usual wandering around and meeting of Mary, John and Christ, and the liberating of sparrows and doves from under Mary's mantle.

At Arzano near Naples the Annunciation is celebrated. First there come three standards, followed by special congregations, then the music and then youths representing angels or characters from the Old Testament. The archangel Michael marches with drawn sword. Gabriel has a flower in his hand: Raphael is accompanied by Tobias. The procession halts, and Tobias shows a fish. Then Abraham passes with Isaac, who carries on his shoulder a bundle of wood. A fresh halt: Abraham proceeds to the sacrifice of his son, but is witheld by an angel. David passes, with warriors and an angel before whom he kneels, reciting the *miserere*. Adam passes with Abel and Cain, and then statues of saints, and then the clergy and people. The procession, returning into the church, mounts upon a stage which represents a mountain, and performs in acts and words what was indicated in the stops along the road. St. Michael walks the stage in martial attitude; then, amid a clanging of chains and flashes of fire, the devil emerges, dressed in red tights with a black crown on his head, and fights with the angel, who overcomes him.

Abraham appears wearing a turban, white tunic, red breeches, red mantle embroidered in gold and trimmed with fur, and polished boots. Then David advances, first as a sinner for love of Bathsheba and then as a penitent. Last comes Adam with his sons. Adam has buskins on his feet, and wears a white tunic and green cloak: Cain has fair hair and a black beard. Abel is younger, with a small moustache; he wears a red turban on his head. Adam relates to his sons his expulsion from the earthly Paradise, and exhorts them to virtue and to sacrifice to the Lord. The murder of Abel follows; and the representation ends with the terror of Cain, affrighted by the voice of the angel.

Elsewhere they celebrate the festivals of the patron saints: at Greci the flaying of St. Bartholomew and the person who acts this part is dressed in a skin which is then torn off him; at Lanciano, the temptation of St. Anthony; at Soccavo, the martyrdom of St. Paul; at Ottajano, the fall of the devil. At Palena, on the last day of Carnival, a man who represents Death takes up his position with a great scythe at the door of the church; and then, thus masked, marches along the country roads. At San Giovanni Gualdo the beheading of the Baptist is represented; and, amid the laughter of the public, Herod, in signing the sentence, dips his pen in a recondite part of the devil, who serves as ink-stand. In Rome on the Day of the Dead, a *rappresentazione* was given in a little chapel of the cemetery of the hospital of S. Giovanni. A stage of boards was set up in the middle, with rural scenery. Upon the stage were set several figures, life-size, representing a sacred event. In front of the stage stood a cleric who, on receiving alms, distributed to the visitors two papers—the one containing an engraved reproduction of the event represented, the other an explanation, with the addition of some devout reflections. At the cemetery of the Hospital of Santo Spirito, at the Oratory of the Confraternity of Death, in via Giulia and other places, like pictures were arranged. Everywhere the people resorted in great numbers to such spectacles. These representations have only recently ceased.

In the Ligurian and Piedmontese country, they still arrange gothic and pagan processions in which the Madonna and the saints appear in masquerade, with their emblems and the signs of their martyrdom. In Piedmont the Nativity, the Passion, the Last Judgment, the Triumph of Penitence, the Chaste Joseph, were represented only few years back. A *Passione* is recited every five years at Sordevolo in the Biella region, being repeated for four consecutive Sundays. The representation is given in a vast space of ground, shut in by a palisade, and is performed with magnificence and solemnity by about four hundred persons. Also in Sardinia like customs survive. Very celebrated in the Veneto is the festival of the *Rua of Vicenza,* usually enacted on the day of *Corpus Domini* with a singular blending of the sacred and profane. At Chioggia, in the evenings of Lent, they celebrate the life of the Saviour with sacred represenations in which are intermingled narrative and drama, the comic and devout. In the Trentino, Good Friday was traditionally celebrated with a figurative procession. In Tuscany, at Lucca, in the church of the *Suffragio,* it is customary to give every year a kind of representation, with painted setting, which lasts three days. It is composed of painted scenery with life-sized painted figures, showing some event from the New or Old Testament, and has the title of *Mistero.*

Celebrated throughout Tuscany is the procession of *Gesu Morto,* which is given at Prato every third year. The church of San Francesco is divided for this occasion into two parts: that in which the High Altar stands remains for the functions of Holy Week; the other is hung with black and, facing the principal door, there is set up a great transparency which represents Calvary, the Crucified, and Mary and John at the foot of the cross. Towards evening the procession comes forth from the neighboring cloister: *il Silenzio* (Silence) dressed in black knee breeches and *cappello a lucerna* (lamp-shaded hat), waving a white handkerchief; a priest dressed in a *tonacella* (short tunic) carrying a cross; the *Cavalleria,* of mounted soldiers in Roman costume, with helmets and swords and purple mantles; the *Fanteria,* a cohort of foot-soldiers led by the Centurian, and preceded by the Roman ensigns; and then another group of horse-soldiers. Afterwards there follow the brothers of the various Companies with torches, and every now and then a priest with the instruments or *Misteri* of the Passion: the cup, the lantern, the spade, the seamless garment, the cock, the pillar, the chains, the purse, the glove, etc. Then the Jews, one of whom bears a manifesto with S. P. Q. R. upon it; others carry manifestoes with *"Crucifige, crucifige";* others with I. N. R. I.; then seven great placards with the seven words uttered by Christ in his agony; the cross;

a chorus of men singing the *Miserere;* the bier upon which lies the dead Jesus, borne under a black *baldacchino;* a chorus of children singing the *Stabat Mater;* the image of the Virgin dressed in black, in the act of wiping her tears with a handkerchief; and finally the musical band which closes the procession. The *Processione di Gesu morto* is still held at Grassina and at Galluzzo, in the neighborhood of Florence.

NOTES

CHAPTER XV

1. In the Sienese vernacular *Bruscello* is also a masquerade of *contadini* who go out for sport with the *frugnolo* (bird-catching lantern), which certainly originated from the wish to imitate and counterfeit the gestures, speech, and the rustic songs of the countryside. The masquerade of the *Bruscello* was born first in the Sienese *Contado* whence it afterwards entered the city, always inclined to turn to jest the peasant customs. In Siena, with the rise of the *Accademia de'rozzi,* which had as its principal aim the giving of performances in rustic style and language, the *Bruscello* became a form of theatrical art. D'Ancona, vol. 2, p. 243.

2. Cars or stands on which the mysteries are set, as at Eboli, where the cars number eighteen and represent all the principal episodes of the Passion.

CHAPTER XVI

SOME CONTEMPORARY ITALIAN DRAMATISTS

SEM BENELLI

Sem Benelli: His reaction from the imitative theatre of the past and the dawn of "Teatro di Poesia": His *La Maschera di Bruto, Tignola, La Cena delle Beffe, L'amore dei tre re, Mantellaccio, L'Arzigogolo* and *Ali*: Giuseppe Giacosa: success of his *La Partita a scacchi*: His *Il Trionfo d'Amore*: His *Tristi Amori* as a picture of Italian provincial life: His most profound and original play, *Come le foglie*: His *I Diritti dell Anima* a psychological play: His *Il piu forte*: Gerolamo Rovetta: His *Romanticismo*, dealing with the Italian *Risorgimento*, a great success: His *Papa Eccellenza*: Luigi Pirandello: Profound change in the Italian post-war drama marked in his plays: His *Six Characters in Search of an Author* with the thesis that personality as generally understood is an illusion: His *Henry IV* preaches the confusion of personality and pretense: His pre-eminence among internationally known Italian dramatists.

WHEN a venerable pile crumbles, when an ancient tree falls, from the decayed roots or upturned stones will sometimes crawl a slimy insect, which has combined with greater forces in the work of destruction. Thus when the regular Italian drama was tottering under the attacks of critics, certain "demolisseurs" came to the front. This noisy mob of Futurists, with blaring trumpets and roll of drums, were eager for battle. The "Grotteschi" used ridicule, and had a definite plan of attack. Opinions solidly rooted and standardized were shaken, and the ground was prepared for the Modern Italian Drama. From D'Annunzio's *Giovanni Episcopo,* to Matilde Serao's *Paese di Cuccagna,* from Verga's Sicilian pictures to that exquisite idealist Fogazzero in *Malombra,* almost all the Italians had been carried away by the wave of realism, a realistic theatre which bore such names as Bracco, Giacosa, and Butti. Ibsen, Suderman, French realism and Italian adaptations were no longer popular. The cry for a National Theatre was answered when D'Annunzio's first plays roused wild enthusiasm and storms of disapproval. It was the dawn of "Teatro di Poesia," poetry as drama, that is to say, the interpretation of reality as transformed by a poet—a reaction against the dogma that the theatre must photograph life; a reaction also against the psychology that presumed to dissect the spirit in medical or physiological terms, a reaction against crude materialism and, above all, a bold assertion of nationalism. Such a program was aided by external circumstances.

The first decade of the century marked a high level of Italian prosperity. D'Annunzio gave poetical expression to national pride. Two other poets rank with him in this "Teatro di Poesia"—Ercole Morselli and Sem Benelli. Benelli has a noble brow, sunken eyes, a chiselled mouth, and pensive expression. An uncommon moral strength lies within his slender and sickly body. Sem Benelli would rank still higher if his achievement were equal to his intentions. It is the Icarian privilege of the elect to fail because they have aimed too high. With *La Maschera di Bruto,* with *Tignola* and *La Cena delle Beffe,* Sem Benelli gained fame. He also acquired a clearer conception of the spiritual problem that dominates his later work— the origin of evil. Why does man sin? Why does the fallen angel become a fiend? Benelli starts with "L'homme est un dieu tombe qui se souvient des cieux." Benelli strives to reconcile this celestial origin of men and the evil which fills the world.

The plot in *La Maschera di Bruto* is the often told story of Alessandro de Medici's murder by his cousin Lorenzo. Lorenzo challenges investigation and eludes it. How did the pale effeminate dissolute youth become a murderer? Benelli's attention converges on the strife in Lorenzo's soul. The originality of Benelli's study is his generalization. It is the complex physiognomy of sinners that he strives to understand and to explain. Lorenzo has assumed the mask of Brutus: the mask of patriotism and the championship of liberty. But will this mask become so much a part of his personality as to change it? Or will it drop and leave him in the desolate nakedness of humiliation and remorse? Chiarelli in *La Maschera e il Volto* had already stated the problem, and avoided it. Benelli asks: Can the sinner so persuade himself and others of his virtuous intent as to meet death hopefully? Or will the mask slip off and discover even to the sinner himself, the blackness of his deed? Lorenzo's last words reveal his agony. Vainly do motherly and sisterly affections strive to comfort him, vainly does his sweetheart bring him the balm of pitying love. He cries out: "Yes, Pity me! Love me for this deep grief of mine; that I am what I am! . . . for my terror of myself!" His is the dying cry, "Our will is not able to lift a feather. . . . Our dreams are more real than our actual living."

While *La Maschera di Bruto* had charmed large audiences for its superficial merits, *Tignola* appealed to the Italians who deemed that a minute representation of everyday life was an essential quality for modern plays. There is the weakling who has a sudden impulse of energy and acts like a hero, only to slip back into his habitual weakness. The bright-winged moth, "la tignola," "may fly out of its shelter of books; but the sunlight, which for a moment lends it the glittering colors of a living gem, will dazzle and shrivel it unless it repairs in haste to its sheltering refuge behind printed dreams and philosophical lore." Thus speaks Giuliano the shopclerk of the bookseller. He has superficially read many books; he has refined his manners, but his essential weakness remains unchanged. He loves a demi-mondaine who is so impressed with his fine speeches that she jilts the wealthy merchant who maintains her. Dazzled by this unexpected *bonne fortune*, Giuliano accepts the post of secretary to a Member of Parliament. With the impulsive haste of weakness masquerading as strength, he leaves the bookshop, scorns his chance of becoming master of the business by marrying the only daughter of Teodoro the owner, and accepts the challenge and fights the duel with the rejected merchant.

The second act finds a Giuliano discouraged in the new situation that he is so unfit to hold. He lacks every requirement for the necessary political rôle. He is even more unfit for the rôle of lover. His mistress and the Member of Parliament discover that they might form a better pair. Giuliano discovers the proof in the slipper dropped by his mistress outside the bedroom door of the Deputy. Holding that eloquent slipper in his hand, shaking it with wrath, he deposits it carefully where he found it. In the third act, Giuliano has returned to the bookshop, has married its heiress, is a ridiculed and betrayed husband in ill-fitting clothes and of seedy appearance. When his late mistress and patron revisit the shop, he attends to their wants with submissive indifference. He has outlived the passing flare of energy and passion and has dropped into his normal self.

Only a few months after *Tignola,* Benelli's *La Cena delle Beffe* roused the enthusiasm of all Italy. The latter play was received in France and in America with favor. It has quick action, an accurate historical reconstruction, and it contains one solidly built character. The plot is taken from Lasca's (Anton Francesco Grazzini) *novello.* The scene is laid in Florence in the time of Lorenzo the Magnificent. Tornaquinci, a noble friend of Lorenzo, is giving a supper in order to reconcile the brothers Neri and Gabriello with Gianetto, a coward whom Neri has had tied in a sack and dropped in the river, and whom he has robbed of his mistress Ginevra, and who now proposes to take his revenge. The most intense situations are developed, and the last act is stupendous. It is the story of one of those practical jokes in which no boisterous merriment can disguise the ferocity of intention. It is certainly no joke for Gianetto to pit his ready wit and sleek manners against the ferocity of Neri Chiaramontese. Gianetto is one more incarnation of the coward weakling who, when frenzied by terror, dares defy his foe, robs him of his mistress, urges him to murder his own brother, and finally to sink into real madness.

With all this list of crimes, Gianetto stirs more pity than repulsion. The fallen angel is there even if his wings are soiled, his hands tainted with blood. He is a coward and a traitor, yet he stands out morally above the evil he has wrought. Man is a puppet in the hand of some supreme fatality that drives him onward to his appointed goal. The Power that has made him such as he is, has also traced the way he shall go. Such sins as he commits are part of his destiny; but that which he cannot avoid he can regret, that which he is impelled to do his divine spirit can denounce. The sin can be expiated by remorse. "It is a drama of action and character, universal in its appeal, original in plot, intense in power."

Sem Benelli in quick succession produced several plays which are meant to contrast the antique Roman civilization with the crushing might of Barbarian invasions. But Benelli was not equipped for the undertaking; he lacked knowledge and he lacked intuition. A poet may tamper with history and use epoch-making events as a background for an amorous episode if only he can bring his readers within the magic circle of his own imagination. But Benelli's historical characters are unsubstantial, his plots inconsistent and always dull.

One of these historical dramas is *L'amore dei tre re* which has also been set to music by Montemezzi; as a libretto it has proved adequate. Time and place are left to the imagination of the public; we are merely informed that the action takes place in the early days of Italian history. The vague stage directions mention a castle, a portico, columns and vaults of divers styles, "che s'incontrano paurosamente." Arcibaldo the blind and aged Barbarian lord, while expecting the return of his warlike son Manfredo, is watching over Fiora his daughter-in-law. Fiora is a symbol of Italy's alluring charm and of woman's perversity. Though only a few months a wife, in the absence of her husband Manfredo, she is receiving in her room at night her lover Avito, a man of her own kin, sleek and soft-spoken but an unredeemed coward. Manfredo the splendid hero, the Northern warrior softened by his Christian education, is also deeply in love with his young wife who does not stint her caresses, though she has but a moment before his arrival, drunk deep in the cup of lust with her lover.

In the second act, on the top of a battlemented tower, Fiora, after listening to Manfredo's affectionate farewell, allows Avito to come from his place of concealment; and while she waves her white streaming veil in tender adieu to Manfredo, Avito embraces her knees, kissing the hem of her skirts. Afterwards Arcibaldo, who guesses dimly that she is faithless, gropes his way towards Fiora and strangles her. In the last act, Fiora's corpse lies in state. In comes Avito to bewail his loss and to kiss once more the lips that were so sweet in life but that now in death distill a deadly poison spread on them by Arcibaldo's order. He staggers and drops just in time to meet Manfredo's irate reproaches, and return them by telling his rival how Fiora loved him. Manfredo, the Christian hero, forgives Avito; he looks on Fiora and guesses that now in death, she has learned to love him, and seeks on her poisonous lips to join her in the realm of death.

Another historical play is the *Mantellaccio* which may have been suggested by that delightful poetical comedy *Le Passant* (François Coppée). The title, translated as *The Mantle,* leaves out the inflexion "accio" suggestive of raggedness; and has further to be explained as being indicative of a society (*Accademia*)—the members of which affected to be in rags, and wore a mantle picturesquely discolored, patched, and weather-stained. This was an emblem of the company's attitude towards the pedantic, purse-proud, pompous *Accademia* which presumed to dictate the laws of Parnassus as transmitted through Petrarchists during the decadent period known in literary history as *secentismo.*

L'Arzigogolo is akin to *Il Mantellaccio.* A reconstruction is planned somewhat like one of Carlo Gozzi's *fiabe,* with a super-abundance of grotesque extravagance, a loose plot and loose language and unblushing lewdness that would never have been tolerated in pre-war times. But under all this grossness and immorality, there is a streak of pure ideality. In a castle somewhere in the misty localization, and at some time in the hazy chronology of *fiabe* resides a debonair lord who has a fair and shrewish daughter Violante. In the manner approved of playwrights of the past, he provides a husband for her. She discards Giano, a high-born and constant suitor, and accepts Floridor, a foolish lout, lately enriched by trade. She will be his wife only in name until she meets a man worthy to be her initiator into the mystery of love, and has been his for "once." Says the prospective husband, "For once or for a few days: let us say five, the usual duration of love-affairs." Floridor accepts the humiliating conditions and Giano retires from the contest.

Act II takes place in another castle equally vaguely located but belonging to Giano, some years after Violante's marriage. All the personages are met; only the Buffoon is not seen. Giano, pleading with Violante, offers as surest proof of his persistent love the evidence of his frenzied evil-doings. Violante dares him to persuade her by such means, and finally entices him to send her the Buffoon that he may plead for his master—each aspiring to meet a kindred soul. Violante grants to the slave that which she has denied to the master. In the third act on the next morning, the Buffoon comes out of Violante's room. Her love has made a man of him. When Giano demands an answer, the Buffoon rushes back to Violante's room and comes forth carrying her in his arms, a corpse, stabbed by him.

In many of Benelli's plays the spiritual thesis is either involved within romantical superstructure, or dimly foreshadowed in contradictory deeds, or uttered in broken confession. In *Ali* (wings)

Benelli has uttered the cry of his soul, has voiced that which has lain deep within his own heart and soul through all his varied production: the unremitting unequal strife forever going on between the flesh and the spirit; the perpetual aspiration of the soul to fly on the wings of adoration and renouncement; the invincible power of earthly attraction which drags down the would-be angel towards "the way of all flesh." Benelli neither adopts nor rejects any formal religious creed. His play is a sermon and yet it contains no religious dogma.

Giuseppe Giacosa

From the medieval brilliancy of Giacosa's *La Partita a Scacchi* to his ponderous drama *Il Piu Forte,* the way is long; but there are characteristic traits that lend to his diversified production a remarkable unity. Giacosa was almost unknown to fame in 1873 when Italy acclaimed his one-act play, *La Partita a Scacchi,* a masterpiece. Many expressions in the prologue are household words. The picture of the Middle Ages in this play is false. The legend borrowed from an ancient *fabliau* is toned down to suit the standard of modern morals. The errant knight of the *fabliau* who on a game of chess stakes his life against one night with his host's daughter, has become the gentle page Fernando. The father foolishly promises his daughter's hand to the chess-player who will checkmate her. Page Fernando is so gentle and modest that "the unconquered chess player Yolanda" needs all her skill to win her predetermined defeat.

The longing for "un teatro nazionale" was flattered by this purely Italian poem. The prologue is a confession and an apology, yet it contains some of the proudest assertions a poet ever traced: "Noi poeti sovente, non siam noi che scriviamo:—E il vento che fa un fremito correr di ramo in ramo. . . ." Thus he reasserts the right of poets to follow their own inspiration without regard to ruling fashion or pronouncements of pretended authority:

O storie di battaglie, d'amor, di cortesie,
Nuvolette vaganti per quelle fantasie,
O sereni riposi dopo l'aspre fatiche,
Voi dell'arte a dei sogni siete i lucenti fuochi.

Which in simple prose means that he will adopt any subject that appeals to his imagination and that he turns to his dramatic art as to a "serene rest after strenuous work."

The great success of *La Partita a scacchi* induced Giacosa to write *Il Trionfo d'Amore*. As in Gozzi's *Turandot,* in the *Merchant of Venice* episode, and in many other plays of Eastern origin, this play rests on the guessing of three riddles. The proud heiress Diana d'Alteno will marry only the man who solves the triple enigma. Ugo di Monsoprano accomplishes the feat, crowns it with another victory by proposing a riddle which she cannot solve, and then spurns her proffered hand. Diana, chastened in her pride, loves the man who has scorned her. *Il Trionfo d'Amore* was less successful than the *Partita*. Giacosa then wrote a series of pseudo-historical plays none of which has obtained the popularity of *La Partita a scacchi*.

In 1888 Giacosa produced his *Tristi Amori*. Unpresuming and but scantily praised by literary critics, these three prose-acts powerfully trace a picture of homely provincial life, and delineate a moral problem. Here is the home of a prosperous lawyer. His modest house is managed by his wife Emma and her servant Martha; his little daughter Giunna is part of the picture. Friendly visitors come and go, and the husband's partner Fabrizio Arcieri becomes one of the family. But a tragedy is sapping the foundation of the family group. The tragedy is the more dramatic for the reticence that characterizes the whole atmosphere. Emma and Fabrizio are lovers; they have drifted into sin; yet they have moral standards and sense of honor. The nobility of the husband's character is fully realized by both of them. Even while they betray him their anguished hearts are torn by a sense of guilt that compels the breaking of their bond. They hesitate; they delay; they suffer. "Who can tell how this thing begins?" says Fabrizio. "It is such a subtle poison. Who can know it at first? It takes so many names. It is pity, it is respect and faith. One does not fear it. It has such appearance of good. . . ." Clear-sighted Emma says, "We are cowards. . . . We had foreseen it all, . . . our conscience told us. . . . Now the only thing we must do is to save Giulio. . . . Our duty towards him now is to deceive him."

Fabrizio's dissolute father knows of this intrigue and has forged the signature of Giulio Scarli. Fabrizio cannot pay. Giulio offers him the sum, a heavy one. Fabrizio refuses to accept; Giulio insists and appeals to his wife to plead with Fabrizio and remove his excessive scruples. Emma sides with Fabrizio. In a beautiful scene the three get entangled in a discussion. Suspicion dawns on Giulio. He understands why Fabrizio refuses to accept the money. The doubt becomes a certainty when he notices that Emma uses Fabrizio's arguments. One agonized cry from the injured husband: "Go! Go! Get out of my house!"

The third act is most original. Emma is weak; she will not elope with Fabrizio; Giulio too is consistent. Since Emma refuses to depart, there shall be no forgiveness for the faithless wife; but the mutual duty of bringing up the child in ignorance of all evil is recognized. It is the everlasting problem that neither law nor social custom will ever settle. Giacosa simply shows what havoc can follow on such a fault when accusing conscience deprives the wrong-doing of any charm, and makes repentance fruitless.

In *Tristi Amori* the passion of the lovers is sacrificed to the honesty of the injured husband; the drama is the triumph of the family tie over the passing pleasure of a miserable infatuation. In *Come le foglie,* an episode of youthful love remains on the second plane, while the problem of character holds first place. "The leaves that the wind drives about—who can stop them?" They are "elegant and graceful; and no one knows where they will be driven." Such "people may never fall into actual wrongdoing; they flutter from meanness to meanness and are lost in universal cowardice." You "miss them some day . . . they are gone." People who allow the storm of circumstances or the wind of petty temptations to drop them into the ditch, are here presented. A whole family is affected with weakness. The Rosanis have been very rich; they are now ruined. Giovanni, the head of the family, accepts a small clerkship. Tommaso his son is more corrupted by indulgence and a vulgar pretense of gentility. He suspects his father of having secretly saved some money. Giulia, Giovanni's young second wife, is also tainted with the same dissipation. Giovanni's daughter Nennele alone shows a stronger moral stamina.

The first act shows the family leaving Milan and starting for the quiet home in Switzerland which has been prepared for them by Giovanni's nephew Massimo Rosani. Giddy Giulia is only concerned with packing her expensive toilets and flowers. Tommy too is careful about tennis equipment and fashionable morning suits. Nennele shows some emotion on leaving her home and an aged faithful servant. Massimo delineates his position as the benefactor and moralist. In fact he loves to make speeches and overflows with aphorisms. The second act, in Switzerland, marks the first steps in the moral downfall of Giulia and Tommy and the gradual rising of Nennele who, besides doing the housekeeping, gives lessons in English. Massimo's preaching gives her heart. Her father earns the family bread as clerk to Massimo, but Tommy gambles at the house of a woman of bad reputation and steals money from Nennele; and Giulia, persuading herself that she has talent for painting, squanders money on subscriptions to art circles, colors and brushes. Thus the dry leaves are driven about by the wind. Tommy accepts money from this woman of ill fame, and promises to marry her. Giulia flirts with a foreign artist, and gives him her portrait in a silver frame which she steals from Nennele's room. There is a slender love-story. Nennele's animosity against Massimo melts into passion; she attempts suicide, but is stopped by her father. The end, however, is happy for the pair of lovers. *Come le Foglie* is Giacosa's most profound and original play. Its characters are true to life. It has been acted in Italian or in translation in France, England, and America.

I Diritti dell'Anima (The Rights of the Soul) is another psychological play. Has a husband the right to investigate the secret recesses of his wife's soul? Has the honest woman the right to conceal an attachment that was never expressed in deed? The problem appeals to every husband and lover. Paolo knows that she has never wronged him in deed, but is tormented by the fear that Anna his beloved wife has wronged him in thought:

And if she did love him. Good God! If she did love him. If she rejected him for virtue, for duty's sake, what becomes of me? If he were alive I could resist him, conquer him . . . but he's dead—he's killed himself for love of her. If she loved him no force can ever tear him from her heart. . . . Why, she is admirable. Even more to be admired if she loved him. Anyone must admire her. . . . So would I if she were some one else's wife. But she is mine. I am not my wife's judge. I am a party, and cannot presume to judge, I am the owner. . . . She is mine, mine. Must I praise her for having defrauded me of only one part, when she could rob me of everything. I look at what she has taken away, not at what remains.

This is no cold, Ibsenite husband but the jealous Italian. After the suicide of this cousin Luciano, a letter is found in his pocketbook which affords the surest evidence of his wife's fidelity. She has written "You write me that if I don't answer you will come back at once. I love my husband, that is my answer. This, this alone, always this. I beg of you not to torment me any more."

Paolo forces Anna to explain not merely her acts but her most secret thoughts, until, driven to exasperation, she avows the secret she had so carefully concealed from her husband, from the man she loved, and also perhaps from herself. Yes! Luciano loved her, yes, she too loved him, and now, when he has killed himself because she denied him, she loathes her husband's investigation. For five long years she has been silent; she has caressed her husband and refused happiness for herself and Luciano. No Ibsenite character, but a Southern passionate woman, she cries this truth in her husband's face, and when he furiously bids her begone, she snatches at the release.

In *Il piu forte* the picture is amply drawn and deeply investigated. Cesare Nalli is aged sixty; by unscrupulous means he has risen to an eminent position in the world of affairs. Elisa is the model wife who does not suspect that the wealth flowing into her household is dishonestly gained. She is the symbol of the many women equally unspoiled and unsoiled, who live and profit from dubious business. Silvio, their only son, is even more uncorrupted. He has been educated abroad, is an artist, and is married to Fiora, a woman who is without scruples. She flirts with Edoardo Falconieri, a nephew of Cesare Nalli's. The important personages are the father and son. Lamais's son has publicly called Cesare Nalli a thief. Silvio would send him a challenge, but no one is willing to carry it; his eyes open to the cruel truth. Father and son stand face to face, Cesare pleading that he does not want leniency. "Money does not hang from the trees. If it must come into my safe, it must come out of the pocket of somebody who was trying to seize mine. It is fair play. Everyone tries to buy for less than real cost, and sell for more—and all business amounts to this: a man must know the real value of things and lie twice. He must lie when he buys, and lie again when he sells. Good faith! Just try it and see how far you go. You will be trampled down at the first step. . . . Everything that the law permits is right."

His son pleads for honesty. "If you wanted me to adopt your standard of morality, why have you brought me up in such a way that I am ignorant of your strenuous logic? You should have instilled it by daily practice. . . . You have taught me only the beautiful things of life, and concealed all that is evil." To which Cesare can proudly answer that, on his own powerful shoulders, he has taken all the load of toil and sin merely to make his son's life pure and noble. Nothing for himself. No pleasure, no dissipation, only hard work, only the making of money to squander on his family. This very delicacy of conscience, this sense of honor, is it not the fruit of the education his money has provided for his son who is now his judge? As a study in psychology and a picture of life, the play honors its author, and is a fitting close to his career.

Gerolamo Rovetta

A journalist, a writer of novels and short stories, author of several plays, Gerolamo Rovetta is remembered for the enormous success of one novel *Mater Dolorosa* and of one play *Romanticismo*. Rovetta is a pessimistic but powerful painter of feminine folly. The gallery of his heroines is interesting. It suggests some bitter personal experience of the havoc womanly folly and egotism can make in a man's life.

In his popular play *Papa Eccellenza*, Pietro Mattei is a Minister of State with an honorable reputation. He holds in check all financial intrigue and speculation. The character of Remigia is drawn with that bitterness and accuracy, that mixture of misogynism and conscientious observation, which characterizes so many of Rovetta's women. Remigia is the spoilt child of a father who constantly grieves over her mother's death. Mattei could not punish the orphan child or oppose her silly marriage. Her husband is a German, stern and positive, who sends Remigia back to her father when she refuses to follow him into the country. Count Alvise Colloredo is of low repute and licentious. Remigia and Alvise are lovers, both are in debt, and a cheque is due. In the waste-paper basket they discover a torn dispatch, translated from cipher by Mattei, and by him jealously kept secret, as it contains a Cabinet decision of the greatest financial importance. Alvise uses this information so as to make a *coup* that will pay all his and Remigia's debts, and also enrich him. Remigia does not realize the meaning of the disclosure; yet she consents to share the profit.

In Act II the catastrophe has happened. A morning paper of the adverse party prints an article about Mattei's expensive establishment and insinuates that large profits have been made out of secret information known only by Mattei. Investigation shows that Alvise is the traitor. The scene between Alvise and Mattei is violent. When Alvise utters the name of Remigia as his informer and accomplice, Mattei, who has heart-disease, drops to the ground in a faint. He has just enough strength to order his friends to stop judicial proceedings against the Journalist.

Rovetta has added a third act of psychological investigation. Remigia is vain and preoccupied with her many gowns for a trip to Milan. Her stern husband tells her the truth. He charges her with having ruined her father and himself by her vanity, her selfishness "because you love no one . . . not even your lover." Remigia in her retorts betrays more despicable sins. Her husband threatens her; she shrieks; her father comes. After telling his daughter "I have given you all, and you take also my life. . . . I cannot forgive you. . . . But I wish to die here near you," he falls to the ground. This emotional conclusion is consistent with the whole play. It is carefully prepared and true to life.

Romanticismo should be read by those who wish to understand the spirit of Italian *Risorgimento*. It is a masterful picture; only the most important lines and the really significant colour is there. The plot is elementary; the author's object is to paint "Un état d'ame" embracing not only the personages moving on the board but also their social world. And the group is almost complete: a degenerate countess devoted to the Austrian rule, attended by her former lover; an Austrian officer; the countess' son Lamberto, the romantical hero; and his wife, sentimental Anna; the scapegrace Giacomino of a gallant and merry disposition who represents the sunny side of this conspiracy. Tito Ansperti, seized by the Austrians, has been tried in Venice and will be sentenced to death. His father and wife allow their shop to be used as a meeting-place for the conspirators. There are stories of traitors, of heroes, and of duels between Italian patriots and Austrian officers. There is a traitor who is described with restraint and a consideration of extenuating circumstances.

The plot is simple, Lamberto and Anna are not one at heart, though they are both devoted patriots. The scene where Anna realizes that the husband whom she suspected of Austrian sympathies is in fact a brave patriot, is a revelation of souls. Lamberto has to conquer the diffidence of those who know by experience that traitors are everywhere and that the slightest mistake may bring about a catastrophe. His mother's liaison is well known, and, before trusting him, the patriots in Ansperti's back-shop must hear him repeat the formula of oath that binds the members of "La Giovane Italia." This oath is "le Clou"; appealing to every Italian heart.

In the third act, the wife of Lamberto is being tempted to betray the names of other conspirators in order to save her husband's life. He comes on the scene in time to release her.

"I will tell you," he breaks out to the inquisitors, "and mind you remember them well. They are the names of all who have hearts and heads, of all who remember and hate. Go out into the streets and the squares. Go into the theatres, the churches; everywhere where people are pretending to amuse themselves or to pray; everywhere where people are suffering and hiding their torn coats. Name . . . the names!" (He laughs aloud.) "Aha! first enlarge your prisons, make them as big as our cities are, and take us there. . . . The name is the name of all. It is the hour—the hour has come! We are all conspirators and rebellious."

Also historical is Lamberto's apostrophe to the gendarme who brutally informs Ansperti's wife of her husband's condemnation: "Lasciate almeno alle nostre donne la liberta di morire di dolore" —"At least leave to our women the liberty to die of grief"—words which were in fact uttered when Tito Speri was sent to death.

Isidore Del Lungo, prefacing the edition of *Romanticismo,* praises its author for having finally composed a really Italian play. Rovetta is not merely well informed as to facts, but so keenly sympathetic that he always presents the most significant detail, and interprets rightly every shade of feeling.

While D'Annunzio, Fogazzaro, Pirandello, and almost all the prominent writers of modern Italy have passed rapidly from one manner to another, Rovetta has held firmly to his original method. It is too soon to determine Rovetta's place among Italian playwrights, but his theatre is a sure guide to the evolution of the Italian people during the period 1870–1900.

Luigi Pirandello

The World War has not only changed the map of Europe but has exerted a profound influence upon the Italian stage as is evident when we contrast the dramatic work produced shortly before 1914 with that of more recent date. The work of the dramatists we have heretofore considered is sufficiently in perspective to warrant a definite verdict as to its value. In regard to these more recent writers the intellectual viewpoint is still uncertain. Philosophic and artistic standards are not the same as before 1914, and the final verdict cannot yet be given.

One noteworthy change in the Italian as in the French theatre is its consideration of a sex-problem. In the older theatre the emphasis was usually on the many variations of the perpetual triangle. But many modern plays either ignore the complication of the intruding lover or give it secondary importance. The truly profound sex-problem is the drama of two, face to face. This is more difficult to depict than the conventional drama of three. Is it possible for a man and a woman to achieve complete union and at the same time preserve their individual souls? Since sex-attraction is uniquely individual and no two lovers are ever the same, may not this most intimate of acts, which all lovers are supposed to understand, sometimes drive the lovers into more complete isolation?

Another characteristic of this modern Italian and French theatre is the absence of dramatic eloquence and the attempt at literary appeal. Men and women as they express themselves in conduct and speech, as they achieve a career, as others accept them in everyday life, are ignored, since words and actions, far from revealing their personality, often obscure and defeat its expression. No message is proposed, no formulas are enunciated, and there is an absence of system and doctrine. But there is much introspection and dealing with the problems of the individual soul—the disappointments, the desires, attractions, repulsions, the unexpressed ideals which are the very substance of every human personality, which, though conscious, are rarely expressed; and the ideals of which we are not even aware and the fact that there is a possibility of their fulfillment —these inarticulate things are indeed the most important things in a man's life.

With Pirandello it is not so much the words and actions of his characters but the implication we draw from them that is significant. He deals with the unexpressed. His men and women seek to extend the limitations of human personality and to discover who and what they really are. They live with illusion and ideals and ignore the destructive commonplace. "Pirandello seeks always for the hidden personality . . . he gives dramatic form and feature to . . . metaphysical abstractions. Problems which press upon every human soul, walk the stage, dramatic, pitiful."

In his play *Six Characters in Search of an Author,* a producer with his company are on the stage of a theatre, when the "Six Characters" enter. They are the characters in a play never finished and never acted. They are looking for an author to present them on the stage, so that they may live the life for which they were created. It is agreed that the six characters shall enact their drama and that it shall then be presented by the producer and his company. The six characters are members of a family whose various relationships are unfolded by each of the characters from his or her own particular point of view. The father enacts his own tragic, personal, pitiful drama; and this is his defense. The shameful act in which he was surprised is not his real self but an aberration. Indeed, personality, as generally understood, is a delusion. With different persons one may be quite a different individual, clinging, however, to the illusion that one remains identical for all persons and in every situation. Nothing could be more false than this illusion, as we realize when suddenly surprised in the midst of some particular action. We realize that we are not wholly committed and expressed in this action, that it would be a cruel injustice if a man were judged solely upon the strength of it, pinned down perpetually to this particular moment as if the whole of his life were thereby summarized and made manifest.

We (he argues) are characters in a story, and as such we have a life of our own and special characteristics. I am always definitely a personality, whereas a man, generally speaking, may in the last analysis, prove to be nobody at all. Are you, for example, as you now conceive yourself to be, similar to the man you were many years ago, with all the illusions which at that time you entertained? Do you not rather, in remembering these illusions, and in realizing that those things which seemed real to you yesterday are to-day no longer the same for you as they were, feel not merely that the boards of this stage, but the solid earth itself, is crumbling beneath your feet? It is that which makes the difference between us. We are not changing, and we cannot change. As characters in a play, we are immutable. You should be struck with terror in approaching us, realizing as you must that your reality of to-day is conditioned by time, that it is a fugitive and passing reality which you take to be one thing to-day and something else to-morrow and which lies at the mercy of chance, of accident, and of impulse.

In *Henry IV* a company of young people were riding through the streets enacting an historical pageant in which the chief character is Henry IV, Emperor of the Holy Roman Empire. The young man who plays the part of the Emperor falls from his horse, strikes his head on a stone, and, when he returns to consciousness, believes that he is indeed the Emperor and insists that all his companions treat him as such. For twenty years this young man has played the part of Emperor although for the last eight years the hallucination has been destroyed and he has been sane. But the world for him has become unreal and he prefers to live within the fiction which for twelve years had been a reality. In compelling all who come near him to play a part in this fiction they are only acting as ordinary men and women do in real life. "It is only when men act as though the comedy they play is really true that it is not a jest and a delusion." His masquerade is deliberate whereas other men confuse their real personality and their pretenses.

"Pirandello is an author for whom human personality is an enigma . . . for whom the public and social life of men and women is a mechanism that obscures the fundamental realities."

Questioning the veracity of the mental and physical accidents of every-day life, Pirandello looks behind them for a deeper reality. He interrogates the passionate spiritual significance of personality and confronts us with riddles. Pirandello was born in Sicily in 1867 and did not produce his first play until he was over fifty years of age. Of all contemporary Italian dramatists he is best known to international fame. His plays have been performed to large audiences and he ha. occupied a large space in dramatic criticism in most of the capitals of Europe, especially in Paris, and also in the United States.[1]

1. For the quotations and for other data in this study of Pirandello acknowledgment is due to *Studies in the Contemporary Theatre* by John Palmer.

INDEX

Abaté, 6, 27
Abbés in Venice, 78, 79
Achille in Sciro, 47
Adelchi, 236, 237
Adelina e Roberto, 218
Agamemnon, 151, 159, 160
Agide, 156
Ajace, 226
Alessandro, 48
Alessandro Farnese, 127
Alfieri, Vittorio, his life, 132–147; a political apostle, 132, 149; his mother, 132; born 17 Jan., 1749, 132; enters the Accademia, 133; enters the army, 133; visits Rome, 133, 134; his amours, 135, 136, 147; meets Countess of Albany, 137; travels in Spain, 144; his tragedies, 148–158; his Life, 158.
Althan Countess d' (Marianna Pignatelli), 5, 14–15
Amore cenza Stima, 239
Amore dei tre re, L', 290
Amori di Ugo Foscolo, Gli, 244
Andreini Francesco (Captain Spavento), 64
Antichrist, 275
Andreini Isabella (Isabella), 64
Antonio Foscarini, 184, 185, 186
Arcadia, 28, 41
Arlecchino, 64
Arminio, 221
Arnaldo da Brescia, 166, 170, 188, 192, 194, 238
Aristocracy, Venetian, 67, 68
Artaserse, 47, 48
Attilio Regolo, Metastasio's greatest drama, 47, 51, 57
Arzigogolo, L', 291
Auge, 127
Azeglio, D', 199, 208

Baccanali, I, 218
Bacciocchi, Elisa, 168, 173
Balbo, 179
Ballata and Ballatella, 44
Bardo, 212
Baretti, Giuseppe, 25, 26

Barnabotti, 68
Bartolommeo, san, 277
Basile, 110
Bassvilliana, 211
Battaglia, Giacinto, 203, 204
Beaumarchais, 82
Beccaria, 116
Bellini, 59
Bernini's statues, 41
Biblioteca Italiana, La, 202, 228
Bonaparte, Napoleon, 168, 196, 197
Bonaparte, Napoleon, 111, 201, 208
Bona presa dai Cavalieri, 273
Bosca Parrasio, 42
Brighella, 64, 110, 113
Bruno, Giordano, 42
Bruscelli, 269
Bruto Primo (Afieri's), 163, 164
Bruto Secondo, compared with Voltaire's Mort de Cesar, 163, 164
Buffonate, 278
Bulgarelli, Marianna, see Romanina, 7
Buon Governo, Il, 168
Burney, C., Memoirs of . . . Metastasio, 62
Burning of Troy, 274

Caccini, 45
Caduta dei decemviri, 61
Caio Gracco, 215
Calamai, Teresa, 130
Calamandrana, Abaté: estimate of Metastasio, 62
Calendimaggio, 270
Calzabigi, Rainieri, de: his estimate of Metastasio's genius, 59
Campanella, 42
Cantilena (slow song), 271, 272
Cantu, 171
Canzonetta, 44
Canzoni a ballo, 270
Capacelli, Albergati, 82
Capponi, Gino, 168, 169, 175, 177, 183
Carbonarism, 198
Carducci, G., 23, 210
Carlo Alberto, 199
Carlo Emanuele III, 143

Carlo Emanuele IV, 143, 144, 196
Carme, Foscolo's, 222
Casanova de Seingalt, 69
Casti's opera *Teodoro in Venezia*, 61
Catholic Church, 78, 79
Catone in Utica, 47, 56
Cause ed effeti, 239
Cavalier servente, 78, 99, 101
Cavour, 199, 200, 201
Cena delle Beffe, La, 287
Charles VI, Emperor, 53
Children neglected, 23
Chiari, 106, 116
Cicisbeo sconsolato, 128
Cimarosa, 59
Cincinnatus, 219
Cisalpine Republic, 212
Città Morta, La, 251
Clemenza di Tito, La, M.'s most admired drama, 49, 57
Cleonte e Isabella, 275
Coloni di Candia, I, 217
Colpo di Martello, Il, 222
Commedia dell' Arte, 60; Andreini Francesco (*Captain Spavento*), 64; Andreini, Isabella (*Isabella*), 64; Arlecchino, 64; Brighella, 64; Cecchini, P. M. (*Frittelino*), 64; Spread all over Europe, 64; Fiorello, S. (*Pulcinella*), 64; Gelosi company, 64; Graziana, 64; improvisation, 64; masks, 107; Pantaloni, 64; Pedrolini, 64; scenic part written, 64
Concari: estimate of Gozzi, 120
Conciliatore, 228
Conferenza (Venetian), 103
Confessioni . . . , Nievo's, 102
Congiura di Milano, 126
Congress of Vienna, 197, 213
Conte di Carmagnola, Il, 233, 235
Contesse di Maggio, 270
Conti, Antonio: his tragedies, 126
Contrasti, 278
Convenienze Teatrali, Le, 32
Convents, 78, 79
Corneille and Metastasio compared, 47
Corradino, 127
Cortellini, Carlotta, 169
Corvo, Il, 99, 109, 110

Council of Trent, 42
Count of Albany, 137, 142, 147
Countess of Albany, 137–142, 144–147

Dafne, first Italian melodrama, 45
D'Annunzio, G., and his plays, 249–268; characters are primitive, 251; characters are puppets, 250; lack human interest, 252; most discussed modern writer, 249; plays are sensual, 252; plays are simple in structure, 251; unsurpassed descriptions, 252; dramatizes himself, 249, 250; *Città Morta*, 251; *Fedra*, 264–268; *Figlia di Jorio*, 260–263; *Francesca da Rimini*, 255–260; *Gioconda*, 252–254
Darbes, 110
Dialogues Critiques, 129
Diderot, 129
Dido first true Metastasian drama, 46
Didone is Virgilian, 46, 47, 57, 58
Diritti dell' Anima, I, 297
Discours sur les trois unités, 233
Doge, 102
Don Giovanni, words by Da Ponte, 61
Donizetti, 59
Don Pilone, Il, 128
Drama, qualities of Metastasio's, 44
Droghe d' Amore, Le, 100
Dryden's *Alexander's Feast*, 154

Edipo, 184
Emanuele III, Carlo, 143
Emanuele IV, Carlo, 143
Eufemio da Messina, 231
Ezio, 48
Ezzelino, Musatto's, 45

FABRE, François X., 141
Fantoni, Giovanni, 150, 172
Farinello, 17
Farina, G. la, 176
Fedra, a classical mosaic, 264–267
Fenzione Abbenturate, La, 60
Ferdinand III, Grand Duke, 168, 174, 175, 183
Ferdinando di Borbone, Don, 127
Ferrari, Paolo, 238–241
Festivals, Venetian, 70–72

Fiabe, 99, 105–114
Figlia di Jorio, La; D'A.'s masterpiece, 260–263
Filicaia, Vincenzo, 167, 172
Filippo, 150, 151
Fils Naturel, 129
Flavia, 277
Foscolo, Ugo, 222–228, 244
Francesca da Rimini, a fiery Amazon, 255–260
Frederic of Hohenstaufen, 194, 195
French tragic theatre, 125
Frugoni, 43

GALIANI, 116
Gambling in Venice was universal, 74, 75
Gamerra, G. de, 129, 130, 131
Garibaldi, 199, 200, 201
Gauthier, General, 173
Gelosi, company of the, 64
Gentili, Cardinal, 33
Gesu Morto, 283
Giacometti, P., 204
Giacosa, Giuseppe, 293
Giannone, Pietro, 42
Giant Goliath, 276
Ginevra di Scozia, 219
Gioberti, Vincenzo, 170, 179, 199, 201
Gioconda, 252–254
Giorno, Il, 240
Giostre, 269
Giovine Italia, La, 198
Giovanni Episcopo, 286
Giovanni di Gascala, 127
Giovanni da Procida, 171, 186, 187, 193
Gismonda da Mendrisio, 246
Giuochi, 269
Gli Eroi etruschi, 273
Goldoni: his honesty and moral standards, 82–84; his opinion of church, 82, 83; his serenity, 84; his use of Venetian masks, 107; his comedies, 84–87; his Pantalone, 85; his female characters: Rosaura, Beatrice, 85, 107; marries Nicoletta Connio, 84; born Feb. 25, 1707, 93; enters college, 93; runs away with actors, 93; studies law, 93; enters college in Pavia, 93; expelled from college, 93; admitted to Venetian bar, 93; writes plays for Imer, 93; love affair with actress, 93; appointed Genoese consul, 94; practices law in Pisa, 94; writes plays for Medebach, 94; signs contract with Vendramin Bros., 94; mother dies, 1754, 94; court poet at Parma, 94; goes to Rome, 94; leaves for Paris, 1762, 94; teaches Italian at French court, 95; Italian theatre in Paris closed, 95; partial blindness, 95; dies in Paris, 1793, 95; statue of Goldoni in Venice, 65; belongs to Venice, 81; Goldoni and "Reform," 87, 88; Goldoni and Gozzi, 88, 107; Goldoni defends actors, 91; praises physicians, 91; loves the lower classes, 91
Goldoni e le sue . . . commedie . . ., 240
Goldsmith's praise of Metastasio, 62
Golt's estimate of Metastasio, 62
Gondola, in Venice, 77, 78
Gozzi, Carlo, 96–104; his plays inspired by jealousy, 96; hated Goldoni, 96, 107; German and English, critics of, 105, 106; a Venetian aristocrat, 96, 97; masks of Gozzi and Goldoni, 107; family misfortunes, 97, 98; goes to Dalmatia, 97; his Venetian plays, 99, 100, 106, 111, 112, 113, 114, 122, 123; returns to Venice, 97; as *cavalier servente*, 99, 101; Ricci, Teodora, 99, 100, 101, 119; Romanticism, 105, 106
Gozzi's plays, analysis of, 118; *Carlo Gozzi*, a play, 119, 120
Gozzi, chronology of the Fiabe, 124; *Amori delle tre Melarance, Gli*, 99, 106, 107, 120; *Augellin Belverde, L'*, 111–114; *Corvo, Il*, 99, 109, 110, 119; *Donna Serpente, La*, 111; *Droghe d'Amore, Le*, 100, 101; *Mostro Turchino, Il*, 124; *Pitocchi Fortunati, I*, 113; *Marfisa Bizzarra, La*, 99; *Re Cervo, Il*, 120, 121; *Tartana degli Influssi, La*, 98; *Teatro Comico . . . Il*, 99; *Turandot, La*, 105, 113, 114; *Zobeide*, 121
Gozzi, Gaspare, 97, 98, 116, 127
Grand Council in Venice, 68
Granelloni, academy of, 98

Gratarol, P. A., 100, 101
Gravina, G., 3–7, 20, 24, 28
Graziana, 64
Gregory XVI, Pope, 198

HENRY IV, 305
Hoole, John; transl. Metastasio's dramas, 62

IMPROVISATION in C. dell' A., 63
Inquisition, 42
Inquisitori di Stato, 217
Italian opera in France, 45
Italian theatre, nationalism in, 201–203

Jacopo Ortis, Le Ultime Lettere di, 213, 223, 244
Jennaro (in Il Corvo), 111
Jesuitism, 42

KINGDOM OF ITALY, Regno d'Italia, 197

LACHRYMOSE DRAMA, 128, 129, 131
La Lande, De, 69
Lamento di Ariana, 45
Landi, U.; his tragedies, 127
Lee, Vernon, 29
Leopold II, 175
Liberation of Vienna, 275
Literature a pastime, 42
Liturgical mystery, 278
Lodovico Sforza, 187, 188, 194
Lorenzini's Il Socrate Imaginario, 59
Louis XVI, 273
Luca, San; Theatre, 65

MADDALENA, 272, 274, 277
Madre Colpevole, 131
Maffei, Scipione, 125, 162
Maggi, 45, 270, 273–275
Maggio, 270–274
Maggio di Bradamante, 275
Maggio of Ginevra, 273
Maggiolate, 270
Maggior Consiglio, 102, 103
Mainetto, 276
Malamani, Vittorio, 123
Malatesta, Paolo; Gianciotto, 256–258, 260

Malombra, 286
Mantellaccio, Il, 291
Manzoni, A., 117, 231–237
Marcello, Benedetto, 31, 32
Marco Polo, by G. Gozzi, 127
Marfisa Bizzarra La, 99
Maria de Medici, Queen, 45
Maria Theresa, 54
Mario e i Cimbri, 171
Martello, P. J., 125
Martinez, Marianna, 16, 18
Maschera di Bruto, La, 287
Maschera e il volto, La, 288
Masi, Ernesto, 123
Masks in C. dell' A., 63–107
Masks in Venice, 107
Mastino della Scala, 217
Mater Dolorosa, 299
Mayer, Enrico, 178, 179
Mazarin, Cardinal, 45
Mazzini, G., 198, 199, 201, 202, 207
Medea, 166, 184
Medicina d'una ragazza ammalata, La, 240
Melodrama, evolution of, 44, 45, 60
Memorie Inutili . . . 97, 101, 120, 123
Menou, General, 173
Merope (by Alfieri), 152
Merope (by Maffei), 45, 125, 126
Metastasio, P. A. D. (Trapassi): first applauded, then neglected, 3; born in Rome, 1698, 3; G. Gravina, 3; adopted by Gravina, 4; required to improvise, 4; improvisation injures health, 4, 5; visits Naples, 5; given title of Abaté, 6; Gravina leaves M. a legacy, 6; studies law in Naples, 6; writes Gli Orti Esperidi, 7; meets actress Bulgarelli (Romanina), 7; lives with her in Rome, 8–9; gives up law, becomes a playwright, 8; love affairs in Rome, 9–10; becomes Poeta Cesareo at Vienna, 10, 58; best work first ten years at Vienna, 11; avoids the court, refuses titles, 11, 38; failing health, 11; Marianna dies, leaves M. her fortune, 13; comforted by Countess d'Althan, 14; grieves over Countess d'Althan's death, 15; refuses to return to Italy,

15; lives with Martinez family, 16; last years unhappy, 16, 39; friendship for Farinello, 17; preserved religious appearances, 18; leaves his fortune to the Martinez family, 19; dies after short illness, over eighty years, 18, 19; his habits, 35, 36, 38; his career is an example of feminine influence, 39, 52; has qualities of a great tragic poet, 53; his only rival is Tasso, 54; his education was classical, 43; his psychological introspection, 43; his lyrics are exquisite, 43; drama explained, 44; poetry is idyllic, 42; letter to Algarotti, 24; did not desert Romanina, 35; an exile from Italy, 36, 37, 38; forerunner of modern romantic drama, 58; his exquisite style, 43; understood good women, 39

Metastasio's plays, 46; *Didone*, 46, 47; *Siroe*, 47, 48; *Ezio*, 48; *Alessandro*, 48; *Artaserse*, 48; *Olimpiade*, 49; *Clemenza di Tito, La*, 49, 50; *Temistocle*, 50; *Attilio Regolo*, 51

Metternich, 170
Millo (in *Il Corvo*), 111
Milton, 105
Minor Italian Dramatists, 209–248
Miollis, General, 173
Mirra, 155, 156
Mocenni, Quirina, 225, 245
Moglie Saggia, 239
Molmenti, Pompeo, 69
Montesquieu, 82
Monteverde, 45
Monti, Vincenzo, 210–215, 242
Morandi, Luigi, 61
Moresca, 272
Morgana; the fairy, 108, 109
Mortorio, 280
Muratori, 42
Musatto's *Ezzelino*, 45

Nabucco, 182, 183, 184
Napoleon I., 168, 209, 210, 212
Narrazione Apologetica, 101
Nelli, Jacopo (his comedies), 128
Neo-guelfism, 170
Niccolini, G. B. (life), 166–180; plays,
181–192; his appearance, 166; his character, 167; his finances, 177; and love, 169, 177, 178

Niccolini a born teacher, 181; classic and romantic, 183, 184; hated Papacy, 188
Niccolini's plays widely translated, 195
Ninetta, Orange-princess, 109
Nozze di Figaro, libretto by Da Ponte, 61
Nuns, abbés and priests in Venice, 78, 79

Obscurantism, Italian, 42
Olimpiade, typical of M.'s first Viennese manner, 49
Oliva, 277
Opera buffa, 60
Opera comica, 59
Oreste (Alfieri's), 152, 160
Oreste (Racine's), 159
Orlando Furioso, 219
Orti Esperidi, Gli, 7, 46

Paese di Cuccagna, 286
Palingenesi, 212
Pantalone, 109
Pantea, by Verri, 126
Papa Eccellenza, 299
Papi, Lazzaro, 209
Parini, 116
Partita a Scacchi, La, 293, 294
Pasqua Veronese, 102
Patriotic societies, Italian, 207, 208
Patro . . . Costa, first opera buffa, 60
Pedrolino, 64
Pellegrino, San, 277
Pellico, Silvio, 228–231, 245–247
Pelzet, Maddalena, 169
Pensées (Pascal's), 221
Perfetti, Bernardino, 26, 27
Phèdre (Racine's), 265
Piccini's *Buona Figliuola*, 59
Piedmont, kings of (1730–1796), 143, 197
Pieri, Jacopo, 45
Pindemonte, Giovanni, 216–220, 248; bibliography, 248
Pindemonte, Ippolito, 220–222
Piu Forte, Il, 293

Poeta Cesareo (Metastasio), 41
Pope Pius VI, 206
Pope Pius VII, 196, 198, 206
Pope Pius IX, 199
Polissena, 182
Poliziano, 45
Pozzi prisons, 69
Presa di Bona, 277
President Des Brosses, praises Metastasio, 62
Priests and Nuns in Venice, 78–79
Priestly education, 42
Processione di Gesu, 284
Programma . . . Musa Italiano, 127
Promenades (Rousseau's), 221
Prometeo, 212
Prussia, 201
Puccini, N., 184
Pulcinella, 64

R*appresentazione Spettacolosa*, 219
Rappresentazione in ottava rima, 279
Rappresentazioni of Contado, 269
Re Cervo, Il, 99, 121
"Reform," literary, 87, 88
Regine, 270
Revolt, spirit of, in Europe, 66
Ricci, Teodora, 99, 101
Ricciarda, 228
Ridicolo, Il, 239
Ridotto in Venice, 75
Ringhieri, his tragedies, 127
Rinuccini, 44
Risorgimento, 41, 208, 238
Ritorno d'Astrea, 213
Roberto Vighlius, 238
Rolli, 43
Romanina (stage name of Marianna Bulgarelli), 7–9; grieves over Metastasio's absence, 12, 13; leaves Metastasio her fortune, 13; collaboration with Metastasio, 30, 31, 46; love affair with Metastasio, 29, 30
Romanticismo, 300
Rome, capital of Italy, 201
Rospigliosi, G., don, 173, 174, 183
Rossini, 59
Rotrou's *Cosroe*, 48
Rousseau, J. J., 69, 82

Rua of Vicenza (festival of), 282

S*acchi*, 99, 100, 109
Sacra rappresentazione, 274
Salotti, Women's, 52
Salvagnoli, Vincenzo, 176
Santa Oliva, 277
Sarpi, Paolo, 42
Satira e Parini, La, 240
Saul, 153, 154, 155, 156
Scala, Flaminio (Flavio), 64
Secentistic musical drama, 55
Seingalt (*see* Casanova), 69
Sentimental Journey, 244
Senza, della, 70
Sepolcri, I, 220, 222, 223, 227
Serbatoio, 42
Serva padrone, 61
Settecento before Alfieri, 125
Settecento Italian morals, 43
Settecento literature considered, 41, 43
Signor dell' Amore, 270
Simoni, Renato, author of *Carlo Gozzi*, a play, 119
Siroe, 47, 48
Six Characters in Search of an Author, 304, 305
Smeraldina, 109
Socrate immaginario, best Italian 18th century musical comedy, 60, 61
Sofonisba, 156, 162, 163
Solitari, 131
Spada di Federico, 212
Stampiglia, Silvio, 61
Stanzas to Virgin Mary, 220
Stanze, 271
Statue of Goldoni, 65
Suicidio, Il, 239
Susannah, 274

T*artaglia*, 108, 109, 113, 122
Tartana degli influssi, La, 98
Tasso, Metastasio's only rival, 27, 54
Teatro comico, Il, 99
Teatro da Arena, 204
Temistocle, Metastasio's most complete character, 47, 50, 57
Teodoro in Venezia; comic opera, 61
Theatre in Venice, 74

Theatrical life, 32
Tiepolo's paintings, 41
Tieste, 226
Tignola, 287
Tirannide, La, 137, 150
Trapassi, F., father of Metastasio, 3, 23
Traversi, C. A., on Metastasio, 23
Trionfo d'Amore, Il, 294
Tristi Amori, 294
Tron, Andrea (el Paron), 100
Tron, Caterina D., 100, 101
Trovatori, 44
Truffaldino, 99, 108, 110
Turandot, La, 99, 105, 113, 114

Ulisses, 220
Ultime Lettere di Jacopo Ortis, Le, 244
Una . . . sere di carnevale, 99
Ursins, Princess of, 68

Valsei . . . l'Eroe Scozzese, 127
Vecchie Storie . . ., 238
Venetian art, 72; dialect, 117; theatres, 32, 33; provinces, 197
Venetian republic, 67
Venice, 201, 207
Venice, city of pleasure, 67; poverty of, 67; oligarchy in, 67; *Barnabotti*, 68; a city of good order, 68; corruption and prodigality, 68; private life in, 72; *La Dominante*, 69; *Liston*, 74; convents in, 78, 79; *Sigisbée*, see *Cavalier servente*, 76; standard of morality in, 86

Venice in 18th century, 67; aristocracy, 67, 68; public spectacles, 70, 71, 72; festival *della Senza*, 70, 71; theatrically inclined, 73, 74; private entertainments, 73; Venetian lady, 73, 74; Venetian masks, 76; *Cavalier servente*, 76; gondola in Venice, 77, 78; nuns and priests, 74–79; abbés, 78, 79
Verdi, 60
Verri, A.; his tragedies, 116, 126
Versi Martelliani, 108
Vico, B., 66
Vico, Giambattista, 28, 42, 223
Vienna, 33
Villeggiatura, 77
Virginia, 163
Vita di P. Metastasio, etc., 22
Vittorio Amedeo III, 143
Vittorio Emanuele I, 198
Vittorio Emanuele II, 199, 200

Wagner, 60
Woman, Italian, 119
Woman's place in Italian society in 18th Century, 51–53
Women actresses forbidden by Pope, 30

Zeno, Apostolo, poet, philologist, 10, 34, 35, 55; prepared way for Metastasio, and recommends Metastasio to emperor, 35, 55
Zobeide, 121